CORRESPONDING LIVES

The History of Psychoanalysis Series
Professor Brett Kahr and Professor Peter L. Rudnytsky (Series Editors)

Other titles in the Series

Her Hour Come Round at Last: A Garland for Nina Coltart
    edited by Peter L. Rudnytsky and Gillian Preston

Rescuing Psychoanalysis from Freud and Other Essays in Re-Vision
    by Peter L. Rudnytsky

Ferenczi and His World: Rekindling the Spirit of the Budapest School
    edited by Judit Szekacs-Weisz and Tom Keve

Freud in Zion: Psychoanalysis and the Making of Modern Jewish Identity
    by Eran J. Rolnik

Ferenczi for Our Time: Theory and Practice
    edited by Judit Szekacs-Weisz and Tom Keve

The Clinic and the Context: Historical Essays
    by Elisabeth Young-Bruehl

Sandor Ferenczi–Ernest Jones: Letters 1911–1933
    edited by Ferenc Eros, Judit Szekacs-Weisz, and Ken Robinson

The Milan Seminar: Clinical Applications of Attachment Theory
    by John Bowlby, edited by Marco Bacciagaluppi

Ferenczi and Beyond: Exile of the Budapest School and Solidarity in the Psychoanalytic Movement during the Nazi Years
    by Judit Mészáros

Looking Through Freud's Photos
    by Michael Molnar

Psychoanalytic Filiations: Mapping the Psychoanalytic Movement
    by Ernst Falzeder

The Abandonment Neurosis
    by Germaine Guex (translated by Peter Douglas)

The Life and Times of Franz Alexander: From Budapest to California
    by Ilonka Venier Alexander

Freud and the Dora Case: A Promise Betrayed
    by Cesare Romano

The Freudian Orient: Early Psychoanalysis, Anti-Semitic Challenge, and the Vicissitudes of Orientalist Discourse
    by Frank F. Scherer

Karl Abraham: Life and Work, a Biography
    by Anna Bentinck van Schoonheten

The Skin-Ego
    by Didier Anzieu, translated by Naomi Segal

A Forgotten Freudian: The Passion of Karl Stern
    by Daniel Burston

CORRESPONDING LIVES
Mabel Dodge Luhan, A. A. Brill, and the Psychoanalytic Adventure in America

Patricia R. Everett

KARNAC

All photographs are courtesy of the Beinecke Rare Book and Manuscript Library, Yale University, unless otherwise indicated. All photographs courtesy of www.AwakeningInTaos.com are in the collection of the Beinecke Library, with the exception of the two portraits of A. A. Brill.

First published in 2016 by
Karnac Books Ltd
118 Finchley Road
London NW3 5HT

Copyright © 2016 by Patricia R. Everett

The rights of Patricia R. Everett to be identified as the author of this work have been asserted in accordance with §§ 77 and 78 of the Copyright Design and Patents Act 1988.

All rights reserved. No part of this publication may be reproduced, stored in a retrieval system, or transmitted, in any form or by any means, electronic, mechanical, photocopying, recording, or otherwise, without the prior written permission of the publisher.

British Library Cataloguing in Publication Data

A C.I.P. for this book is available from the British Library

ISBN-13: 978-1-78220-340-7

Typeset by V Publishing Solutions Pvt Ltd., Chennai, India

www.karnacbooks.com

*For Zael and Django,
who always bring me back to myself*

*And for Ann Stokes,
who loves and writes letters
and offered me a place to return to, over and over*

CONTENTS

ACKNOWLEDGMENTS	xi
ABOUT THE AUTHOR	xv
SERIES EDITOR'S FOREWORD	xvii
LIST OF ABBREVIATIONS	xxii
INTRODUCTION	xxiii
CHAPTER ONE Illustrations	1
CHAPTER TWO Early psychoanalysis in New York	31
CHAPTER THREE From lonely child to salon host	39

CHAPTER FOUR
A jealousy complex   49

CHAPTER FIVE
"Let's go and get married!"   59

CHAPTER SIX
Lawrence: "Is Taos the place?"   71

CHAPTER SEVEN
"An irrevocable step!"   77

CHAPTER EIGHT
Lawrence again   83

CHAPTER NINE
Flirtations   97

CHAPTER TEN
Abreaction   105

CHAPTER ELEVEN
Another analysis   113

CHAPTER TWELVE
Lorenzo   119

CHAPTER THIRTEEN
Intimate Memories   127

CHAPTER FOURTEEN
New York memories   149

CHAPTER FIFTEEN
Brill in Taos   163

CHAPTER SIXTEEN
Psychoanalysis again in New York   179

CHAPTER SEVENTEEN
Back in Taos   189

CHAPTER EIGHTEEN
The Jeffers affair					201

CHAPTER NINETEEN
Money and a novel				213

CHAPTER TWENTY
Dreams, ups and downs			223

CHAPTER TWENTY-ONE
Notes Upon Awareness				237

CHAPTER TWENTY-TWO
Myron						249

CHAPTER TWENTY-THREE
A salon revived					265

CHAPTER TWENTY-FOUR
Surgery in New York				275

CHAPTER TWENTY-FIVE
Mabel's birthday				285

CHAPTER TWENTY-SIX
Final years					293

CHAPTER TWENTY-SEVEN
After Brill's death				301

APPENDIX
Psycho-Analysis with Dr. Brill			307
by Mabel Dodge Luhan

REFERENCES					313

INDEX						319

ACKNOWLEDGMENTS

It was in 1986 that I first became aware of the very existence of letters between Mabel Dodge Luhan and her psychoanalyst, A. A. Brill. I was then immersed in research at the Beinecke Rare Book and Manuscript Library, Yale University, for my book of correspondence between her and Gertrude Stein. The letters between Luhan and Brill were sealed until the year 2000—an impossibly distant date. At the time, I was in graduate school for psychology and was immediately intrigued when I noticed a clause in the catalogue entry for these restricted letters making an exception for psychiatrists. I spoke with Patricia Willis, then curator of American literature at the library, and she offered to consider allowing access to psychologists as well. Thus, soon after receiving my doctorate, I returned to the Beinecke and the letters became available to me. I am forever grateful to Pat for her creative approach to the early unsealing of this correspondence, and for the indescribable experience of being one of the first to open the large manila envelope of letters from Brill to Luhan, a woman whose life and work I had studied for years and now could view through the words of her analyst. As a psychologist, I was exquisitely aware of both the delicate nature of these confidential documents and the privilege in being able to hold and read them.

Central to my research on this book were many visits to the Beinecke Library where, in addition to first seeing the Brill letters in 1989, I learned from Michael Forstrom in 2004 of the existence of supposedly destroyed letters from Luhan to Brill. For his thorough recataloguing of the Luhan archives resulting in this discovery, I will never forget Michael's essential contribution or my shock and delight at this news. Nancy Kuhl, curator of poetry, has been an inspiring resource, extraordinarily generous in her research support. From the moment I met her, I was compelled by the energy and brilliance she brings to all projects. As one of the events for her co-curated exhibition in 2011, "Psyche and Muse," Nancy hosted a reading from this correspondence between Brill and Luhan, while also elegantly serving as its narrator. For the staff at the Beinecke Library, I have great appreciation for making the archives so available and for their genuine interest in this project.

Other libraries have also been incredible resources and refuges. I am grateful to the Manuscript Division of the Library of Congress, particularly Leonard Bruno who, on a lead of mine, patiently searched for and found a document on Brill's interest in birds. The A. A. Brill Library at the New York Psychoanalytic Institute held a trove of information, and I thank Nellie Thompson for her assistance with my inquiries. I am greatly indebted to Mark Gordon who, practically serving as a library himself, made his vast collection of images of Mabel and Tony Luhan readily available, and also introduced me to Tony Luhan's great-grandson, Blue Spruce Standing Deer, who spoke with me at length about his memories of Tony and Mabel.

My research into this rare collection of letters between a psychoanalyst and his patient has drawn me into contact with many people who have been generous with their time and interest. John Burnham answered my questions quickly and fully, gamely joining me in 1996 on a Division 39 panel, "Letters in Psychoanalysis" (where I first presented a paper on this correspondence), and believing in me enough to ask me to chair a panel at a 2009 conference commemorating the centennial of Freud's 1909 visit to the United States. There I met George Makari and James Anderson, who both graciously extended invitations to me. George Makari had, in fact, just returned from the Luhan house in Taos, New Mexico, and asked me to speak about the Luhan/Brill letters to his Richardson History of Psychiatry Research Seminar held at the DeWitt Wallace Institute for the History of Psychiatry, Weill Cornell Medical College. With his characteristic inquiry and curiosity, James Anderson became fascinated by Mabel Dodge Luhan's connections with early psychoanalysis. He invited me to write a paper for *The Annual of Psychoanalysis* on her 140 dreams recorded during her psychoanalysis with Smith Ely Jelliffe (also in restricted files at the Beinecke). Jim consistently expressed interest in my manuscript of the Luhan/Brill letters and championed my efforts towards their publication. In this spirit, he introduced me to Peter Rudnytsky, whose initial enthusiasm for this project was immensely gratifying, and whose steadfast availability for reading early drafts and offering invaluable guidance has been a genuine incentive.

For time and places to write, I am indebted to a number of people. Ann Stokes, in her dedication to provide a retreat for women on her New Hampshire mountaintop, has hosted me over twenty times in her cabins, becoming a dear friend and correspondent. Debra Boltas and Hanlyn Davies offered me a place to stay in New Haven, where I enjoyed their kindness and good company. Olivia Bernard bigheartedly opened her lakeside home and deck to me. For extended writing time and support, I am honored to have received two fellowships from the Beinecke Library, in 1995 and 2005, for work on this project, allowing me two spacious months of immersion in the Luhan archives.

Over the years, these letters between Luhan and Brill have been presented and discussed many times. I am very grateful to the Western Massachusetts and Albany Association for Psychoanalytic Psychology for offering a number of such opportunities, including two readings of a play based upon this correspondence. I will always remember reading as Mabel with my good friend and colleague Paul Lippmann reading as Brill. Paul characteristically embraced this project with depth, passion, and humor, giving a voice to Brill that came from his heart.

While seeking permission to publish A. A. Brill's letters, I had the great pleasure of corresponding with both his children before they died. Edmund Brill, whom I also spoke with by phone in April 1996 (when he said Mabel Luhan "became a friend of my father's; they both knew the same people"), initially agreed that I could publish a few selections from A. A. Brill's letters. After Edmund's death later in 1996, Gioia Bernheim and I corresponded until 2000, when, after a number of refusals, she eventually granted permission to publish all of her father's letters to Luhan. Her own engaging letters are filled with vivid memories of Mabel's visits to their home, as well as comments about her father and early psychoanalysis.

For permission to publish the letters and reproduce photographs, I am grateful to the Yale Collection of American Literature, Beinecke Rare Book and Manuscript Library, Yale University. I also want to thank Mark Gordon at www.AwakeningInTaos.com for his photographs.

Edward Burns at the Carl Van Vechten Trust was generous with his permission to publish Van Vechten's photograph of Mabel on the cover, and Emily Olson at the Amon Carter Museum of American Art was gracious in granting permission for Laura Gilpin's photographs.

At Karnac Books, editor Rod Tweedy was always available to answer my many questions, and Constance Govindin, Cecily Blench, Kate Pearce, and copy editor James Darley were responsive and helpful in guiding my manuscript through each stage towards publication.

This writing project has spanned three decades, serving as a home I could return to throughout the years. During this time, I have had two sons, Zael and Django Ellenhorn, and now they are writers themselves, loving words and the singular pleasure of lingering over great phrases. My friends have sustained and supported me with their enduring patience, interest, and questions about my book. Amrita Basu was forever there to offer guidance at a moment's notice; Julie Westcott was the first to read my compilation of Mabel Dodge's annotated dreams and to confirm what a treasure they are; many others—including Audrey Alton, Janet Zuckerman, Renée Price, Vicky Lowry, Carol Kostik, Nan Salky, Andrea Keins, Ruth Kane-Levit, Margaret Babbott, Jane Kristal, Lyndy Pye, Lynn Matteson, Judy Goldman, Adin Thayer, Olivia Bernard, Oriole and Sid Feshbach, Laurie Herzog, Clare Ellis, Amy Glynn, and Laura Vogel—have lovingly kept track of me through this long process. My late father, William Everett, always inquired about my writing and shared my love of letters. Over the last eight years of his life, we archived family correspondence and I read aloud to him hundreds of letters, including weekly missives he had written to his parents during his two years in Japan. Others in my family—Gintare Sileika Everett, Jim Everett, Richard Halverson, Barbara and Lew Ellenhorn, Maureen Ellenhorn—often asked, too, and I hope they know how much this has mattered. To dear Gary Bivona, special thanks for making it easy for me to take time and space for writing.

Here at the end belongs a heartfelt acknowledgment of the person who first taught me to write and edit: I remember, as a child, my mother sitting on the couch with a red pencil, correcting her students' English papers. I grew up somewhat edited myself, always aware of language and good writing. Over the past year, my mother, Jean Halverson, read every single word of this book, helping me edit and condense. Without her loyal company and her fierce devotion to getting it right, these last months would have been quite lonely. I am blessed to have her deep involvement in this project.

ABOUT THE AUTHOR

Patricia R. Everett is a psychologist in private practice in Amherst, Massachusetts, and the author of *A History Of Having A Great Many Times Not Continued To Be Friends: The Correspondence Between Mabel Dodge and Gertrude Stein, 1911–1914* (University of New Mexico Press, Albuquerque, NM, 1996). Since 1983, she has researched the Mabel Dodge Luhan archives at the Beinecke Rare Book and Manuscript Library, Yale University. Her current writing projects include an annotated collection of the dreams of Mabel Dodge and the unpublished correspondence between Brill and Freud.

SERIES EDITOR'S FOREWORD

If every book is a wager, Patricia R. Everett has taken a great risk and been most handsomely rewarded. In *Corresponding Lives* she weaves together three distinct strands into one seamless and sweeping narrative. Her book is at once an invaluable edition of the "complete existing correspondence" between her two protagonists, spanning the years 1916 to 1944 and comprising forty-six letters by Mabel Dodge Luhan and seventy-six letters by Abraham Arden Brill, a masterly dual portrait of the lives of an extraordinary woman of letters and the preeminent American psychoanalyst in the first half of the twentieth century, and an illuminating study of the reception of psychoanalysis in the United States in its intertwined public and private aspects as a cultural phenomenon and a multidimensional human and therapeutic relationship between a single analyst and a single patient. To do any one of these things would have been a commendable achievement; to have done them all qualifies Everett's book as at least a minor masterpiece.

To say the name of Mabel Dodge Luhan is immediately to think of Taos, New Mexico, where in 1918 she purchased a home that became an artists' colony and, five years later, married her fourth husband, the Pueblo Indian Antonio (Tony) Luhan. In the most impressive display of her charismatic power, Mabel in 1921 wrote to D. H. Lawrence, then living in Sicily, inviting him and his wife Frieda to come to Taos, where they materialized the following year. It epitomizes Mabel's role as a nexus between the worlds of literature and psychoanalysis that the manuscript of *Sons and Lovers* (1913), which she had received from Frieda Lawrence in 1924 as recompense for a ranch north of Taos, Mabel in turn gave to Brill in 1925 as payment for his professional services to her paramour, the writer Everett Marcy. The manuscript was sold in 1963 by Brill's heirs to the University of California for the paltry sum of $17,000. Both Mabel and Lawrence penned accounts of their tempestuous relationship: Lawrence in his short story "The Woman Who Rode Away" (1925), described by Patricia Everett as "a murder by literary means," and Mabel in *Lorenzo in Taos* (1932), cast in the form of a letter to Robinson Jeffers, to whom she turned after the debacle with Lawrence as the poet who she hoped would vicariously fulfill her desire to "give a voice to this speechless land."

A woman does not have four husbands (the last three of whom were infected with syphilis, which she eventually contracted from Tony) and at least two affairs even after her marriage to her would-be soulmate without having a complex inner life. Everett, without resorting to heavy-handed strokes, traces Mabel's struggles to her origin as Mabel Ganson in Buffalo, New York, in 1879, the economically advantaged but emotionally starved only child of a father of whom, as she claimed in *Background* (1933), the first of her four volumes of *Intimate Memories*, she remembered only his "dark looks and angry sound" and a mother who never gave her "a kiss or smile of spontaneous affection." What is more, as she revealed in the same book, her "first kisses" were from the "perfumed Latin lips" of her Uncle Carlos, the husband of her mother's younger sister. At the age of twenty-one she secretly married Karl Evans, with whom she experienced for the first time, in the words of the ensuing volume, *European Experiences* (1935), "the amazing explosion of the internal fireworks ... silent, fiery fountains falling on black velvet." As she confessed in an unpublished work, *Doctors* (1954), however, this orgasm occurred while having sex with her husband but fantasizing about her gynecologist, Dr. John Parmenter, with whom not only she but also her mother would soon embark on an affair. Indeed, Mabel was in doubt as to the paternity of her only child, John Evans, born in 1902, of whom she wrote in *European Experiences*, the baby "didn't seem to be mine" nor did she "feel any love for him." Not surprisingly, John repaid his mother for this intergenerationally transmitted traumatic legacy by becoming estranged from her and publishing a novel, *Shadows Flying* (1936), in which the central male character repels his mother's sexual advances with the cry, "If you ever so much as touch me again, so help me God, I'll murder you!" Meanwhile, Mabel, after the death of her mother in 1933, upon viewing the body said to herself—as she recorded in the unpublished manuscript *Family Affairs* (1933)—with the twisted logic of an abused child, "Forgive me, Mother, that you couldn't love me!"

Conveniently enough, Karl Evans died in a hunting accident in 1903, but it was rather to extricate her from her entanglement with Parmenter that Mabel and her young son were dispatched by her mother to France in 1904. Wasting no time, Mabel met her next husband, the wealthy Bostonian Edwin Dodge, on the transatlantic crossing and they were married by October of that year. Almost as rapidly, Mabel became miserable, finally reaching the point, as she put it in *Movers and Shakers* (1936), her third volume of memoirs, where she felt "a sort of nausea at the sight" of Dodge with his "persistently debonair, hard-shelled, American aplomb" and "refusal to look below the surface of life." But she found a creative outlet first in 1905 by acquiring and restoring a villa outside Florence and then in 1912 by relocating to New York where her apartment at 23 Fifth Avenue became the gathering place for the glitterati. It was in 1915, which, as Everett documents, "featured the first significant popularizations of Freud's ideas" in America, that Brill held forth for the first time in Mabel's salon and in 1916 that she began her own analytic treatment, first on January 3 with Smith Ely Jelliffe (with whom she continued to correspond for the next twenty-three years) and then on October 23 with Brill. (In 1928, she likewise obtained analysis from the Jungian Frances Wickes.) Remarkably, during her six-month analysis with Jelliffe, Mabel kept a record of 140 dreams, about which Everett has published a paper in the *Annual of Psychoanalysis*. What impelled Mabel to seek analysis to begin with was her passionate but tormented affair with the artist Maurice Sterne, who, after her divorce from Dodge in June 1916, became her third husband in August 1917.

The story I have sketched out here is told by Everett in all its intricate twists and turns. It is the story of a woman privileged by virtue of her race, wealth, and social class who, perhaps stirred by the memory of her exotic uncle's kisses, as she recalled in *Family Affairs*, "had a sense of drowning horror at having done the impossible act" when she "crossed to the other side to stand with these dark men, their river of blood dividing me forever from my own kind." It is likewise the story of a woman who not only lived an emancipated life but also wrote with astonishing frankness about her "intimate memories" of all kinds, including her experiences of orgasm and menopause, but who at the same time found in Brill an analyst who conventionally insisted, in Everett's words, that "motherhood was the primary fulfillment for a woman" and who herself proclaimed the virtues of a "return to earth, the mother whom we had almost forgotten and from whom alone we get our life." These complexities, if not outright contradictions, are reflected in the range of intellectual influences on Luhan—from the occult and Christian Science to Freud and Lao-Tzu—and the parade of illustrious people who crossed her path, and therefore appear in Everett's pages, is positively breathtaking. In addition to those already mentioned, they include Gertrude Stein, Alice B. Toklas, Carl van Vechten, Myron Brinig, Lincoln Steffens, Leo Stein, Max Eastman, Mary Austin, Hans Prinzhorn, Sándor Radó, George Gurdjieff, Theodore Dreiser, Thornton Wilder, Isador Coriat, John Reed, Walter Lippmann, Leopold Stokowski, Bobby Jones, Margaret Sanger, Jiddu Krishnamurti, and Lillian Gish.

For devotees of psychoanalysis, however, the most fascinating aspect of *Corresponding Lives* is bound to be the insight that Everett provides into Luhan's relationship with Brill and, by extension, into how psychoanalysis was practiced in the United States in the first half of the last century. What stands out above all from the correspondence that Everett characterizes as the most "extensive and elaborate written conversation between patient and analyst" of which we have a record is just how unorthodox and even casual Brill's treatment methods were. He openly opposed Mabel's marriages to Dodge and Luhan, told her to "give up that ridiculous mystical Indian business," assured her "I love you just as much as I did before," visited her twice in Taos with his Leica camera always at the ready, invited her to his apartment for lunch after their analytic sessions, and put her up when she came to New York. In an appendix, Everett makes available for the first time the 1938 manuscript, "Psycho-Analysis with Dr. Brill," a stirring depiction of what Mabel terms "the peculiar and infinitely variable course of a psychoanalytic ordeal" as she, a woman with "no self-confidence ... no self," experienced it with "a good gardener"—a Robert Moses of the soul, tending to his patients like the trees in Central Park—who was "able to bring to life the arrested growth" and so to help his charges come to terms with the painful realization that "one has been stunted—and that now all one can do is to make the best of the remains." Still, Mabel concludes her account by noting that a session might end with Brill getting up and saying, "'Well, let's go home and have some lunch,'" a revelation that led Brill to worry about the effect on his reputation were it to be published and to admonish her, "A psychoanalyst does not act that way and does not go to luncheon with his patients," even though, as Everett irrefutably observes, "he *is* a psychoanalyst and he apparently *did* act that way, resuming her analytic treatment and their lunches together."

As in her fully limned portrait of Luhan, therefore, complexities and contradictions abound in Patricia Everett's profile of Brill, the "trusted and significant confidant" whom Freud in 1921 praised to his disciple's wife Rose as "the same good boy I knew him before" and in 1932 to Brill himself as "the only one who can always be relied on, who never lets a person down," and who viewed psychoanalysis as a "branch of psychiatry" that needed to "be taken away from the quacks" but who was after his own fashion an intrepid free spirit and whose decades of unflagging devotion enabled Mabel Dodge Luhan to discover the writer in herself and who taught his patients, like the birds he loved, to sing.

Professor Peter L. Rudnytsky
Series Co-Editor
Gainesville, Florida

LIST OF ABBREVIATIONS

Manuscript collections

CVVC: Carl Van Vechten Collection, Beinecke Rare Book and Manuscript Library, Yale University.
GLSC: Gertrude and Leo Stein Collection, Beinecke Rare Book and Manuscript Library, Yale University.
SFA: A. A. Brill Papers, Sigmund Freud Archives, Library of Congress.
MDLC: Mabel Dodge Luhan Collection, Beinecke Rare Book and Manuscript Library, Yale University.

With no exception, all referenced letters from or to Mabel Dodge Luhan, Smith Ely Jelliffe, and A. A. Brill, as well as Jelliffe's notes on Mabel Dodge's analytic treatment, are in the Mabel Dodge Luhan Collection, so no citation is indicated in the text.

Books

Full citations are provided in the References.

B: Luhan, *Background*
Doctors: Luhan, *Doctors: Fifty Years of Experience*
EE: Luhan, *European Experiences*
ETD: Luhan, *Edge of Taos Desert: An Escape to Reality*
FA: Luhan, *Family Affairs*
JIS: Leo Stein, *Journey Into the Self*
LIT: Luhan, *Lorenzo in Taos*
M&S: Luhan, *Movers and Shakers*
NUA: Luhan, *Notes Upon Awareness*
S&L: Maurice Sterne, *Shadow and Light*
Statue: Luhan, *Statue of Liberty*
URT: Luhan, *Una and Robin in Taos*

INTRODUCTION

This book of letters between a spirited and cultured woman and her prominent New York psychoanalyst came unbearably close to never existing—literally saved from the fire by a mysterious decision. My communications with the analyst's daughter on the fate of her father's papers revealed that, after he died, his wife "... collected all correspondence between my father & his patients & had it all destroyed. Many of his patients were still living at the time & worried about their histories being exposed." His daughter, in fact, said her husband took "tons of cartons over to his tannery in Hoboken N.J. where they were destroyed in large ovens that were used to tan leather. Thus a lot of important material was destroyed" (Gioia Bernheim, personal communications, November 31, 1996; July 2, 2000).

For over fifteen years, I periodically transcribed and annotated the existing letters from Abraham Arden Brill to Mabel Dodge Luhan, archived in a formerly restricted file at the Beinecke Rare Book and Manuscript Library at Yale University. I longed for Mabel's side of the correspondence, but resigned myself to Brill's daughter's assertions. I also believed his son, Edmund Brill, who proclaimed to Mabel in 1951 after she herself asked about her letters: "All of Dad's personal letters from you were destroyed ... thoroughly burned upon his death." A prophetic handwritten note, however, passed quietly to me at a luncheon, suddenly gave me dim hope. In 1996, after I presented a conference paper on this correspondence and repeated Edmund Brill's claim, the psychoanalytic historian John Burnham wrote to me: "I am skeptical that any of Brill's papers were actually burned."

And then, unexpectedly, in 2004, Mabel's letters to Brill, as well as eleven additional ones from Brill to her, were discovered among unsorted material during a recataloguing of the Luhan collection. A miraculous escape from the fire thus gave rise to this book of correspondence.

* * *

Mabel Dodge Luhan, an only child raised in Buffalo, New York by desperately unhappy parents, became a perpetual seeker of stimulation and meaning and an influential salon host: first in 1911 in Italy at her Villa Curonia outside of Florence, inspired by meeting Gertrude and Leo Stein in Paris and attending their famous salons; next in New York from 1913 to 1917 with gatherings of revolutionaries from the art, literary, and political worlds at her 23 Fifth Avenue apartment; finally in Taos from 1917 on at her sprawling adobe home, Los Gallos, where she attracted writers and artists, most notably D. H. Lawrence. There she met Antonio Luhan, the Pueblo Indian who was to become her fourth husband in 1923, a radical union that forever altered her turbulent life.

During the fall of 1916, in her fervent search for understanding, Mabel entered psychoanalysis with A. A. Brill—the first American psychoanalyst who tirelessly devoted himself to English translations of Freud after meeting him in Vienna in the winter of 1907–1908, and walking with him there, discussing psychoanalysis and interpreting each other's dreams. She was analyzed by Brill until she moved to Taos in December 1917, returning to New York for several periods of treatment with him until 1938.

Mabel first wrote to Brill in 1916, and he soon replied. Their correspondence lasted until 1944, four years before his death, spanning crucial periods of development for each—a rare archival treasure of letters back and forth for almost thirty years, preserved by both intention and chance. No other such extensive and elaborate written conversations exist between patient and analyst. They offer an uncommon opportunity to understand the complex relationship between patient and analyst during the early practice of psychoanalysis in the United States.

* * *

This collection of letters represents the complete existing correspondence between Mabel Dodge Luhan and A. A. Brill: forty-six letters from Mabel to Brill, and seventy-six from Brill to Mabel, all located at the Beinecke Library. I transcribed each letter from the original, remaining loyal to the written words therein, not correcting or deleting misspellings, typographical errors, or repeated words (although corrections or acknowledgment of errors appear in brackets). Letters from Brill that are signed with "[A.A.B.]" indicate transcription from a typed carbon that was not signed. In editing the letters, I have used ellipses to indicate where I have deleted material I deemed unessential to the storyline.

This book is not just a chronological presentation of the correspondence between Mabel and Brill, but a narrative organized around the letters, with passages introducing and linking them to provide background and context. It is a story of one woman's sustained connection to her psychoanalyst through writing and a revelation of the vital role that an analyst can play years after formal treatment. Mabel wrote to Brill about her emotional states and conflicts, seeking his advice and understanding. In return, Brill offered opinions, affection, and his particular grasp of her character and struggles. Their letters illuminate a continually developing relationship, humming with the quality of an ongoing analysis.

In her letters, as in life, Mabel was despairing, insightful, inspired, questioning, talented, willful, creative, and insecure. Brill met her with warmth and frankness, humor and authority. He did not shy away from delivering strong interpretations when replying, and he wrote *to* her in an intensely personal manner. He encouraged her to keep their communication alive and acknowledged the importance of their bond: "There must have been something wrong in your conscious relationship to me. Let's hear about it" (April 9, 1928). And he combined these interpretations with expressions of love: "Well stop brooding over some of your putative transgressions. You have no real cause to complain ... At any rate I love you just as much as ever" (c. July 25, 1940). These exchanges between Mabel and Brill are stirring in their portrayal of an analyst and patient who not only maintained but deepened their emotional connection over many years.

People have always been grateful to me for my ability, since I was a child, to put myself in their places, to sense, without knowing causes, the multitudinous fluctuations of the human psyche. This natural sympathy that I could feel was not voluntary exactly, any more than the changing colors of the chameleon who takes on the tone of whatever he comes in contact with are voluntary. I was just naturally fluctuating and flowing all the time, wherever I found myself, in and out of the people I was with. I have always been myself and at the same time some one else; always able to be the other person, feel with him, think his thoughts, see from the angle in which he found himself ... It is the only genius I have ever had but it has been enough.

Mabel Dodge Luhan, *Background* (1933, pp. 200–201)

The psychoanalytic therapist must not only be well versed in the whole gamut of human emotions and understanding, but he must be capable of empathizing himself into his patient's past, be he a child or a sage. Psychoanalysis is thus the only science which shows how human beings feel and think. The more I have worked with it, the more fascinating it has become.

A. A. Brill, "A Psychoanalyst Scans His Past" (1942, p. 542)

CHAPTER ONE

Illustrations

This collection of illustrations offers a visual record of Mabel Dodge Luhan's life, as well as photographs of A. A. Brill and reproductions of their letters to each other, with the flourishes of their handwriting and signatures. The images include Mabel in her New York apartment, a painting she made for Brill, her transformation upon arrival in Taos, New Mexico, and Antonio (Tony) Luhan, the Pueblo Indian who became her fourth and final husband. Not only was Mabel widely photographed herself—as Mabel Dodge, Mabel Sterne, and Mabel Luhan—but she also embraced photography as a medium, meeting and purchasing prints from such masters as Edward Weston and Ansel Adams, commissioning photographers such as Laura Gilpin to capture her Taos estate and her beloved Tony, and sitting for portraits by her close friend Carl Van Vechten. Also shown are photographs of her friends, among them D. H. Lawrence and Robinson Jeffers, and pictures that Brill took of her Taos home during his 1938 visit. Considered together, these images speak about one woman's daring pursuit of deeper understanding during the early years of psychoanalysis in America, her sustained and sustaining connection with her analyst through letters, and the inspiring world that she continually created around her.

1. Mabel Dodge at 23 Fifth Avenue, New York, 1915.
(Photograph courtesy of www.AwakeningInTaos.com)

This photograph shows Mabel Dodge in the apartment where she held her celebrated salons. (She is flanked by metal candlesticks that also appear in the 1916 photograph of the interior of 23 Fifth Avenue, on a bureau at the back right.) She may have donned this dress and turban for the occasion of one of her evenings.

2. Mabel Dodge and son, John Evans, Buffalo, New York, 1916. (Photograph courtesy of AwakeningInTaos.com)

In this photograph from Mabel Dodge's hometown of Buffalo, John Evans is fourteen years old. At this time, Mabel was separated from her husband Edwin and romantically involved with the artist Maurice Sterne, whom she would marry in August 1917.

3. Interior of Mabel Dodge's apartment, 23 Fifth Avenue, New York, 1916. (Photograph courtesy of AwakeningInTaos.com)

This was the setting where Mabel began hosting her famous evenings in late January 1913, providing a place for animated dialogue among intellectuals and activists. The atmosphere of these gatherings was described by the critic and writer Carl Van Vechten in his novel, *Peter Whiffle* (1922), a fictional account of Mabel and her circle: "The crowds flocked to her place and she made them comfortable. Pinchbottles and Curtis Cigarettes, poured by the hundreds from their neat pine boxes into white bowls, trays of Virginia ham and white Gorgonzola sandwiches, pale Italian boys in aprons … Arguments and discussions floated in the air, were caught and twisted and hauled and tied, until the white salon was no longer static. There were undercurrents of emotion and sex" (p. 122).

4. Abraham Arden Brill, n.d.
Courtesy of the National Library of Medicine.
(Photograph courtesy of AwakeningInTaos.com)
Inscribed below in Brill's handwriting: "Abraham A. Brill."

This photograph of A. A. Brill by Theodore C. Marceau, who ran two successful photography studios in New York, was taken before 1922, the year Marceau died. By this time, Brill was well established as a leading psychoanalyst in New York, where he had founded the New York Psychoanalytic Society in his living room in 1911 and maintained a full schedule of teaching at hospitals, working at clinics, and seeing patients in his private practice. He first consulted with Mabel Dodge in 1916.

5. Mabel Dodge, *Tulips in Vase*, watercolor on paper, c. 1916.
Inscribed bottom right on the wooden frame in Mabel's handwriting: "For Dr. Brill from Mabel Dodge."

This painting is in the collection of the Beinecke Rare Book and Manuscript Library. Brill's daughter, Gioia Bernheim, recalled: "As for Mabel, she went through a stage of painting. We had two different paintings of red tulips in vases that were hung on the walls in our home in N.J. They were quite amateurish & I always felt I could do as well. These were collected at her death & I think are in the archives" (personal communication, November 31, 1996).

6. Mabel Dodge Sterne, Taos, New Mexico, c. 1918.
(Photograph courtesy of AwakeningInTaos.com)

As reported in her memoir, *Edge of Taos Desert* (1937), soon after she arrived in Taos, Mabel asked her son to cut her hair—"Just straight around—just below the ears"—resulting in a style that she believed made her look more Indian. She remembered: "Soon it was all off. Straight across my eyebrows, then down a few inches and hanging heavily over my ears in an angular bob. I had no precedent for this kind of hair-cut. No one I knew or ever saw wore short hair like this" (p. 73).

8   CORRESPONDING LIVES

7. Antonio (Tony) Luhan, Taos, c. 1918.
(Photograph courtesy of AwakeningInTaos.com)

In *Edge of Taos Desert*, Mabel described Tony's face as "like a noble bronze—rather full and ample, with a large nose and a generous mouth" (p. 102). This photograph is possibly the one that Mabel referred to in this memoir when she recalled that Tony was taken by "someone" to the studio of Jimmy Fraser in New York: "Jimmy photographed him in his blanket, looking very down in the mouth and ill, really" (p. 213).

8. Tony Luhan and John Evans, Niagara Falls, 1918.
(Photograph courtesy of AwakeningInTaos.com)
Inscribed on bottom in Mabel's handwriting: "1918 / Tony Lujan—Taos, N.M./ John Evans—Cody, Wyo."

This photograph was taken during a trip that Tony made to New York with a friend of Mabel's, Julia (last name unknown). As reported in *Edge of Taos Desert*, when they arrived in Chicago, Julia became aware of the unusual way Tony appeared, in his striped blanket and long braids wound with ribbon, and she insisted he buy another outfit at a department store. As she related to Mabel: "It was terrible, Mabel! ... He picked out a kind of light green suit, and a blue shirt—and the hat! Well! The clerk took him off to put them on, and when he came back, I wouldn't have known him" (p. 211). On their journey, they stopped in Buffalo, most likely meeting up there with John Evans. This photograph shows Tony in his new suit and hat.

9. Los Gallos, Mabel Dodge Luhan's residence in Taos, c. 1935. Photograph by Laura Gilpin. ©1979, Amon Carter Museum of American Art.

This photograph shows the Big House at Los Gallos—the name Mabel gave her home because of the Mexican ceramic chickens mounted on the roof. In June 1918, she purchased an adobe house in Taos along with twelve acres of land and immediately began adding to the structure, expanding it over the years into a sprawling estate with many outbuildings. In her memoir, *Winter in Taos* (1935), Mabel described the main living quarters of the Big House, eventually comprised of seventeen rooms over 8,400 square feet: "The house grew slowly and it stretches on and on. At one end it piles up, for over the Big Room there is the bedroom where Tony sleeps, next to my room, and a big sleeping porch off of it; and from this room one climbs a steep little stairway up into a kind of lookout room, made of helioglass set in wooden columns on all four sides, where one has the views of all the valley … There is nothing on this bare, blue-painted floor but some serapes, and up here under the sky, winter and summer, one can lie in the sunshine and bathe in it until 'untied are the knots in the heart,' for there is nothing like the sun for smoothing out all difficulties" (p. 66). This photograph also shows the second-floor bathroom windows that were painted by D. H. Lawrence when he was reportedly shocked by Mabel's lack of modesty in having clear panes of glass in such a room.

ILLUSTRATIONS   11

10. Los Gallos logo, n.d.
(Photograph courtesy of AwakeningInTaos.com)

This logo from Mabel's stationery features a red and white drawing of a chicken surrounded by a circle of type. In a letter to Mabel from November 9, 1929, Brill begins: "Like a voice from the desert when I looked at the hand-writing on this peculiar-looking envelope, I mean the peculiar design with the symbolic Los Gallos. I said to myself, is it possible that Mable [sic] thought of me again."

11. D. H. and Frieda Lawrence, c. 1923.
(Photograph courtesy of AwakeningInTaos.com)

This photograph was most likely taken in Taos during one of the Lawrences' visits. At Mabel's invitation, D. H. Lawrence arrived in Taos in 1922 with his wife, Frieda. It was his travel writing in particular that inspired her to urge him to New Mexico, believing that he could help articulate her surroundings. As Mabel reported in her memoir about their relationship, *Lorenzo in Taos* (1932): "I wanted Lawrence to understand things for me. To take *my* experience, *my* material, *my* Taos, and to formulate it all into a magnificent creation. That was what I wanted him for" (p. 77).

ILLUSTRATIONS   13

12. Mabel Dodge Luhan, c. 1920s.
On verso in Mabel's handwriting: "Mr. Knopf—To be used between Part II & Part III if you wish—with poem 'Ballad of of [sic] a Bad Girl[.]' Seperate [sic] from text of book by blank page before and after."

"The Ballad of a Bad Girl" was written by Mabel in 1924 for D. H. Lawrence, and was published with an illustration by Lawrence in the May 1924 issue of *Laughing Horse*, a small magazine founded by writer Walter Willard "Spud" Johnson. In her note to Alfred Knopf, it is most likely that Mabel is referring to *Lorenzo in Taos*, published by Knopf in 1932, when suggesting that he include this portrait with her poem. However, neither this photograph nor her "Ballad" appeared in the published version of *Lorenzo in Taos*.

> DR. A. A. BRILL
> 1 WEST SEVENTIETH STREET
> NEW YORK
> PATIENTS SEEN BY APPOINTMENT · TELEPHONE TRAFALGAR-8010
>
> April 12, 1932.
>
> Mrs. Mabel Dodge Luhan
> Taos, New Mexico.
>
> Dear Mabel:
>
> I was very glad to hear from you, and I am very intrigued about the volume of 1915-1917, l'affaire Maurice. But, alas, alack! by the time it will be ready, I shall probably not be interested in it!
>
> As for LORENZO, as I said to you before, I believe it is a great book. My feeling is that the reviewers who are not even slightly conversant with your life would not be so interested, but I am sure that those who know about you, and surely those who know you personally, would be fascinated by it. But, aside from the personal element, I would say that literarily it is a great success. As for arguments, it would take so long to argue about these matters, that I would rather not start. Some day when we meet again, and have plenty of time, we shall discuss matters.
>
> With my kindest wishes to you and Tony, in which Mrs. Brill joins me, I am
>
> Affectionately yours,
>
> AAB:LB

13. A. A. Brill letter to Mabel Dodge Luhan, April 12, 1932.

14. Mabel Dodge Luhan, New York, 1934.
Photograph by Carl Van Vecthen. © Van Vechten Trust. Stamped on verso: April 12, 1934.

Mabel Dodge had been introduced to Van Vechten in New York in 1913 and soon invited him to visit her at 23 Fifth Avenue. As she reported in her memoir of that period, *Movers and Shakers* (1936), "He was the first person who animated my lifeless rooms. He entered the exquisitely ordered and prepared apartment and he enjoyed it so much that he seemed to give it a gently vibrating awareness of itself … There was an instant response from all those inanimate things and the place became alive for us and for all others who ever afterwards entered there" (p. 16). They immediately established a close friendship and she supplied him with a letter of introduction to Gertrude Stein, who became his lifelong friend. In 1932, Van Vechten began his career as a celebrated photographer, taking portraits of many influential figures over the next thirty-two years, including singers Marian Anderson and Billie Holiday, prizefighter Joe Louis, artist Georgia O'Keeffe, and Gertrude Stein. Van Vechten took this photograph of Mabel during her visit to New York in April 1934.

16 CORRESPONDING LIVES

15. Mabel Dodge Luhan with Adrian and Robinson Jeffers, 1934.
(Photograph courtesy of AwakeningInTaos.com)
Inscribed on bottom in Mabel's handwriting: "1934/Mabel/Adrian/Robin."

Mabel and Tony traveled to Carmel, California in February 1930, where they were introduced to Robinson Jeffers, the famous poet whom she then succeeded in luring to Taos that same year, along with his wife, Una. As she explained in *Lorenzo in Taos*, narrated in the form of a book-length letter to Jeffers, Lawrence failed to satisfy her literary demands, so she asked Jeffers to take his place: "Well, Jeffers, that is all I have to tell you about Lawrence in Taos. I called him there, but he did not do what I called him to do. He did another thing. Perhaps you are the one who will, after all, do what I wanted him to do: give a voice to this speechless land" (p. 255). Robinson and Una Jeffers became frequent guests in Taos and came to know Brill well during their 1938 visit, when he was also staying with Mabel. Also shown in this photograph is Adrian, the clothes designer for Hollywood stars, whose styles Mabel embraced at this time.

16. Myron Brinig on horseback, Taos, mid-1930s.

Mabel first met the novelist Myron Brinig during his 1934 visit to Taos. At times, she was obsessed with him—as she had been with D. H. Lawrence, yearning for an intimate bond with a creative man, whose inspiration she craved for her own liveliness—and admitted in a letter to Brill from September 16, 1938 that her barely disguised autobiographical novel, *Water of Life* (c. 1938), "is a romantic-psychological one & I suppose it is an attempt to sublimate the Myron fixation." Her book tells the story of the relationship between a powerful and unfulfilled woman named Gaza and an artistic, detached homosexual writer named Gendron, inspired by Myron Brinig and, most likely, Lawrence. On September 30, 1938, Mabel wrote again to Brill: "Much of the time I am alone for no one interests me & I am so negative at such periods, I interest no one. I turn to thoughts of Myron believing that if he were here I would be alright yet I know this is only rationalizing & seeking a solution."

17. A. A. Brill, c. 1936.
Courtesy of the National Library of Medicine.
(Photograph courtesy of AwakeningInTaos.com)
Inscribed on bottom right in Brill's handwriting: "With greetings, A.A.B."

This photograph of Brill appeared on May 25, 1936 in *Time*, alongside a photograph of Smith Ely Jelliffe, to illustrate an article in the "Medicine" section called "Damage & Defense" that described furious attacks upon psychoanalysis at a meeting of the New York Neurological Society. The caption under Brill's photograph read: "Psychoanalyst Brill. He was told to keep his hands off children." One physician "began by denouncing the $10 an hour fee which psychoanalysts ordinarily charge" and another, Dr. Bernard Sachs, who, coincidentally, had been Mabel's first psychiatrist in 1913, addressed Brill harshly after his disparaging pronouncement: "Psychoanalysis more often prolongs and engenders mental disorder than it cures it ... Dr. Brill, I want you to keep your hands off the children. Your doctrines already have done outrageous damage" (p. 31). In fact, Mabel Dodge had invited Dr. Sachs to one of her salons at 23 Fifth Avenue for a psychoanalytic evening where Brill spoke about Freudian theory, thereby providing many of her guests with their first glimpse of psychoanalysis. At the time of this photograph, Brill and Jelliffe were ardent defenders of the current relevance of psychoanalysis.

18. A. A. Brill letter to Mabel Dodge Luhan, October 11, 1937.

19. Mabel Dodge Luhan letter to A. A. Brill, Thursday [before April 8, 1938].

20. A. A. Brill letter to Mabel Dodge Luhan, April 14, 1938.

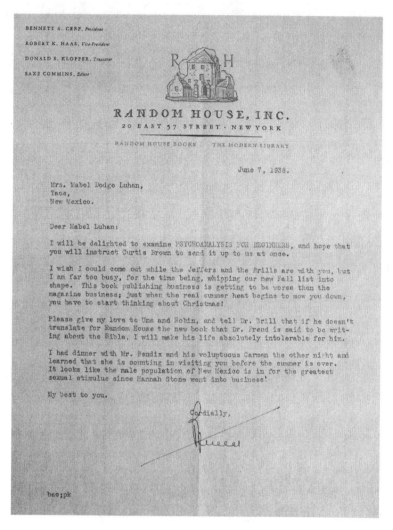

21. Bennett Cerf letter to Mabel Dodge Luhan, June 7, 1938. (Photograph courtesy of AwakeningInTaos.com)

Cerf, co-founder of Random House, was friendly with both Mabel and Brill and encouraging about her psychoanalytic writing. In a letter from June 24, 1938, Mabel asked Brill if Cerf intended to publish her psychoanalytic treatise, *On Human Relations,* also called *Psychoanalysis for Beginners.* Brill replied to her on June 28, 1938 and July 12, 1938 about his attempts to contact Cerf, who was out of town for two weeks. Her manuscript was never published.

22. Mabel Dodge Luhan on horseback, Taos, 1938.
(Photograph courtesy of AwakeningInTaos.com)
Photograph by A. A. Brill. Inscribed on bottom right in Mabel's handwriting: "By Dr. Brill/1938."

Brill and his wife, Rose, visited Mabel and Tony in Taos in June 1938, at a time when Robinson and Una Jeffers were also guests. In an unpublished memoir of this summer, *Una and Robin in Taos* (1938), Mabel recalled: "Dr. Brill photographed everybody as was his custom in the country. The man never moved without his Lieca [i.e., Leica] kodak [*sic*] hung on his shoulder and he took us all several times" (p. 13). During this visit, Brill photographed Robinson and Una Jeffers, as well as Tony Luhan. In a letter to Brill dated July 5 [1938], Mabel wrote: "Thanks for the fine photographs! Very, very good, aren't they!" This was Brill's second and last visit to Taos, during which Mabel honored him with a large party complete with Indian dancing. Brill also presided over a number of animated conversations that included one of his favorite topics: sex.

23. and 24. Mabel Dodge Luhan's Los Gallos residence in Taos, c. 1938. Photographs by A. A. Brill.

There are two other photographs of Los Gallos by Brill in the Luhan archives, as well as two of the town of Taos.

ILLUSTRATIONS 25

25. A. A. Brill letter to Mabel Dodge Luhan, July 25, 1938.

26. Mabel Dodge Luhan, Frieda Lawrence, and Dorothy Brett, near Taos, c. 1938.
(Photograph courtesy of AwakeningInTaos.com)
Photograph by Cady Wells.

The year after D. H. Lawrence's death in 1930, Frieda began returning often to Taos, where she owned a ranch north of town (acquired in 1924 from Mabel with the handwritten manuscript of *Sons and Lovers* serving as payment for the deed to the land). In 1938, Frieda bought a house six miles outside of Taos, where this photograph on her porch was likely taken. She remained friends with Mabel and the painter Dorothy Brett, who had written her own memoir of her relationship with D. H. Lawrence, *Lawrence and Brett: A Friendship* (1933).

ILLUSTRATIONS 27

27. Mabel and Tony Luhan, c. late 1930s.
(Photograph courtesy of AwakeningInTaos.com)

This photograph shows Mabel and Tony in heavy winter coats, most likely in Taos. Their union was a constant source of fascination to others, as revealed in *The New Yorker's* "Talk of the Town" column on February 3, 1940, featuring a piece on "Mabel's Tony": "We dropped in on Mabel Dodge Luhan, who … is back in town reviving her salons of yesteryear, largely to ask about her celebrated, and fourth, husband, Tony, a Pueblo Indian who is due to come to New York from their home in Taos, New Mexico sometime in February. Mrs. Luhan … told us that Tony, who, like herself, is over sixty, will probably not have too good a time here; he's visited the city before and, as a confirmed outdoors man, objects to having everything go on under roofs" (p. 14).

1009 N. Rexford Drive, Beverly Hills.
Dec — 5. [1938]

Dear Dr. Brill —

The old malaise returns. I guess I have to move on soon. Everyone is angelic to me but nothing helps. I am alone too much & there is no one here I like enough to go out after — Being alone turns my thoughts too much to Tony who now does not write to me. I suppose this "depression" will pass like others have but I do not feel very sociable while it is going on. Also Brett is arriving too this week to stay & I guess I'll get irritable. Tony will let me know his plans soon. He is in San Antonio with the dancing boys. We may meet soon in Taos. I really should stay home when I'm like this. I have been here 3 weeks today & my ticket was for 1 month so it will be next week. I try to exercise & I am working some. I am writing out the Una story — Its ugly of course I cannot use it — But to get it out of my system! Love to you both. Mabel.

28. Mabel Dodge Luhan letter to A. A. Brill, December 5, 1938.

29. Mabel Dodge Luhan, 1948.
(Photograph courtesy of AwakeningInTaos.com)
Photograph by Laura Gilpin. © 1979, Amon Carter Museum of American Art.

This photograph shows Mabel the year that Brill died. She is considerably older and had just published her final book, *Taos and Its Artists* (1947), a tribute to the artists who thrived on her beloved New Mexican landscape, including Dorothy Brett, Andrew Dasburg, and Marsden Hartley. She had hired Laura Gilpin, as well as John Candelario, to come to Taos and take photographs of the artists included in the book, who were presented with short biographies and reproductions of their work.

30. Mabel and Tony Luhan, Taos, 1949.
(Photograph courtesy of AwakeningInTaos.com)

In her unpublished memoir of her relationship with Tony, *The Statue of Liberty* (1947), Mabel wrote: "Yesterday I told Tony our lives are so divided from one another by different interests and activities that we do not pass an hour or the day or night together ... He linked together the fingers of both his hands and trying to tear them apart again he groaned, 'I can never get away from you. Every minute no matter where I am, my heart is with you.' And I said, 'I know it ... I guess we are together no matter what we do'" (p. 6). Mabel and Tony remained deeply connected for the rest of their lives: "We have truly always loved one another and nothing can come between us—not even death. I am sure" (p. 183). Mabel died in 1962, still married to Tony, her fourth and final husband, who died the following year.

CHAPTER TWO

Early psychoanalysis in New York

In the early days of psychoanalysis in the United States during the 1910s, the movers and shakers of Greenwich Village in New York were willing and enthusiastic participants in this radical approach to understanding human behavior and emotions. As championed by Sigmund Freud in his groundbreaking writings such as *The Interpretation of Dreams* (1900) and *The Psychopathology of Everyday Life* (1901), the unconscious was a compelling force that these pioneers embraced in their struggle towards deeper knowledge. Among the most devoted practitioners of this new psychology in New York were A. A. Brill and Smith Ely Jelliffe. And among the most outspoken and literary of their patients was Mabel Dodge (later Luhan) who seriously immersed herself in this new treatment, first with Jelliffe in January 1916 and six months later with Brill. She was an ardent popularizer of psychoanalysis through her weekly salons and Hearst newspaper columns, becoming a persuasive force who encouraged others to be analyzed.

Mabel Dodge Luhan (who acquired her last name in 1923 from her fourth and final marriage in Taos, New Mexico to the Pueblo Indian Antonio Luhan) left behind vast archives that contain voluminous unpublished psychoanalytic writings along with a wealth of letters from her active correspondence with both of her analysts, beginning in

1916 and continuing until close to the end of each of their lives. Most dramatically, the letters between Brill and Luhan document an often inaccessible aspect of early analytic relationships, revealing striking discrepancies between theory and actual practice. (Brill was not shy about self-disclosure and even visited Luhan in Taos in 1937 and 1938, while Mabel stayed with Brill and his wife, Rose, in New York earlier that same year.) The correspondence includes intensely personal exchanges, strong interpretations, and forceful advice from Brill, and provides evidence of a closely maintained emotional connection between patient and analyst for almost thirty years, well beyond the time of Luhan's formal analysis. The very existence and survival of this epistolary record of a psychoanalytic relationship and its evolution over time is unparalleled in analytic archives.

* * *

Brill: the first American psychoanalyst

Abraham Arden Brill, born in 1874 in Kańczuga in the former Austro-Hungarian Empire, was a psychiatrist who had immigrated to the United States on his own at the age of fifteen, purposely fleeing his strict and dominating father, a minor commissary officer in the Imperial Army who wanted his son to be a doctor (while his mother hoped he would be a rabbi, in keeping with the family's Jewish faith). As Brill recalled to Jelliffe on December 4, 1940: "Before I was thirteen, I became obsessed with the idea of leaving home and coming to America … My home environment literally stifled me" (Hale, 1971, p. 390). He arrived in New York in 1889, penniless but determined to pursue, against all odds, his goal of becoming a physician. Over his lifetime, Brill offered almost no details about his early home life or the struggle of his first years on the Lower East Side in New York, a striking omission for a man whose career was dedicated to what lies beneath.

After completing medical school at Columbia University's College of Physicians and Surgeons in 1903, Brill worked at a state hospital and took intensive courses with Adolf Meyer, the director of the New York State Pathological Institute on Ward's Island who was committed to teaching psychoanalysis to newly graduated psychiatrists. As Brill explained in his autobiographical essay, "Psychotherapies I Encountered" (1947a), after four years in the state hospital system, "[H]aving become disheartened at the hopelessness of mental treatment, I went in search of something better" (p. 575). He decided that French psychiatry promised the most learning in his search for other psychotherapeutic approaches, so he traveled to Paris in June 1907, visited the clinic at the Salpêtrière Hospital where Freud had studied hypnotism under the famous neurologist Jean-Martin Charcot, and then worked in the Hospice de Bicêtre with neurologist Pierre Marie. In August 1907, again dissatisfied, Brill went to the Burghölzli psychiatric clinic in Zurich where he studied with the psychiatrists Eugen Bleuler and Carl Jung, who opened his eyes to the Freudian psychoanalysis that was being applied in work with psychotic patients.

Brill described his immediate interest in the psychoanalytic method, which did not strive to "simply classify" a patient but rather pursued with active curiosity the meaning of the patient's symptoms: "They took his hallucinations, one by one, and tried to determine what each meant, and just why the patient had these particular delusions ... To me, that was altogether new and revealing" (1908, p. 223). Brill related an experience in his initial exposure to ideas at the Burghölzli clinic that further committed him to psychoanalysis. Bleuler presented the case of a woman in her fifties who had "poured red wine into her bed before retiring ... After prolonged questioning, this act was construed as an effort on the part of the patient to re-establish her discontinued menstrual flow" (1944, p. 29). Brill described yet another surprising and clarifying moment in this same case:

> I noticed also that while talking to the patient, Bleuler raised her hands to his nose and smelled them. I was mystified by his action, but being a stranger I did not dare ask for an explanation. It soon turned out, however, that there was a question whether the patient was masturbating and that the odor of her hands might give the clue. I was naturally much impressed by the novelty and frankness that characterized the whole procedure. In New York we rarely discussed sex at staff meetings and if we had to do it sometimes, we all reacted to the situation with a certain amount of reserve, if not disgust ... I naturally contrasted this with the matter-of-fact approach to the sexual life of the Zurich case. When I spoke of it later to Jung, he said: "The trouble with you is that you know nothing about Freud and his concepts on sex." (1944, p. 29)

Brill's positive reaction to straightforwardness about sexuality reveals an uncharacteristic openness not readily shared by many of his New York colleagues.

In contrasting the Zurich approach to practices in New York, Brill underscored the radical nature of this new treatment, fiercely dedicated to uncovering what lies underneath the expression of symptoms. He attributed his eager embrace of psychoanalysis to his earlier immersion in the teachings of Baruch Spinoza, the philosopher who had become his "spiritual father" when at age sixteen he rejected his Jewish religion. For Brill, Spinoza's imperative to make sense of human behavior—as captured in his dictum: "Human actions should not be laughed at, should not be shocked at, nor held in disdain, but should be understood" (1931a, p. 244)—fit perfectly with the teachings of Freud, whose slogan, "Please refrain from all criticism," Brill exalted (1931a, p. 244).

Brill described another particularly compelling instance of his acquired insights and conversion to this new psychology while he was at the Burghölzli clinic: the process of realizing that all human beings, including even himself, share certain basic experiences and instincts, thus blurring the distinction between abnormal and normal:

> I was captivated by the case histories because the patient no longer represented something entirely foreign to me, something insane, as I had hitherto regarded him when I merely described his strange behavior. Now even his most peculiar expressions as I traced them back to his former normal life struck familiar chords in me.
>
> At first this slightly alarmed me. I feared lest there be something wrong with me; but I soon discovered that what I found in a patient, even while deciphering obsessions or delusions, was only an exaggerated or distorted expression of that which exists in every normal person. Since nothing is so convincing as that which one finds in oneself, my faith in the Freudian mechanisms was soon established. (1944, p. 33)

In a crucially personal way, Brill now accepted the universality of the unconscious, the power of an individual's needs and motives, and the importance of understanding oneself in order to understand the patient. This time in Zurich proved decisive for Brill's professional development, strengthening his commitment to psychoanalysis as he saw the powerful success of its approach to treating patients and believed it offered a "microscope for the study of the mind" (1942, p. 539).

While in Zurich, Brill also met Ernest Jones, a neurologist who was the first in England to use psychoanalysis with a patient in 1905. Brill and Jones traveled to Vienna together to meet Freud in the early winter of 1907–1908, an experience that had a profound effect on Brill's career. Although no letters dating from before their initial meeting have been found among the Freud and Brill papers at the Library of Congress, Brill reported: "As we had been corresponding for some time, we knew each other fairly well by the time we met. It was then that we arranged that I should be his English translator, a work to which I devoted almost all my spare time for a period of more than ten years" (1944, p. 46). Brill returned to New York and began his work as the first American translator of Freud, starting in 1909 with the publication of Freud's *Selected Papers on Hysteria and Other Psychoneuroses* (originally published in 1895), thereby making available to American psychiatrists and others Freud's revolutionary ideas about the unconscious.

Fresh from his experiences in Zurich and Vienna, Brill began practicing in New York during the fall of 1908 as the first American psychoanalyst. He described the circumstances of his work:

> I said that I would have preferred to practice psychoanalysis when I first entered private practice, but ... I could not have earned a living on psychoanalytic practice. I earned $37 the first month of private practice and only a small part of it through psychoanalysis ... In time I gradually built up a fair psychoanalytic office practice, but in the clinics I administered whatever therapy the situation permitted ... But whenever I found an interesting psychoanalytic case in the clinic, I made special morning appointments with the patient when the clinic was ordinarily closed ... I charged nothing for these visits; at times I even paid the patient's carfare ... Within about six months I had a full office practice, that is from 8 a.m. to 1 p.m. and from 5 p.m. to any hour thereafter. I worked daily except Sunday from 2 to 4 p.m. in some clinic or hospital. (1947a, pp. 575–591)

Brill's description of his methods of building a psychoanalytic practice is fascinating in its details and in his willingness, frowned upon by his colleagues, to accept no payment in order to have the experience of treating a patient psychoanalytically.

In September 1909, Freud delivered his historic lectures at Clark University, in Worcester, Massachusetts, where he formally introduced his revolutionary theories to an American audience, a pivotal event that inspired the beginnings of a more organized psychoanalytic movement in the United States. Brill had accompanied Freud and his disciples Jung and the Hungarian Sándor Ferenczi from New York to Worcester. In March 1910, Freud, at Ferenczi's urging, founded the International Psychoanalytic Association, appointing Jung as president. Freud then wrote to Brill on April 14, 1910, proposing that he organize a branch of the association in New York: "Now it is probably the time for you in New York and perhaps Jones in Boston to propose founding local groups ... You, as the only one with experience, will take on the intellectual leadership" (SFA). In 1911, Brill founded the New York Psychoanalytic Society, holding the initial meeting at his home at 87 Central Park West, and remaining for years in various roles from president to secretary, with his last presidency in 1935.

Brill and Freud maintained a lifelong correspondence that attests to the intimacy sustained throughout their uninterrupted friendship and provides convincing evidence that Brill was a more trusted and significant confidant of Freud's than has been recorded in psychoanalytic history. The letters between Freud and Brill revolve around the development of the psychoanalytic movement in the United States, with its many struggles and personality conflicts. They also detail the ways that Freud helped Brill establish the early reception of psychoanalysis in the United States and directed him in his personal relationships. Throughout the letters, Freud's affection for Brill remained constant. He felt they shared "an intimacy of the kind present in blood relationships" (April 25, 1923, SFA). In fact, Brill's first child, Gioia, born in 1911, was Freud's goddaughter, and, according to her, both she and her brother were named after Freud: "Gioia, pronounced Joya, means joy in Italian which was the language my father was studying when I was born. Freud also means joy in German. Hence I was named after Freud who was my godfather. The same for my brother, Edmund (Sigmund)" (Gioia Bernheim, personal communication, November 31, 1996).[1] And Brill's earlier renunciation of his own father opened the way for Freud to occupy that crucial space (Fass, 1969, pp. 25–26, 46). Freud acknowledged Brill's central role in spreading the word about psychoanalysis—"The great pains you are taking with the translations touches me deeply" (May 25, 1909, SFA)—and appreciated his steadfastness: "You are indeed the only one who can always be relied on, who never lets a person down" (June 17, 1932, SFA). Until his last days, Brill championed Freud's cause with the fierceness of a devoted son.

* * *

Jelliffe: conversion to psychoanalysis

In addition to his private practice and clinic work around 1909, Brill was actively engaged with students of psychoanalysis, among them Smith Ely Jelliffe, a successful neurologist in New York who, when he first met Brill, was already established as the initial force behind psychosomatic medicine in the United States. In 1910, he and Brill were both working at the New York Neurological Institute. Jelliffe described his conversion to psychoanalysis in his article, "Glimpses of a Freudian Odyssey" (1933): "After our clinics three times a week, Brill and I walked homewards together through the park, and … we argued and he persisted and thus I became a convinced Freudian" (p. 325). These walks while talking about psychoanalysis are reminiscent of Brill's long walks with Freud in Vienna only a few years before. Brill had his own version of these early discussions, recalling their first meeting when Jelliffe "showed at that time definite resistances to psychoanalysis" (1947a, p. 582). Brill then wrote of his successful plan to convert Jelliffe:

> … I conceived his attitude towards psychoanalysis as a direct challenge and forthwith decided to change his mind. That I succeeded in my efforts is well-known … However to give you a more intimate view of Jelliffe's conversion to Freud, let me read the following quotation from a letter which I received from him, April 2, 1943: "Our walks through the park started something in me of inestimable value … I felt that bottom rock had been reached and we could then build with confidence. I had been reading Freud, but you made it vital and real for me." (1947a, p. 582)

In 1913, Jelliffe was actively practicing this new psychology and founded the *Psychoanalytic Review* with psychiatrist William Alanson White. Brill, however, despite his influential role in Jelliffe's professional development, had reservations about Jelliffe's particular version of psychoanalysis, as he wrote to Freud in a letter dated December 12,

1913: "Jelliffe is a very ardent worker for psychoanalysis, but of course he is thoroughly Jung. He is one of these persons who can make believe that he knows it all when as a matter of fact he knows very little. I have occasion to see one of his cases and I am satisfied that he had no idea what he was doing" (SFA). Brill's criticism of Jelliffe's work in 1913 is a somewhat uncanny precursor to his future inheritance of Mabel Dodge as a patient in 1916, when she consulted with him while Jelliffe was on vacation and chose to leave Jelliffe to pursue analysis with Brill.

Note

1. Brill occasionally mentioned Gioia in his letters to Freud, as on January 11, 1914: "Gioia is rapidly becoming a little girl & watching her develop I more and more realize the infantile sexual theories" (SFA). When the Brills were again expecting a child, Freud wrote to Brill on November 16, 1914: "If wishes still have any trace of omnipotence, everything will go well and a son will be a source of gratification for your homosexuality" (SFA). On January 10, 1915, Freud offered: "Our warmest congratulations on the birth of your son. You know how important it is for a man to have a son or sons" (SFA).

CHAPTER THREE

From lonely child to salon host

Born into a wealthy family in Buffalo in 1879, Mabel Ganson was an only child whose parents were drastically unhappy and deeply estranged, their vast economic privilege derived solely from inheritance. Her father's despair and violent moods permeated her childhood years, and the atmosphere in her home was barren of any closeness or warmth. As she described in *Background* (1933), the first volume of her memoirs, "I have no recollections of my mother's ever giving me a kiss or smile of spontaneous affection, or of any sign from my father except dark looks and angry sound." She continued: "There never was a sense of life in our house. No one cared to be in it. Really no one *lived* in it, you might say. My father was in it the most of any of us, but he was usually up in his room," and concluded, "So there we were, the three of us, separated into our different modes of loneliness—a family" (pp. 23, 49, 36). Mabel's father was plagued by mental and physical illnesses that were expressed in both silences and rages. Her mother was characteristically absent, both when she was actually home and when she was away, leaving her daughter to fend for herself in her dreaded state of inactivity. Mabel searched for excitement outside her house, determined to flee its emptiness and secrets, as well as "escape the *fear* of the pain of idleness" (p. 42). In a passage that follows a description of Mabel's discovery of her mother's unhappiness, she explained: "My mother, a speechless woman herself, had set an example of mute endurance and I had modeled myself upon her. So it was, in our house, as though we believed that by ignoring and never speaking of the misery we caused each other we would thereby blot it out from our hearts" (p. 37). These two early themes, of flight from boredom and of silence about anguish and melancholy, were central to Mabel's life struggles and her eventual turn to psychoanalysis.

Mabel emerged from this upbringing as a determined and highly spirited young lady, a rebel against the Victorian values of the society in which she was raised. In 1900, she secretly married Karl Evans, surprised into a wedding by his luring her to a country church near Buffalo where a minister was waiting. With no protest, she acquiesced to the brief ceremony, which she later described in her memoir *European Experiences* (1935) as "one of the few things I have ever had done to me in my life" (p. 33). The sexual component of her marriage was passionless on her part for months until the moment when she had her first orgasm, as she reports quite differently in two autobiographical accounts. She remembered that she and Evans were in her parents' house where:

> ... for the first time I experienced the amazing explosion of the internal fireworks. I had never heard of that gentle transformation that is, in sensation, as though the nerves expressed themselves in the manner of silent, fiery fountains falling on black velvet ... No one had ever told me about this definite, so definite and surprising thing. And I had never read of it. (*EE*, p. 36)

Here, Mabel Ganson Evans writes daringly and openly of a female's sexual experience, a radical step for a woman of her time, thereby providing an opportunity for others to "read of it" and foreshadowing her receptivity to psychoanalysis with its inquisitive approach to sex. In her memoir, she then described her intense preoccupation with her newly awakened sexuality and how it completely altered the way she viewed her world.

In another autobiographical work, *Doctors: Fifty Years of Experience* (1954), an unpublished account of her medical history, Mabel recalled her first orgasm occurring during intercourse with her husband while fantasizing about her gynecologist in Buffalo, Dr. John Parmenter, with whom she was infatuated and would soon have an affair: "I invented a new method for myself. I closed my eyes and pretended it was the doctor I was with. And for the first time since we had been married the strange, unknown miracle occurred in my body" (p. 15). Certainly, these two accounts are not necessarily mutually exclusive. Mabel reported that she became pregnant on this first occasion when she thought of Dr. Parmenter, and immediately thereafter entered into a sexual relationship with him. He evolved for her into "the motivation and the cause for living" (p. 17) and was a constant presence in her life, throughout this first pregnancy that apparently ended in miscarriage (*EE*, p. 44), and then during her next full-term pregnancy. At this same time, her doctor was also involved in sexual liaisons with Mabel's mother, a fact Mabel discovered one day when she opened her mother's bedroom door to discover them together (*Doctors*, pp. 18–19). One can only imagine the intense feelings of betrayal Mabel must have experienced. Her mother, so emotionally unavailable to Mabel, was yet literally enjoying the same sexual pleasure and partner as her daughter. Mabel's unquestioning trust in Dr. Parmenter was shattered, her relationship with him compromised, her world thus diminished.

* * *

A baby: "that stranger"

In 1902, Dr. Parmenter nonetheless delivered Mabel's baby, a son named John Evans. He arrived into the world, resented by his mother who complained: "I had been torn from giving birth to that stranger" (*Doctors*, p. 20). Mabel's distancing reception of her infant is in sharp contrast to her descriptions of the joys of pregnancy, a time when she reported being deeply content: "I myself was of the greatest value to this fruitful earth that I have ever been before or since … All my feelings about myself and my own needs and wishes, all my strong egotistical will, and the mental life, sank out of sight" (*EE*, p. 47). For Mabel, pregnancy became an opportunity to give herself permission to disengage from tiring and tedious aspects of the world. In an eloquent passage, she praised the advantages of pregnancy for a woman like her, as she surrendered to the process and experienced an irrefutable merger:

> And this, I suppose, is maternity. All in the womb. There we possess and are possessed by our own. Ever after birth there is the tug

and the pull: but in the reciprocity of the womb, there is unity and peace and the only legitimate contentment we are ever allowed to know in this world ...

Do women realize, I wonder, how precious these days are when they need not take any notice of any living person? ... All the rest of the time we have to continue the weary and awful, adorable, never-ending traffic and exchange of souls in the outer world. (*EE*, p. 48)

Mabel's experience of pregnancy underscores the psychological toll she suffered from intimate exchanges with the world. She felt liberated while bearing a child, free to disconnect and be less vulnerable to the demands of both her own will and the wills of others.

As soon as her son was born, however, Mabel reported a drastic internal shift as she was jolted back to her previous self: "Before I opened my eyes I knew there was a change of consciousness. The baby was gone and my soul had returned to my body. Ah! Melancholy awakening!" She looked at her baby and suddenly became aware of the "pathos and the pity of life and I thought, 'I don't like it,' and my heart shut right up then and there." She was impenetrable to this new experience of motherhood, impervious to any feelings beyond deep sadness, and instinctively wanted him away from her: "I didn't feel anything for it. I saw it was a nice baby, but it didn't seem to be mine ... It seemed to me I didn't want a baby after all" (*EE*, pp. 50–51). Her disturbed perceptions of her baby continued and she felt guilty in his presence.

Mabel's rejection of her son may have been related in part to questions about his paternity, whether the father was her husband or her gynecologist, as she lamented: "Finally, the time came to face the issue. I hardly knew whose baby I was going to have" (*Doctors*, p. 19). Clearly, Mabel's preoccupation with this affair during the early days of her son's life must have added enormously to her distaste for motherhood. She wrote that eventually, "My curious reluctance to see the baby dwindled away and though I had ceased to feel sadness, neither did I feel any love for him, and I felt sorry for us both on this account" (*EE*, p. 52). John Evans's early days were defined by the company of a detached and disaffected mother, the bad luck of being born to a mismatched pair who rarely saw each other, and nourishment through bottle-feeding since Mabel did not produce any milk.

Restless and unfulfilled in her roles as wife and mother, Mabel Evans was released from one of these bonds when her husband died in a hunting mishap in 1903. Then, her continuing affair with Dr. Parmenter so severely threatened her physical and emotional health that Mabel's mother (reportedly on Parmenter's advice) forced an end to the relationship, putting Mabel and John Evans on a steamer bound for France in July 1904 (*Doctors*, p. 28).

* * *

Edwin Dodge: "persistently debonair"

During the crossing, Mabel met Edwin Dodge, a wealthy young man from Boston who tirelessly pursued her until she agreed to marriage in October 1904. Although he willingly acted as father to John and provided his wife with her accustomed luxuries, Mabel Dodge again found herself discontented with the confines of marriage and motherhood. Her silent depression isolated her from her son and new husband and it was only when they moved to Italy in the fall of 1905 that she felt stimulated by the possibilities available to her. At the Villa Curonia outside Florence, she devoted her energies to elaborately restoring the fifteenth-century building and hosting generous feasts, gathering together such celebrities as actress Eleanor Duse and writer Gertrude Stein with her companion Alice B. Toklas. However, the appeal of these activities predictably waned after a number of years and the Dodges returned to New York in November 1912, soon moving into a second-floor apartment at 23 Fifth Avenue.

As she had done with the Villa Curonia, Mabel Dodge immersed herself in a dramatic transformation of her new home. But once the redecorating was completed, she fell into a deep depression and was left again with the despair of estrangement from her husband. As she described in her memoir of this period, *Movers and Shakers* (1936), when she looked at Edwin Dodge she experienced "a sort of nausea at the sight of his persistently debonair, hard-shelled, American aplomb" (p. 12). She articulated the fundamental differences that she perceived between them and underscored elements in her nature that eventually led her to seek psychoanalysis as a way towards deeper understanding:

> This continued good cheer of his that came, I thought, from a refusal to look below the surface of life, from a constant outward

> gazing that never looked *within*, made me so furious at times that I wanted to hurt him ...
>
> I was always seeking for the causes and meanings of things under the surface, myself, feeling my way into the depths, and groping among the terrible and abhorrent shapes that live below the pretty aspects of ten o'clock in the morning, but Edwin had always seemed curiously unaware of the possibilities lurking in the soul ...
>
> This made me wish him away. I persuaded myself that he stood between me and real life ... that Edwin blocked my growth, and my need for new ideas and that the life of ideas could never flourish in his company. (pp. 12–13)

Mabel's impassioned curiosity about the meanings beneath surfaces certainly links her to Brill's devotion to psychoanalytic understanding. She convinced her psychiatrist at the time, Bernard Sachs, that Edwin was at the root of her depression and fatigue, resulting in her doctor's recommendation that Edwin move out of the apartment into a nearby hotel until her condition improved.

With her husband banished, Mabel's mood lifted and she began to engage creatively and expansively with the world around her. She developed close friendships with journalist Hutchins Hapgood and writer and critic Carl Van Vechten, who introduced her to many of the radical thinkers of the time. She regularly visited Alfred Stieglitz's 291 gallery, a central meeting place for avant-garde writers and artists, and became an early patron of modernist art. It was at 291 that Mabel met the artists Andrew Dasburg and Marsden Hartley, who were to be her friends for years.

* * *

23 Fifth Avenue: salons

Located near the northern border of Greenwich Village, 23 Fifth Avenue was ideally situated to be the home for Mabel Dodge's famous salons, which attracted the intellectual, political, and artistic circles of New York between 1913 and 1917 (see Illustrations 1 and 3). In late January 1913, inspired by a suggestion from the author Lincoln

Steffens, she began hosting gatherings that provided a setting for the lively exchange of ideas. As she reflected: "Perhaps intuitive people like Steffens have sometimes seen the possibilities before I knew them myself ... and by suggesting the activity already preparing to express itself, have helped to bring it to the surface. Certainly this is what skillful psychologists try to do" (M&S, p. 81). Her salons were populated by a wide range of guests, listed by Mabel as: "Socialists, Trade-Unionists, Anarchists, Suffragists, Poets, Relations, Lawyers, Murderers, 'Old Friends,' Psychoanalysts, I.W.W.'s, Single Taxers, Birth Controlists, Newspapermen, Artists, Modern-Artists, Clubwomen, Woman's-place-is-in-the-home Women, Clergymen, and just plain men" (M&S, p. 83). Many evenings had a specific topic and a chosen speaker.

At one of her salons at 23 Fifth Avenue in 1915, Mabel Dodge held a psychoanalytic evening where A. A. Brill spoke about Freudian theory, thereby providing many of her guests with their first glimpse of psychoanalysis. Mabel described the reception that he received: "Dr. Brill had begun his Freudian analysis before that time, and it was thought to be just as queer as all the other attempts people were making to achieve some kind of social adaptation. We had him come down and talk to us one of the Evenings and several guests got up and left, they were so incensed at his assertions about unconscious behavior and its give-aways." Dodge then recalled her first psychiatrist's response: "Although I had invited Dr. Sachs to come on the Psychoanalytic Evening, he repudiated my invitation with the tone of an admiral who has been invited to tea on an enemy submarine. He said he was not at all in sympathy with the subject or with the manner of presenting it to the public, and, he added, he considered the subject a dangerous one for me" (M&S, p. 142). In his autobiography, Steffens credited Dodge with first exposing him and others to psychoanalytic ideas:

> It was there and thus that some of us first heard of psychoanalysis and the new psychology of Freud and Jung, which ... introduced us to the idea that the minds of men were distorted by unconscious suppressions, often quite irresponsible and incapable of reasoning or learning ... There were no warmer, quieter, more intensely thoughtful conversations at Mabel Dodge's than those on Freud and his implications. (1931, pp. 655–656)

Mabel's early captivation with psychoanalysis and her eagerness to share her discovery with others resulted in innumerable psychoanalytic treatments. She herself was soon to enter analysis with Smith Ely Jelliffe.

* * *

Embracing Freud

Freud's theories about the unconscious, hidden motives driven by primitive or sexual desires, and dreams as conveyors of meaning were of enormous appeal to the American avant-garde, who were in search of the newest trends in thinking and of underlying meanings. Mabel Dodge was an outspoken example of the American intellectual who embraced this new method of investigation to examine her own psyche. Her memoirs and letters are filled with interpretations and analyses of the thoughts, feelings, and behaviors of herself and her friends. To those so inclined, Freud offered a way of explaining how hidden motives affect a person's ways of thinking and acting through concepts such as condensation and symbolization, as revealed in dreams and slips of the tongue. Although writings about psychoanalysis began to appear soon after Freud's Clark lectures in 1909, it was several years before these radical ideas were more widely accessible through journals and books.

The year 1915 featured the first significant popularizations of Freud's ideas. The writer and editor Max Eastman published two articles in *Everybody's Magazine*: "Exploring the Soul and Healing the Body" and "Mr. Er-er-er—Oh! What's His Name?" *Good Housekeeping Magazine* featured "Diagnosis by Dreams" by writer Peter Clark Macfarlane. In addition, three books targeted for lay readers appeared: psychoanalyst James Jackson Putnam's *Human Motives*, professor Edwin B. Holt's *The Freudian Wish and Its Place in Ethics*, and psychoanalyst Isador H. Coriat's *The Meaning of Dreams* (Burnham, 1991, p. 120). These publications reached the movers and shakers of the time who were eager to uncover motives and explore their own unconscious and that of others.

Mabel proved to be a pioneer in her early fascination with psychoanalysis, and her involvement took a variety of forms, initially as a patient in 1916, and later as proselytizer and informal student. In her role as a bi-weekly columnist for the *New York Journal*, she added to the popularization of psychoanalysis with articles such as "Mabel Dodge Writes About the Unconscious" and "Love and Ownership: The Art Lover's Desire; Seeing is Possession; The Desire to Own; The Power of Instinct." Mabel wrote these columns from August 1917 to February 1918, a job that Brill, in his role as her psychoanalyst at the time, had urged her to take for therapeutic reasons.

Many American intellectuals fervently adopted Freud's view of the world and began analyzing everything about themselves and those around them. The aim of such activity was often the discovery of a real or authentic self, stripped of dishonest facades and hypocritical stances (Burnham, 1991, p. 123). The influence of psychoanalytic teachings was inescapable in the Greenwich Village of the teens. As the writer Floyd Dell recalled, "Everyone at that time who knew about psychoanalysis was a sort of missionary on the subject, and nobody could be around Greenwich Village without learning a lot about it" (Burnham, 1991, p. 120). Striking a different note, Hutchins Hapgood described the climate of frequently excessive analysis that developed out of enthusiasm for the new psychology:

> Psychoanalysis had been overdone to such an extent that nobody could say anything about a dream, no matter how colorless it was, without his friends' winking at one another and wondering how he could have been so indiscreet. Freud's scientific imagination certainly enriched the field of psychology and was a great moment in our knowledge of the unconscious. But every Tom, Dick, and Harry in those days was misinterpreting and misapplying the general rules underlying analysis. (1939, pp. 382–383)

Although Hapgood claimed he had no use for his own psychoanalysis, he reported in his memoir: "Mabel, of course, tried it, as she tried everything" (1939, p. 383).

In Mabel's correspondence with others from this time, there are numerous references to both Jelliffe and Brill. Also a patient of Brill's, Dasburg once signed a letter to Mabel, "Still trusting in Brill and Jesus" (Luhan, *Intimate Memories, Vol. 7*). In another letter, c. fall 1916, Dasburg wrote: "It's so long since we have seen each other that I almost forgot where we left off. You had just begun with Brill ... I haven't seen Brill all summer" (Luhan, *Intimate Memories, Vol. 6*). Mabel also shared a deep interest in psychoanalysis with Leo Stein, a writer, art critic, and brother of Gertrude Stein. In 1915 and 1916, Stein consulted first with Brill and then Jelliffe for analysis. As he reported in his autobiography, *Journey Into the Self* (1950), Leo wrote to Gertrude on February 15, 1916: "I see a good deal of Mabel Dodge ... Everybody is occupied more or less with psychoanalysis" (pp. 71–72). References to analysts, psychoanalysis, and the unconscious were rampant in correspondence and conversations at this time, partially due to the range of Mabel's contacts and influence.

CHAPTER FOUR

A jealousy complex

In a letter simply dated January 1916, Mabel Dodge, clearly conversant in contemporary psychoanalytic jargon, wrote to Smith Ely Jelliffe in New York requesting treatment:

> Dear Dr. Jelliffe—
>
> I want very much to see you to discuss the possibility of your analyzing me. I am obliged to admit to having a jealousy complex which has produced an anxiety neurosis with an increasingly compulsory action on my behavior. I am living in the country now … but I will be in New York on Wednesday, and I will call up your house and try & get an appointment with you if you will have time to see me that day …
>
> Sincerely,
> *Mabel Dodge*

At the time she entered psychoanalysis with Jelliffe, Mabel was living at Finney Farm, a country estate in Croton-on-Hudson, which she had leased for two years. With a main farmhouse and a number of outbuildings, this became a refuge for her and her friends. Her companion during this period was artist Maurice Sterne, whom she had met at a dance recital in 1915 and found irresistible due to "his handsome look of suffering" (*M&S*, p. 350). She had been separated for two years from Edwin Dodge, would divorce him in June 1916, and eventually marry Sterne in August 1917. The relationship between Mabel and Sterne was characterized by extremes of passion, jealousy, destructiveness, and distance, as well as her intense and violent ambivalence. The "jealousy complex" she referred to in her letter to Jelliffe was often fueled by Sterne's looking at other women or by Mabel's misperceptions of his actions. The "compulsory action" she mentioned often had her searching for clues to his betrayals, but also refers to her own driven sexual behaviors with him that seemed intended to solidify their bond, however temporarily.

According to Jelliffe's case records, Mabel had her first session with him on Monday, January 3, 1916. He assigned her a diagnosis of "psychoneurosis," the current term for emotional conflict made popular by Freud that considered symptoms as symbolically expressing early childhood conflicts. Jelliffe's notes seem to read as a verbatim account of Mabel's evaluation of herself: "An only child never in possession of my kingdom: Root of my character. Main trouble: Jealousy—much in love at present, with a man, with compulsory sex possession ... At menstrual period + +, resistance less: issues greater, suffering intolerable ... Contact with life only through an individual: absorbed in or through some man." In these notes, Mabel is revealed as an obsessively self-reflective woman, aware of the impact of her upbringing on her possessive character and on her sense of longing for others to complete her. She also appears to understand her cycles of despair and repair and, quite remarkably for this era, the negative effect on her mood of hormonal changes during the time of menstruation.

Jelliffe's next entry is from January 5, 1916, with subsequent notes indicating that Mabel saw him for analysis between two and four times a week until June 2, 1916. His case records contain forty-eight separate entries from January 3 to October 23, 1916, as well as her written recordings of 140 of her dreams.

After a month in treatment with Jelliffe, during which he reportedly instructed, "[I]t was customary during an analysis ... for the patient to be separated temporarily from the family," Mabel banished Sterne from Croton in February 1916—"At Jelliffe's request, then, I got him off to Pottsville to paint" (*M&S*, p. 446). She remembered her resulting feelings: "For me it was exactly like a holiday, as though Maurice had been a tremendous job from which I was granted a vacation ... It seems to me I never loved him with any ease except when we were separated, and then tenderness and a kind of compassion entered into me" (M&S, pp. 447–448). They struggled along in their relationship through the spring and early summer months of 1916, while Mabel continued her analysis and tried to convince Sterne to consult with Jelliffe. In a letter from Finney Farm in the spring of 1916, Dodge wrote to Jelliffe: "I hope you will do your best to come out tomorrow night because I notice a little change in Sterne today & you might be able to 'get' him now." Mabel's efforts to urge Sterne into treatment with Jelliffe were ultimately unsuccessful.

By the summer of 1916, Mabel had been ambivalently involved with Sterne for a year, serving as his lover, model, muse, and generous benefactor. She predictably longed for Sterne when he was away, but their reunions were regularly followed by her inevitable departure or a renewed banishment of him. Mabel remained depressed and confused, uncertain where to find her identity: "But empty of my love for Maurice I was empty indeed!" (M&S, p. 482). She despaired: "I was alone: I had to have help and I thought of Dr. Brill. He had helped Andrew [Dasburg] ... and others I knew of, and I could not go back to Jelliffe, for I didn't want to *talk*, now, I wanted to live" (M&S, pp. 497–498). Looking to yet another man for definition, at a time when Jelliffe was quite conveniently on vacation, Dodge reached out to Brill.

* * *

"A very bad Oedipus complex"

In emotional disarray, Mabel contacted A. A. Brill, who agreed to a consultation: "He saw me and told me he could not take me until later in the fall; but I told him I was badly in need of something ... I was frightened, for I felt I could not endure my terrible burden of melancholy. He said, oh, yes, I could, and he turned me away" (M&S, p. 498). She wrote to Jelliffe on July 1, 1916 to explain her defection to Brill:

> I told him [Brill] I had unwisely stopped my analysis sometime ago & asked if I could continue it with him. He said that was impossible—that he couldn't help me by continuing another man's

analysis—that he wouldn't take me as your patient, the way a general practitioner might do, temporarily.

I said that naturally I would probably have gone back to you had you been on the spot ... He said he would take me as a patient if I begin an analysis with him & continue it—& I told him I would.

In this letter, Mabel does not betray her conviction that she could not return to Jelliffe, but rather attributes her leaving to his unavailability. In *Movers and Shakers*, Mabel offered another explanation for leaving Jelliffe. At first, she considered her treatment a form of intellectual entertainment, "an absorbing game to play with oneself, reading one's motives, and trying to understand the symbols by which the soul expressed itself" (p. 439). However, after several months, she reported that the amusement had lessened and she was depressed again. Although she concluded this analysis believing that "Jelliffe couldn't really help me to understanding" (p. 467), Mabel maintained a correspondence with him for the next twenty-three years, a testament to the value she placed on their relationship, particularly on shared intellectual interests, as they continued to exchange ideas, book recommendations, and news of mutual friends.

Jelliffe's case notes from October 23, 1916 reveal that Mabel returned to him for one session, apparently to explain her decision to work with Brill: "Wanted to see you very much after you went on your vacation./ Brill./can't wait ... He would take me only if I promised not to come to S.E.J. I promised. I [i.e., Jelliffe] told her that it was duress. I had no quarrel c. M.D. but I did not take it right in part of A.A.B. & would have nothing to do c. him. He had done the same thing for several patients & I was through c. him." At this time, Brill's dismissal of Jelliffe's technique as "thoroughly Jung," expressed in his December 12, 1913 letter to Freud, was apparently being acted out in his taking patients away from Jelliffe, including Mabel.

In her memoir, Mabel recalled that analysis with Brill was strikingly different from treatment with Jelliffe:

"I have a very bad Oedipus complex ..." I began, but he interrupted me.

"Never mind about that," he said. "I want your dreams. I want you to organize your life so that you have plenty of occupation and I want you to bring me in at least one dream every time you come."

"But I hardly ever dream," I protested.

"Well, you will."

"How do you mean, 'organize' my life?" I went on, somewhat impatiently.

"Make a program for yourself and stick to it. How do you occupy yourself at home? ... Do you like to paint or write? My impression is you are out of place in the country. I think you should be working with a number of people. I may be wrong, but I believe *people* constitute your best medium." (*M&S*, p. 505)

Mabel's protest about not dreaming, intriguing in its untruthfulness, strangely belies her recording of 140 dreams during her analysis with Jelliffe. For Brill, dreams were a crucial tool for understanding the psyche, a conviction born from his reading Freud's *The Interpretation of Dreams* and his dedication to dream analysis as essential to psychoanalytic training, a position advocated by Freud himself. Brill recalled:

My own dreams were analyzed mostly by Jung, some by Bleuler, and later by Freud and Ferenczi. I had still other dreams which I analyzed myself following my return from abroad, later sending them to Freud with all the associations as well as with my interpretations. Invariably he pointed out many things that I had overlooked. As this occurred in every one of my dreams, despite the fact that I had already had considerable experience in both practice and theory, I became convinced that no one wants to look at himself as others do. (1944, p. 42)

This devotion to the dream as an opening to deeper understanding and dialogue was an approach Brill strongly valued in his work.

According to Mabel, "Brill was certain from the first that I had no use for the country, that I was wasting my life in Croton," and argued with her about her professed preference for the quiet of country life. When Mabel complained "I hate the city!" he replied:

"That doesn't make any difference. Perhaps you belong in it just the same. Why do you hate it?"

"Oh, the noise and the smells—the hurrying around after nothing! I can't stand it ..."

"It is the *norm*—the usual environment of the period you are living in. If you can't stand it, you are maladjusted. That's why you are here this morning. We're going to see about that." (*M&S*, pp. 505–506)

Brill's forceful opinions and interpretations are evident in this exchange, revealing a strong will that prevailed throughout his relationship with Mabel.

Many years later, an article by Brill asserted his firm belief in the value of city living, despite commonly held views to the contrary. "What's Wrong With Cities?" appeared in *The Saturday Evening Post* on October 17, 1931, where he proclaimed "The city is the best, the most healthful place to live" (p. 50) and "Only neurotic people are uncomfortably aware of city noise" (p. 20). With patients such as Mabel likely in mind, he defined a neurotic: "… a person who is mentally at least average, but who is incapable of controlling his emotional flow. No human being can allow his emotions full expression—the world is against this—so that the average person has to direct some of his emotions to other channels. The neurotic, because of his nature, is unable to do this properly" (p. 44). Brill was convinced that "Such people usually forget their noisy environments when they become absorbed in something fundamental, in something which deals with the primary instincts, such as hunger and love" (p. 21). Here Brill promoted his strong belief in the power of work for improving mental health, a view he pressed upon Mabel over the years with the same force and confidence he employed in his letters to her. His fierce insistence upon constructive outlets for emotions inspired Mabel's four-volume *Intimate Memories*, her extraordinarily creative and candid memoirs published in the 1930s.

In his first existing letter to Mabel Dodge, in response to lost letters from her, Brill finally conceded that the retreat offered by Finney Farm's setting in Croton was beneficial to her state of mind and creative output, despite his convictions about the city as a superior environment. As Mabel admitted, "For more than any other reason, I began to write to appease Brill, and get him off that idea of my return to town!" (*M&S*, p. 507). She had been working on two short stories about her tumultuous relationship with Sterne ("A Quarrel" and "The Parting") at the urging of Max Eastman, who published them anonymously in September and October 1916 in his journal *The Masses*. This kind of engagement with writing was work Brill clearly supported.

δ

[c. fall] 1916

Dear Mrs. Dodge,

Your letters—plus those enclosed—interested me very much. I am very glad that you are keeping away from the crowd and are assuming a healthy attitude towards the world; I feel certain that the work will do you much good in more than one way. Living alone with your son and taking a rest from the "antiquity shop" is what you really were in need of. I was naturally pleased to read Eastman's letter[1] as I think much of his abilities as a critic etc. After hearing your "Parting" I felt that you have the material, and I do not doubt that once your inhibitions will be gone you will be able to put your thoughts on paper with the same freedom as you can put them in speech. Everything depends on you. I'll do my share if you'll cooperate.

I cannot see how I can get S. to come to me for analysis. I repeatedly asked him to call on me and he promised to do so. Should he keep his promise, or rather, should he feel inclined to see me again I shall naturally indirectly urge him to be analyzed. Watchful waiting is the best and only modus operandi in this case. We shall see.

With best wishes I am,
Very Sincerely,
AAB

δ

It is interesting to read here that Brill himself had urged Sterne to consult with him. In *Movers and Shakers,* Mabel wrote: "Maurice did not feel the antagonism for Dr. Brill that he had felt for Jelliffe, and after a time he actually began to go and be analyzed himself" (p. 512). She revealed: "He seemed at times so nervous and distraught that I persuaded him to go to Dr. Brill for analytic treatment. In the course of this procedure, Dr. Brill found from Maurice's dreams that he had syphilis. He had never known that he had contracted it when he was on the island of Bali, drawing and painting" (*Doctors*, p. 34). Mabel had already been exposed to syphilis by Edwin Dodge, who admitted to her before their marriage that he was afflicted with the disease, although not "in the infectious stage" (*Doctors*, p. 33). There is no evidence to suggest that Mabel was infected at this time.

In his memoir *Shadow and Light* (1952), Sterne recalled an appointment he reluctantly scheduled with Brill around this period: "During one of my crises with Mabel, she, as usual, had blamed all our problems on my emotional difficulties and had insisted that I consult Brill. I had no money for stiff consultation fees and Brill agreed to accept a painting in lieu of payment ... After one session, Brill said to me, 'There's nothing wrong with you. All you need is a new cow'" (p. 152). If this account is accurate, it is noteworthy that Brill was so direct in his opposition to Sterne's involvement with Mabel and also that he consulted with Sterne at the same time he was seeing Mabel in analysis, exactly what Mabel had hoped Jelliffe would do, revealing a relaxed attitude about such boundaries during these early years of psychoanalysis. (In fact, Andrew Dasburg and his wife Grace Mott Johnson, a sculptor, apparently each saw Brill during their marriage.)

In his next letter to Mabel, Brill seems to be warning her against being too financially charitable with Sterne, whom she provided with room and board. In his memoir, Sterne admitted, "My financial dependence on Mabel was a terrible thing for me. However, an important reason for it was that during the short period we were together, she had antagonized not only my friends, but also those acquaintances who were potential buyers of my work" (*S&L*, p. 158).

δ

[c. fall 1916]

Dear Mrs. Dodge,

I was too busy to answer sooner and I preferred to let you solve your problem without any interference from me. When I read the first letter (you sent) of Mr. S. I felt like telling you that you should not give up any more than he wants to give and that you should appear no more anxious than he. It seemed to me that he wanted much more than he could offer and that it was a very poor bargain, to use a commercial term. I changed slightly after reading his other letters but I still think that you should be careful and not so generous. I shall discuss things more fully when I see you. The fact is that I feel that you are beginning to see things as they are and that you yourself are undergoing a change. I may be wrong. It is a pity that you have to keep right on with the complication when I thought that you were going to have a rest ...

I am always pleased to hear from you and if you receive no answer you must not stop writing. I answer when I am able and when I should.

Sincerely,
A. A. Brill

P.S. I am keeping S.'s letters for you.

δ

Brill's encouragement of Mabel's wish to correspond with him was a compelling suggestion on his part, urging her to express herself to him at any time, but also telling her he might not always respond, due to his full schedule and measured judgment of which letters merited a response. He did not turn away from this contact outside of analytic sessions but indeed supported it. This correspondence between Brill and Mabel is not unique: Freud and other pioneers in psychoanalysis maintained friendships and corresponded with patients, thereby deviating from Freud's (1912e) own recommendations about anonymity and neutrality. Freud himself wrote many letters to individuals currently or formerly in analysis with him, among them Ferenczi, H.D., and Marie Bonaparte.

Note

1. Mabel printed Eastman's letter to her in *Movers and Shakers*: "Thank you a thousand times ... You owed it to me, anyway, for didn't I tell you to do it? You have a gift and energy of creation that ought to be more sacred to you than any personal thing ... This is an intense and compelling work of art, and I hope you know it" (p. 435).

CHAPTER FIVE

"Let's go and get married!"

Mabel described Brill's assessment of her relationship with Sterne: "Dr. Brill did not seem to try to remove me from Maurice; the most he did was to insist that my feeling for him was aesthetic and not sexual, and that in that sense it was not real and direct. However, he did not press this point, for he trusted to the analytic method itself to bring a final clarification and readjustment in my ideas and feelings" (*M&S*, p. 512). However, despite the unstable and often destructive nature of their relationship, public enough for many to behold and judge, Mabel and Sterne were married on August 23, 1917. As Mabel reported, she proposed one morning:

"Let's go and get married!" I said, raising one eyebrow.
"But dearest! Why this morning? Are you sure you want to?"
A flush broke over his face and a look of pleasure.
"Yes, I want to …"
"Oh, darling! I hope we are doing the right thing!"
"Well, we're doing it anyway," I replied succinctly, getting out of bed. (*M&S*, pp. 524–525)

Sterne remembered that Mabel was watching him pack for his upcoming trip to Wyoming and offered: "Let us finish this impossible impasse and get married." He agreed, thinking she meant upon his return, but she said, "Let's get married today!" When he asked if she would join him on his travels, she responded, "Of course not!," encouraging him to go nonetheless (S&L, p. 127).

Sterne acknowledged warnings they had received about getting married and quoted from Mabel's letter to him on July 30, 1916, following her initial consultation with Brill: "Could we marry and be all in all to each other, do you think? When I write of getting over it or not being with you again it is on account of my suspicion that you don't love me truly and deeply. Brill thinks it should be worked at sensibly." Even Mabel's close friend Hutchins Hapgood expressed strong doubts, cautioning Sterne: "Watch out for that witch. In order to remake you, she will try to destroy you first" (S&L, p. 125). Despite these serious concerns, however, they impulsively chose to marry. As Mabel reported, an announcement in the *New York Herald* read: "Mrs. Mabel Dodge secretly married to Russian Artist ... 'No romance,' says Maurice Sterne, 'we just decided to wed'" (M&S, p. 526).

Brill's next letter to Mabel, reprinted in *Movers and Shakers*, is in reply to a lost letter of hers announcing her marriage.

δ

August 27, 1917

Dear Mabel,

Your letter was interesting but not surprising. For some time I anticipated the good news and I will confess that a few weeks ago I was sure that you were married. Now please accept my most cordial wishes and congratulations. You did not have to ask me to wish you luck; you realize I hope that both you and Maurice are very near my heart and that my objections were purely academic. I never said that I disapprove but I counselled [sic] waiting a bit longer. I have no doubt that you will be very happy as Maurice is a very fine fellow and as far as I know has always tried his very best to please you. I wish you to convey my best wishes to him and would like to see you soon.

As ever,
A. A. Brill

δ

Although he professed congratulatory sentiments in this letter, Mabel's account of her next meeting with Brill revealed quite opposite feelings on his part, along with his protest about making sudden decisions during analysis:

> When I motored down to my appointment with Dr. Brill ... I was very much on the defensive. I entered his office ready to fight, for I expected him to attack me. Instead, he looked at me sadly and without animosity.
> "Couldn't you have waited?" he asked.
> "Waited for *what*?" I asked in a hard voice.
> "To finish your analysis," he answered. "Then you would never have taken this step."
> "Oh, I don't know ..." I began.
> "Well, we will not argue about it. The thing is done. We will continue our work. Have you any dreams to tell me?" (*M&S*, p. 528)

His objections overruled by Mabel's strong will and impulsivity, Brill insisted on resuming the routine of their meetings.

Sterne left for what he termed his "rather novel honeymoon," recalling: "I was sure that I had not wanted to marry Mabel and that Mabel had not wanted to marry me" (*S&L*, p. 127). When he returned to New York, Mabel once more found reasons to be jealous and, according to her, banished him yet again, this time to New Mexico. She explained: "It's no use, Maurice. We can't make a go of it here. One of us must leave. And *I* want to stay here. I'm going to send you out to the Southwest. I've heard there are wonderful things to paint. Indians" (*M&S*, p. 532). Sterne, however, remembered the initiative behind his departure quite differently. Rapidly becoming disillusioned about the stability of his new marriage and having difficulty working, he consulted with Brill, who advised a "temporary separation" (*S&L*, p. 131). At the urging of a friend with acquaintances in Santa Fe, Sterne decided to travel to New Mexico, where he believed the Pueblo Indians might inspire his creative work.

After Sterne left, Mabel reported that she became ill with a swelling in her thyroid and her dreams then ceased. Brill apparently advised her to suspend treatment until she was well, but when she recovered she did not return to him, exploring instead other forms of mind cure like New Thought and mediums: "I did not resume my analysis. I was off that. It seemed to me I had gone as far as I could with Brill, and away from him I began to resent his interference with my fancies about the unseen powers and influences that appear to guide us and that are not *all*, as he would have me believe, the promptings of our own unconscious wishes" (M&S, p. 533). Mabel's adventurous spirit and passionate curiosity at times led her to more mystical approaches towards understanding human behavior, a practice Brill condemned and judged harshly, as indicated in some of his later letters.

Sterne wrote to Mabel from Santa Fe encouraging her to join him there: "Dearest Girl—Do you want an object in life? Save the Indians, their art-culture—reveal it to the world!" (M&S, p. 534). She was hesitant to leave New York and replied on December 12, 1917: "Dr. Brill told me I was not to go West—not being well enough. 'Stay here until he comes back,' he said. 'He cannot stay away from his best good forever—he knows it himself'" (S&L, p. 136). However, five days later, Mabel wrote to Sterne again, determined to make the journey against medical and psychoanalytic advice: "The plain truth is I am just dying of loneliness without you and I have to come to you … I'm no good away from you. We must learn the secret of being together" (S&L, p. 136). In her characteristic flight towards a man to secure her sense of herself—recalling Jelliffe's intake notes: "Contact with life only through an individual: absorbed in or through some man"—Mabel left New York, as well as her analysis with Brill, to be reunited with Sterne in New Mexico.

* * *

"And it was right"

Mabel joined Sterne in Santa Fe in December 1917, but reflexively disliked the city and instead chose Taos for her new home. Soon after, Mabel met Antonio Luhan, a Pueblo Indian from the Tiwa community, whom she recognized immediately from a dream she had after Sterne left for New Mexico (see Illustration 7). As she recalled in her autobiography of this period, *Edge of Taos Desert: An Escape to Reality* (1937): "[Luhan] looked at me for the first time, with a quick glance that penetrated to the depths with an instantaneous recognition, and I saw his was the face that had blotted out Maurice's in my dream—the same face, the same eyes, involuntarily intense, with the living fire in their depths" (p. 94). Mabel invited Luhan for a visit, during which he made a strong and enchanting impression with his singing. A slow courtship followed as Luhan, called Tony, introduced her to the wonders of his country and the ways of the Indians. Mabel found her new world expanding profoundly as she learned to embrace the spirituality and community of Native American life, a psychic immersion that competed with and at times replaced the psychoanalysis that Brill fiercely defended and even prescribed.

In June 1918, Mabel purchased an adobe house in Taos along with twelve acres of land (see Illustration 9). Her growing relationship with Luhan drove Sterne back to New York in August. Mabel revealed her feelings about his departure:

> I had not the courage ... to see Maurice go away. I knew it was forever, and I knew to what world he was returning. I felt I had been delivered from it and that he was still condemned. I somehow knew that I would never have to pretend to be a part of that old world again and that the need to conform to that environment, as Brill had tried to teach me to do, was really not a necessary exercise. (*ETD*, p. 320)

Considering herself newly released from the emotional and spiritual constraints of the world she had left behind, Mabel thereby refuted Brill's previous judgment that she was "maladjusted" in her aversion to the city.

Soon after Sterne left Taos, Tony Luhan and Mabel began their affair, described in the following passage that concludes *Edge of Taos Desert*:

> He bent a firm, gentle look down upon me and held out his hand, and I took it.
> "I comin' here to this tepee tonight," he said, "when darkness here. That be right?"

"Yes, Tony," I said, "that will be right."
And it was right. (p. 334)

In this moment, Mabel stepped over many boundaries in her continual search for meaning and identity. She acknowledged the crucial role of Tony's gaze as she sought her place in this new world: "Tony was working upon me continually and his influence upon me apparently came from the way he saw me, how he looked at me. From his eyes came the magnetic drag that pulled up the sleeping spirit out of the depths. As he saw me so I was slowly becoming; he saw me into being" (*ETD*, p. 321). This last evocative sentence could certainly be applied to the role of an analyst with a patient. Under Brill's gaze, Mabel had once experienced such a transformation, and would again on the several occasions she returned to him for treatment years later. However, for the moment, Tony Luhan had replaced Mabel's need for Brill.

In *The Statue of Liberty: An Old Fashioned Story of Taboos* (1947), an unpublished account of her relationship with Tony and her immersion in Native American culture, Mabel included this next letter from Brill, introducing it with: "It was not calculated to influence me!" (p. 47).

δ

March 18, 1919

My dear Mabel,

I have not written to you for a long time because, as you know, I am very busy and I really had nothing to write to you. What induces me to write to you now are all kinds of rumors that I heard, which I am inclined to lend credence to. You may not like my butting in but I know that if you will realize you will know that my doing so is purely in a friendly spirit and that I have no other interest in the matter except my friendly regard for both you and Maurice. Incidentally I wish to say that I have not seen him until last Saturday when I asked him to call on me so as to see whether he could give me any information. He was in very poor spirits and as he put it: "all I hear are rumors. I am the last man to whom people would come and tell things"; but from my own information I feel that you are making a great mistake, and as you know me to talk straight from the shoulder I shall talk frankly to you, realizing fully well that you are <u>not</u> going to take my advice.

Now don't you think that you ought to have some regard for the future and give up all that ridiculous mystical Indian business. Everybody thinks you are crazy and if everything that I hear is really so, as an alienist, I would agree with them; the game is too dangerous if not altogether crazy. I again wish to assure you that I am telling you that in the friendliest of spirit, and am very anxious to hear from you if you will take it as it is given. On the other hand, I will feel that I have done my duty to an old friend.

Very sincerely yours,
A. A. Brill

δ

In his letter, Brill forcefully declared Mabel "crazy" and derided as "ridiculous" her current adoption of an Indian way of life. Mabel, however, was far beyond Brill's influence at this moment, for she had entered into a full embrace:

> How I envied tribal life!
>
> Although all my life I had made every effort to break away, and successfully, away from my family, my schools, my group of girl friends, and finally away from one husband after another; yet my longing had always been some kind of social unity. Somehow to escape the solitary hours, the <u>lonesome</u> aloneness I always felt when I was by myself …
>
> When I reached Taos the life of the tribe seemed at last, perfect to me. All these people living in their closeness had the fulfilled look I had missed in other places and particularly in my own! (*Statue*, pp. 41–42)

In stark contrast to this tribal life, Mabel decided hers was "empty and meaningless" and realized that Indians, unlike her, "did not rely upon their sex life to make them whole and satisfied" (p. 45). She resolved to complete her conversion in her characteristically appropriating style: "'This will be mine,' I thought when I crossed the barrier between Tony and myself and I sought in every way to become like one of them as I turned away from my own kind. I wore a shawl and moccasins and I sat upon the roof in the sun and adopted the repose and the calm of the

"The beating heart of the world"

Not unexpectedly, given the vagaries of her emotional life, Mabel's familiar depression eventually returned. She may well have taken Brill's advice in his last letter when she returned to New York in April 1919 to explore from a distance her new life and involvement with Tony Luhan. In *An Intimation* (1929), Mabel's fictional account of their relationship, her character Martia is urged by Tony's counterpart Jose to visit New York:

> Finally the gentle elation of her life began to leak away and she grew depressed as so often in the past. She tried to hide it from Jose as best she could, but it was impossible to hide anything from one who knew things through the pores of his skin! They had small need to talk or to tell, between them ... Though she grew depressed, she did not grow less loving now ...
>
> He who was so wise, told her to go away for a little while. To go back to New York and see her friends for a short visit. She did not want to go. In her depression she did not want anything much. But she went. (p. 11)

It is uncertain whether Mabel met with Brill during this visit. She may have been disinclined to see him, as she noted: "The way of life of the Indians had banished the schematic solution of Psychoanalysis and left me without any theories or methods but only a nameless wonder that defied analysis" (*Statue*, p. 67). While in New York, however, and in dramatic opposition to psychoanalysis, Mabel did consult with Mrs. Lotus Dudley, an occultist who insisted she had something to communicate. At their first meeting, Dudley pulled her own sleeve back and showed Mabel her bare forearm:

> The blue veins on her wrist formed a small pulsating heart ...
> "Do you know," she went on with more hesitation, "that Taos is the beating heart of the world?"

> I started a little for I remembered Tony's words had been the same, and all at once I was drawn back from <u>nowhere</u> and I became present and aware again. (*Statue*, p. 68)

Dudley spoke about Taos as the home of "a particular truth that has been kept alive on earth for centuries" by the Indians "until the time when they can hand it over to the white man." She insisted Mabel had a significant role to play in Taos when the secret was to be revealed: "When the time comes … a bridge will be needed between the Indians and the white people, and *you have been chosen to be that bridge*" (p. 69, emphasis added). Mabel soon returned to New Mexico, emboldened by this encounter and resolved to lure important figures to Taos. Among those who came and sometimes stayed were Andrew Dasburg, social worker and activist John Collier, and writers Mary Austin and D. H. Lawrence. Strengthened by imagining herself as fulfilling a purpose, Mabel settled back into life in Taos. She supervised additions to her adobe home while dedicating herself to the preservation of Pueblo culture and lands, as well as development of an artistic community.

Mabel also deliberately deepened her relationship with Tony Luhan. As she reported, she took a decisive step towards him and his world:

> "Tony! You know if we come together now there's no turning back. Do you feel that?"
>
> "Yes." He nodded. "I know this not play. This forever."
>
> "I mean, I know it is like going across a deep gulf on a bridge that goes with me, is gone when I reach you. I will not be able to return because you will make all of my own kind of life unreal for me. It has always been more or less unreal—you will make it impossible."
>
> "I give you a new life, a new world—a true one, I think." (*ETD*, p. 331)

The profound implications of Mabel's decision cannot be minimized. For a white woman at that time to leave behind her culture and background to cross a racial barrier was a revolutionary and daring step.

* * *

Although no letters exist between Mabel and Brill after March 18, 1919 until August 11, 1922, her letter to Jelliffe on September 24,

1921 indicated that she was seeking contact with Brill: "Also I want to hear what Brill says ... & I want you please to post this to him after answering it—to save me copying it all out." Mabel described to Jelliffe in very specific and elaborate details the sexual problems of her childhood friend from Buffalo, Nina Witt, asking for his opinion: "She has a pronounced skin eroticism & is unable to experience orgasm except with a terrific strain ... This however is very rare—she usually only craves & allows caressing of the skin over the body. Any further act is repulsive to her." Jelliffe replied on December 3, 1921, concluding Witt was "woozy." Mabel was apparently satisfied with Jelliffe's dismissive explanation, answering on December 10, 1921: "You corroborated what I had already made up my mind to—that the lady is poco loco." There is no evidence that Brill ever received Mabel's letter; no response from him has been located. It is striking that Mabel wrote so frankly about the particulars of sex and freely sought consultation with her former analysts about the intimate problems of another woman, thus revealing the current climate in some circles of more open dialogue about very personal matters.

Since Brill's last surviving letter to Mabel in 1919, he had been to Europe and visited Freud, as indicated by a postcard from both men, sent to his wife, Rose, on September 2, 1921: "Had a delightful meeting and talk with the professor and feel like a new man. Love Abe" and "Glad to see your husband and find he is the same good boy I knew him before. My best love to you and the children. Freud" (SFA).

A lost letter from Mabel in 1922 invited Brill to Taos. He replied, saying that he was boarding a ship to Europe, and then wrote again from Geneva.

δ

August 11, 1922

Dear Mabel,

I did not answer your letter sooner because it actually drew me to Taos, and if I could have been able to make any arrangements I certainly would have come; but I am sailing on the 19th of this month, and it was absolutely impossible to take sufficient time for a trip of this kind. I am sure that I will be in Taos sooner or later, in order to enjoy all the nice things that you have at your disposal.

With my personal regards to all your friends, I am,

As ever,
AAB.

δ

September 4, 1922

Dear Mabel,

This is a wonderful place and I enjoy it immensely ...

Kindest greetings,
Yours,
A. A. Brill

δ

In this correspondence, Brill has abandoned his former critical stance towards Mabel's behavior in Taos and even considered visiting New Mexico himself, which he will eventually do in 1937.

CHAPTER SIX

Lawrence: "Is Taos the place?"

In November 1921, Mabel had written to D. H. Lawrence inviting him and his wife, Frieda, to Taos after reading his *Sons and Lovers* (1913), *Psychoanalysis and the Unconscious* (1921), and, most influentially, *Sea and Sardinia* (1921). As she reported in her memoir about their relationship, *Lorenzo in Taos* (1932):

> It was after reading *Sea and Sardinia* that I wrote to him to come to Taos. That is one of the most actual of travel books, I think; for in it, in that queer way of his, he gives the feel and touch and smell of places so that their reality and their essence are open to one, and one can step right into them ...
>
> I wrote him a long letter. I told him all that I could about Taos and the Indians—and about Tony and me. I told him how much I wanted him to come and know that country before it became exploited and spoiled. (p. 16)

Lawrence's travel writing in particular inspired Dodge's attempt to lure him to New Mexico, where she believed he could help articulate her experience with Native American culture, thereby broadening the scope of her audience: "I wanted Lawrence to understand things for me. To take *my* experience, *my* material, *my* Taos, and to formulate it all into a magnificent creation. That was what I wanted him for" (p. 77). She strongly believed that Lawrence would prove to be an impassioned and accurate observer of Taos, and that his words would eloquently describe its ineffable qualities.

Lawrence replied to Mabel's letter on November 5, 1921 from his home in Sicily: "Truly, the q-b [Queen Bee, Frieda's nickname] and I would like to come to Taos … I believe what you say—one must somehow bring together the two ends of humanity, our own thin end, and the last dark strand from the previous, pre-white era. I verily believe that. Is Taos the place? … I want to leave Europe. I want to take the next step. Shall it be Taos?—I like the *word*" (*LIT*, pp. 17–18). By the time Lawrence arrived in Taos almost a year later, he and Mabel had exchanged many letters about ideas, artists, and psychoanalysis.

Mabel had been powerfully drawn to Lawrence's writings about psychoanalysis, an enthusiasm she shared in her correspondence with both Jelliffe and Brill. In a letter to Jelliffe on October 9, 1921, she had written about *Psychoanalysis and the Unconscious*: "Have you read D. H. Lawrence's remarkable book? I am having Brentano [New York bookstore] send it to you. It seems to me to establish at last the great, clear distinction between the mental unconscious where we suppress our ideas about desires & things, & the true unconscious, source of desire." Later, however, Mabel began to have serious doubts about Lawrence's views. In a letter to her on December 4, 1921, he wrote: "I rather hate therapy altogether—doctors, healers, and all the rest. I believe that a real neurotic is a half devil, but a cured neurotic is a perfect devil. They assume perfect conscious and automatic control when they're cured: and it is just this conscious-automatic control that I find loathsome … I would prefer that the neurotics died." Mabel then reported: "Now in this letter I had my first shock from that man. He whom I was trying to draw to Taos because he seemed to me to have more consciousness than anyone alive was inimical to conscious activity! I was unable, then, to understand what he meant." Trying to grasp Lawrence's meaning, she wondered: "Could one really live, then I wondered, by impulse, by letting 'It' decide, as I had believed years ago until the Freudian analysts had deprived me of my faith in 'hunches' and in intuitions?" (*LIT*, p. 25). In her memoirs, Mabel referred to ways she believed her analysis with Brill had deprived her of a connection with her instincts: "Gradually coming under his influence, I altered my convictions and lost a good deal of color out of my life along with the surplus of tension. It took me some time to recover my indisputable realization of the Force that may be directed, but that, directed or not, rules all life" (*M&S*, p. 512). It seems that Mabel's passionate immersion in Tony Luhan's world was a kind of antidote to the flatness or colorlessness she experienced at times in her work with Brill.

In the early fall of 1922, D. H. and Frieda Lawrence (see Illustration 11) arrived in Taos as guests of Mabel Sterne and Tony Luhan. From the beginning, the relationship between Lawrence and Mabel was intense and stormy, full of conflict and drama, yet at the same time contained a validation of Mabel's initial goal for his visit: "I had been right about one thing in him: He *could* see and feel and wonder" (*LIT*, p. 16). Mabel, who was going through menopause at the time, believed that in her transformed state she could serve as a preferred muse for Lawrence, a compelling alternative to the influence of his wife. In *Lorenzo in Taos*, Mabel described her early observation of the dynamic between Lawrence and Frieda: "He felt things through her and was obliged to receive life through her, vicariously; but that he was irked by her vision; that he was impatient at being held back in the sex scale … She was the mother of orgasm and of the vast, lively mystery of the flesh. But no more. Frieda was complete, but limited. Lawrence, tied to her, was incomplete and limited" (p. 45). This perception of life lived through another bears an uncanny resemblance to ways Mabel characterized her younger self with Jelliffe and also in her autobiographical writings, thus leading her to a powerful identification with Lawrence: "Can it be possible that it was in that very first instant when we all came together that I sensed Lawrence's plight and that the womb in me roused to reach out to take him? … I longed to help him with that—to be used—to be put to his purpose" (*LIT*, p. 45). Mabel strove to insert herself into his world.

To further this goal, Mabel wrote Lawrence a poem about her experience of menopause, a gripping illustration of both her emancipated state and willingness to openly acknowledge female sexuality. Entitled "Change," written around 1922 and published in *Palms* in 1924, her poem begins with a lengthy mourning of the loss of bleeding—"Languidly dying month by month/Recedence of life in every cell … / Gradual fatigue of the pigment/And departure! Departure everywhere!"—and describes her despair over the drain of color from her life: "Scarlet days fading out to white,/What shall I do in white days, God?" Although she initially agonizes over her inevitably pale and parched existence, towards the end of the poem, Mabel discovers a hidden blessing in the end of her fertility and her subsequent sense of empowerment: "Blessed change!/You see, my own, how the heart opens/To the new occupation?/ ... This is the happy time" (pp. 136–138). Mabel felt liberated by the end of menstruation, newly available for exciting artistic and spiritual endeavors.

Under the strain of her intense striving for a creative marriage of minds with Lawrence, combined with Frieda's jealousy, Lawrence's own role in the rivalry, and his violently ambivalent feelings about Mabel, Lawrence and Frieda left Taos after only two months, moving to Mabel's ranch in the mountains north of Taos in order to live further away from her control and gaze. They eventually traveled to Mexico in the spring of 1923, not to return until the following spring.

Soon after Lawrence's departure, Mabel became deeply reengaged with Indian political affairs, actively working with her friend John Collier. In 1922, she had become fervently involved in opposing the Bursum Bill, introduced that year into the United States Congress as a measure that would likely strip the Pueblos of tens of thousands of acres. This was the first time in the history of the United States that the protection of Indian lands, cultures, and rights developed into a national movement. Mabel was swept up in the controversial cause and sought support from many of her old connections in New York. She had helped Collier, who was vigorously working to defeat the bill, to gather signatures for the "Protest of Artists and Writers Against the Bursum Bill." Mabel had been reluctant to attract too much publicity to her own role in opposing the bill, concerned that her affair with Luhan would create serious controversy and jeopardize their efforts. As early as November 21 of a year noted by Rudnick as "1922?," she wrote to Collier that she would marry Tony if doing so "will make it more convenient from the worldly standpoint" (Rudnick, 1984, p. 179, n. 66). After the Bursum Bill was defeated in January 1923, its supporters sponsored another bill also aimed at depriving Indians of their land. In this next campaign, Collier advised Mabel that those supporting the new bill would likely target her and that public knowledge of her relationship with Luhan would be damaging to the cause. Mary Austin learned that an attorney for the United States government was warning of threats against Mabel's friends for their support of Indian rights, causing her and others to support Mabel's marriage to Tony (Rudnick, 1984, pp. 175–182). Mabel recounted this story:

The Department of Justice came into the embroilment. Inspectors arrived to size up the Taos situation and decided that my house was the centre of disturbance; that I was instigating all the trouble for the government ... When Tony and I were found living there unmarried, they tried to use that weakness to quell me, to drive me away from the Indians and Taos. Tony was a ward of the government. Very well ...

I do not suppose it occurred to them that I was not the kind they could manage. Tony and I were quietly married. Nothing could make me give him up, nothing will ever make me give him up. (*LIT*, p. 113)

Mabel's resolve not to be influenced by intimidating threats is a striking illustration of her firm belief in her right to marry whomever she chose and consequently to lead an unconventional life.

* * *

Brill's next letter is in response to a lost letter from Mabel that likely reported on her current emotional collapse in response to her embittered relationship with Lawrence: "Life was too much for me. One morning when I was lacing my shoe, I lost consciousness and remained away from myself for twenty-four hours—having a vacation from it all, lying on the bed with a smile on my face while doctors worked round, giving me all kinds of medicine, and Tony sat on the floor praying" (*LIT*, p. 112).

δ

March 15, 1923

My dear Mabel,

I was very delighted to receive your letter. It shows me that you are alright, that you have no aphasia; but I am, however, a bit alarmed over the fact that you had a temporary aphasia. If the doctors find absolutely nothing wrong with you organically, then I think that you ought to be looked after mentally, because if one shows a tendency to such temporary aphasia it means that there is something there that must be thoroughly cleared out. I realize all the stress and strain that you have gone through, but even so, you should not have reacted to it in this fashion.

Again I must withhold my approval of another marriage. I see no reason for it, and it will simply involve you in something else. You know I also strenuously objected to your Sterne venture. However, I am quite willing to see the other side of it. I do not think that Collier is any judge to advise you in such matters.

I am very pleased to know what you are doing, and hope that you will keep me informed.

As ever,
A. A. Brill

δ

CHAPTER SEVEN

"An irrevocable step!"

Despite Brill's opposition to a union between Mabel and Luhan, they were married in Taos on April 23, 1923, with Andrew Dasburg and his companion the feminist and artist Ida Rauh as their only witnesses. An article in *The New York World* from April 28, 1923 quoted Mabel explaining that "business considerations" had played a role in her decision to marry. The headlines in papers across the country revealed the intrigue that her marriage generated. On April 29, 1923, *The New York World* announced: "Patron of Arts, Indian's Bride, Enjoying Her Fourth Honeymoon: Mabel Evans-Dodge-Sterne-Lujan Now Dwells in Radical Art Colony in New Mexico, After Spectacular Career in Italy and New York." In "Why Bohemia's Queen Married An Indian Chief" from the *Pittsburgh Post* (June 19, 1923), the story is somewhat cattily told that Mabel "enjoyed the companionship of the Pueblos more than that of many of her civilized friends and is said to have often expressed the wish that she were really one of them" (in Luhan scrapbook, *Untitled*).

Before their marriage, Mabel had contracted syphilis from Tony. Her abrupt awareness of infection was preceded by an evocative and painful memory triggered by smelling a blood-streaked sheet Tony had draped over himself when he returned home one night after sex with another woman. As Mabel recalled, when she perceived the odor, "... an old memory rushed back to me":

> There was a dream I had had years ago and told to Dr. Brill. The dream was overwhelming, yet it was only about an odor. A strange unknown effluvia that assaulted me with menace and threat and it was accompanied by a voice I had never heard before that uttered meaningly [sic]: "That is the odor of evil."...
>
> So on that night, lying in the darkness beneath the pillow I lived again through the same terror and despair of the first dream experience. For I recognized then for the first time what the nature of that odor was ... For me now the primitive, physiological character of the smell of the seminal fluid was evil, deadly and destructive. (*Statue*, pp. 166–167)

Mabel explained: "Tony and I came down with the inevitable sign of syphilis on the intimate parts of our body. Three times and out. The third husband who had syphilis, all of them dignified and rather eminent men in their various situations" (*Doctors*, p. 44). They were both treated with weekly shots of Salversan 606 (arsenic), the standard treatment at that time, with a recommended length of eighteen months of shots to cure the disease when detected in its early phases (Rudnick, 1984, p. 347, n. 59). However, according to Mabel's account, she and Tony received injections only for the summer and winter months and "At the end of this winter we considered ourselves cured. Anyway, we avoided by the treatment the other phases of the disease" (*Doctors*, p. 45).

In Brill's next letter, his concern about Mabel's health and his mention of the "best works in some diseases" may refer to his knowledge of her syphilis. The persecution that Brill addresses likely has to do with Mabel's recent experiences of being threatened because of her support of Indian rights and her relationship with Luhan.

δ

May 1, 1923

My dear Mabel,

My most cordial congratulations to you and Tony [and] may your troubles now be over for all times. My objections to marriage were based in all probabilities on ignorance of all the facts involved but I meant well. I am sure Mabel that you understand me. Besides I felt a bit worried over your physical constitution and I wanted you to come here. I am not altogether unprejudiced in this matter but I can't help feeling that the best works in some diseases are done in this section of the country and I wanted you here. I still feel so especially as you are somewhat susceptible to some of the medicine. Moreover I'll be frank to tell you that I wanted to do a bit of investigation about your so[-]called "break down[.]" I am not satisfied to let such things go after a superficial patching particularly when it concerns a sensitive being like you. In brief there are many moral (not theological) and physical reasons for my attitude. I felt that all of you are either persecuted or are suffering from delusions of persecution and I thought that it would be best to get you out of there for a while, at least, and put you at rest as far as your psychic and physical make[-]up is concerned. When I received the message from Andrew [Dasburg] I was debating it for days but when I found that it could mean at least 3–4 weeks I could not make up my mind to do it. I have to finish my courses at the University[1] and examine my students by the middle of the month. I am involved in 3 hospitals[2] and last but not least I could not do it financially. You see Mabel I could more than double my income if I acted like the others but I cannot do it. If I find a person worth while [sic] I treat him money or no money, consequently although I am a good earner I have to stay on the job. But had it been in June I would have come. Your marriage as such is not at all wrong but I was not sure of the other matters and I still feel that if you could come here and be a little bit overhauled it would do good.

My family joins me in wishing you good luck happiness and health.

As Ever,
Brill

P.S. Not knowing Tony's name I am forced to address you as Sterne.

δ

Although Brill suggested in his letter that Mabel "get out of there" and come to New York to get "a little bit overhauled," his serious consideration of making a diagnostic and therapeutic trip to visit her in Taos is a striking illustration of the more relaxed attitudes that existed at this time in psychoanalysis. Freud and other early analysts also had contacts with patients outside of their offices. Freud met with patients on his vacations (Gabbard, 1995, p. 1124), Ferenczi took a patient with him on holiday to continue her analysis, and during vacation Melanie Klein occasionally analyzed patients on her hotel bed (Fortune, 1993, p. 108).

Others were not as kind as Brill about Mabel's marriage to Tony. Gertrude Stein, who enjoyed any scandal about Mabel, wrote to Van Vechten on May 31, 1923, responding to the clipping he had sent from *The New York World* citing her "business reasons": "Dasburg said that Antonio deserted Mabel two days after the wedding, that might account for one's not hearing from her but it does not sound very likely does it. Business reasons are business reasons." And again on August 5, 1923: "Not a word from Mabel at all. Lo, the poor Indian" (CVVC).

In *Family Affairs* (1933), an unpublished and strikingly frank autobiographical account of her family relationships, Mabel wrote about the effect of her marriage to Tony on both her son and mother: "It had almost crushed John, and John told me it had almost crushed my mother" (p. 16). John had always been strongly and ambivalently connected to Mabel, as revealed in letters and poems he sent her over the years, and was often jealous of her relationship with Tony. (John himself had recently married Alice Henderson in Santa Fe on December 20, 1922.)

Mabel was highly aware of the monumental leap she had taken in marrying Luhan: "An irrevocable step! To pass across from one's race to another is an irrevocable step" (*Statue*, p. 3). In her poem, *Inevitable* (c. 1923), she acknowledged: "What incomprehensible aloneness for the white woman/Who crosses over into the indian [sic] heart!" However, Mabel also realized the profound and unique rewards of entering such a different world, a transformation she had once fervently sought through psychoanalysis:

> With Tony I could change into something more acceptable in my own eyes, and I was changing slowly, though the world sought to separate us and made life difficult ... When I identified myself in imagination with my race and knew I had broken its barrier and left it and crossed to the other side to stand with these dark men, their river of blood dividing me forever from my own kind, I had a sense of drowning horror at having done the impossible act.

> But when I was just myself and disentangled from my family, I knew I had done what I was meant to do, and I had a deeper feeling of rightness than I had ever had before ...
>
> This right action in marrying Tony, never lost its validity in my judgment. I have always known it was right, nothing can ever make me think or feel otherwise. (*FA*, pp. 12, 17)

Mabel's instincts proved accurate: Tony Luhan was her fourth and final husband. They remained together until her death in 1962, and Tony died the following year.

Severing her racial identification with her family proved a life-changing decision for Mabel, as she began to experience a crucial shift in her sense of herself, a feeling that things were as they should be, a hard-won and previously elusive state. *Inevitable* ends with her celebrating the safety she feels in Tony's presence: "No security for me like the certainty of this unknowable man./He is more than father ... /I am at home." Mabel also told "how we suc[c]eeded in spite of conflict and terror, of mishap and misadventure until finally everyone gave in and agreed: 'You have put it over,' and Dr. Brill conceded: 'You are in the saddle now. No one can unseat you'" (*Statue*, p. 3).

In Brill's next letter, in response to lost correspondence from Mabel, he acknowledges her rejuvenated circumstances.

δ

September 26, 1923

My dear Mabel,

Your letter and telegram came while I was away, and as to you, I was very pleased to hear of your state, and was not at all surprised when you told me you are well adjusted; I expected you to do so, and I have a great deal of confidence in your recuperative powers. I was extremely sorry that I could not visit you last Spring; this season is the hardest time for me when it is a question of going for any vacation; there are all those so-called medical Spring meetings which one has to attend; and last but not least, I felt that a quick psychoanalytic dose is not effective enough. As you are aware, my idea of the work is to give it time, and unless one gives it time one cannot get very much out of it.

What you say about Nina [Witt] interested me; it did not really occur to me that she is going to come; I know her changeable disposition, and I am not enthusiastic about having her as a patient; I had a taste of them [Nina and her husband, Lee Witt] last year, and was quite pleased when they stopped coming. The only way I would take her would be if she would come alone, without him, and guarantee that she would stay at least six months, otherwise I think it would be a waste of time and money.

I had a nice but short trip to Europe, and have gained a great deal by it. Everything here is just as of old, as I suppose it is with you.

With my kindest regards to you all, I am,

As ever,
AAB

δ

Sharing with Mabel his feelings about former patient Nina Witt, Brill revealed an apparently more casual approach to confidentiality that existed towards the beginning of psychoanalysis in America. As a physician, Brill would have been expected to honor the Hippocratic Oath, which includes the obligation to guard the privacy of information: "What I may see or hear in the course of the treatment ... in regard to the life of men, which on no account one must spread abroad, I will keep to myself holding such things shameful to be spoken about" (Edelstein, 1943, p. 3). However, as illustrated by his letters to Mabel, Brill sometimes divulged intimate details about patients. In correspondence with Brill, Freud also mentioned names of patients, as in a letter from February 20, 1920: "I am now treating a New York dentist, whom you also know, Dr. Bieber. He is making very good progress." And when Brill's daugher, Gioia, was in analysis, Freud revealed to Brill, in a letter dated November 25, 1934, that her analyst, Lillian Delger Powers, was a former patient of his whose "interest at the time was devoted entirely to squirrels" (SFA).

Notes

1. Most likely New York University.
2. Brill was on the staff of the New York Psychiatric Institute as well as, over the course of his career, Bellevue, Beth Israel, Neurological, Bronx, and Post-Graduate hospitals.

CHAPTER EIGHT

Lawrence again

No longer able to tolerate their rupture, Mabel wrote to D. H. Lawrence in Mexico and he replied immediately on October 17, 1923: "Yes, I was pretty angry. But now let us forget it. At least I will forget, forget the bad part. Because also I have some beautiful memories of Taos. That, perhaps, is what makes the sting burn longer" (*LIT*, p. 117). Renewed contact with Lawrence was crucial for Mabel: he championed her efforts at transformation and understood her opportunity for meaningful change from her union with Tony. In this same letter, he suggested: "You have striven so hard, and so long, to *compel* life. Can't you now slowly change, and let life slowly drift into you. Surely it is even a greater mystery ... to let the invisible life steal into you and slowly possess you." He also observed: "When I say in my book: 'one cannot go back,' it is true, one cannot. But your marriage with Tony may even yet be the rounding of a great curve; since certainly he doesn't merely draw you back, but himself advances perhaps more than you advance, in the essential 'onwards'" (*LIT*, p. 118). Lawrence's ability to speak so directly to Mabel about her character and her marriage is reminiscent of the forceful ways Brill advised her in his letters.

When Lawrence arrived in London in December 1923, he sent Mabel a letter reassuring her of their connection: "Remember I am depending on your spirit at the back of me ... I am glad when I hear you feel relieved of the old tension" (*LIT*, p. 126). Mabel wrote of their resumed friendship: "My heart was lightened by being in touch again with Lorenzo" (*LIT*, p. 121). In this intervening time before Lawrence returned to Taos in the spring of 1924, he and Mabel exchanged frequent letters and reached a truce. She then began to write, largely attributing to him—as she once had to Brill—the drive behind this renewed engagement: "His gradual influence upon me was ... to make me more conscious, more careful, and more understanding! I was writing in these days, painfully, yet, but how it helped me to clear up in my mind the turgid and unexpressed volume of energy that was so hard to carry along!" (*LIT*, p. 131).

Mabel wrote poems for Lawrence and sent them to him in January 1924, including the highly autobiographical "The Ballad of a Bad Girl." She abandoned her former efforts to seduce him into collaboration and took a new approach: "I submitted my will to him and told him so. I luxuriated in submission for a change and hoped I pleased him by it" (*LIT*, p. 128). "The Ballad" is a direct expression of this shift and an appeal to Lawrence. It begins:

> When I was a baby, Mother pushed me from my cradle,
> But I didn't fall! Oh no, sir! Tho' it's odd, odd, odd.
> I snatched up in the hall Father's silver-headed walking-stick
> And, a-straddle it I hastened after God, God, God. (p. 1)

The poem then describes the girl's ascent into the heavens, learning secrets along the way while "Father died raving, and Mother? Mother married again." When she reaches God, the girl approaches him cautiously and is about to "plunge my eager hand within his burning breast,/When out of his heart there up and jumped a very, very angry man,/With blue, blue eyes and a red, red crest." This man, identifiable as Lawrence by both his appearance and her intended audience, yells at her to leave: "Quit that! Get out of here! Down, down, down you go!/Back, back to earth where you belong./This is no place for women here! Don't you know your business?" (p. 2). He kicks her down to earth and along the way she learns a secret: "That a Woman can be saved by a fall, fall, fall!" The poignant last two lines reveal the painful absence of a maternal figure in Mabel's own life: "Then I lay down in the pansy bed and whispered: 'Mother! mother me,/And teach me how to mother and that's all, all, all!'" (p. 3). This poem illustrates Mabel's sudden rejection of her previous stance on feminism, as well as her independence as a woman with liberated life choices. In an undated letter to Carl Van Vechten, Mabel explained that her poem was "an indictment against all Feminism & an earnest appeal to women to leave off trying to steal the world away from men—& to return to their original function—motherhood. Whatever that is" (CVVC). This abrupt change is best understood in the context of Mabel's current efforts to please Lawrence by being less forceful, more accommodating to his way of seeing her, as explained by him: "Your poems do amuse me. But I am not going to think of you as a writer ... the essential you, for me, doesn't know and could never write" (*LIT*, p. 130). Lawrence preferred his Mabel more passive and less knowing.

Mabel sent "The Ballad" to Brill and Jelliffe, as well as to Leo Stein and Van Vechten, and Brill replies with a critical interpretation.

δ

February 26, 1924

Dear Mabel,

Your ballad, which I have read with a great deal of pleasure and interest, is certainly clever. Perhaps, I cannot see altogether through it, but I feel that I understand it.

The basic ideas and symbolisms are very good and altogether I was surprised at your display of poetic talent. There is only one thing that I did not like and that is probably the reason why I did not write to you before. It seems to me that you are trying to get a great deal of what we call 'grim humor' out of a serious situation. Now, do not say to yourself "there he is again with his Jeremiad [i.e., complaint]," but you asked me to tell you what I thought of it, so here it is.

I confess that I do not see as much mysticism and other stuff in it that others might; I naturally read it in terms of yourself.

As ever,
A. A. Brill

δ

But Mabel received much praise for her poem—published with an illustration by D. H. Lawrence in the May 1924 issue of *Laughing*

Horse, a small magazine founded by writer Walter Willard "Spud" Johnson—from other sources. Leo Stein wrote in an undated 1924 letter: "It's bully! Write some more"; Jelliffe replied on March 13, 1924 that he "enjoyed it very much ... I think you must have had a pretty good scream. I chuckled over a number of the stanzas myself"; and Van Vechten was particularly enthusiastic, writing on June 13, 1924: "It has vigour, glamour, and interest—all the essentials of ART. I love the moral and aesthetic ending of the fall—not into Hell but into the pansy bed. More than all it seems to be the complete solution of the Oedipus Complex—and should therefore be <u>required reading</u> at any Institution where the elements of psychoanalysis are taught." So Brill's critique must have been particularly troubling. In his next letter, answering a lost missive from Mabel, Brill reassures her of his friendship, encouraging her to see his response as an honest reflection of his concern for her.

δ

[c. spring 1924]

Dear Mabel,

Your letter tells me how you were affected by my letter. I feel sorry that you should feel, what shall I say, so agitated over it. No, it is not the situation in the Ballad as a Ballad that I had in mind but the ballad as a production by Mabel. I mean by this that no one is capable of writing ballads or anything else without putting oneself into it. All inspirational literature is fundamentally a conscious or unconscious expression of one's own conflicts. Now I really believe that you are describing your own life in this ballad and that you truly believe that your life, considered in terms of present standards, has not been a success. But you cleverly, I might say, forcibly reject this and strive to make a success out of a failure. And when I say this I do not necessarily mean Tony. Perhaps Tony represents "the redemption through falling." I don't know but that you [are] perfectly right when you say that he is the only one that could move you. Now Mabel please remember that I never "make hateful insinuations." I am known to talk straight from the shoulder, and surely I always did this when it concerned you. Now let me review: I strenuously objected to Maurice and to Tony. In both cases I felt that you were descending to a lower level in your flight from reality. In the case of M. you'll probably admit that I was right. In the case of Tony, you surely will not. I wished you well when you married M. and certainly also when you married T. That has nothing to do with my convictions. I have a strong affection for you and wish you well whether you take my advice or not. But when it comes to telling facts it is a different matter. As far as I know I am unbiased when it concerns you. I have no axe to grind nor do I wish anything. I always liked you for your sake although you rarely ever listened to me. Nor do [I] recall ever obtruding myself with advice and suggestions. You ask why not leave well enough alone? I certainly did and cannot help if my remark stirred your complex in this rather forcible way, had I anticipated it I would not have have [sic] said it. But as I did stir you to resentment etc. I feel sorry and wish to say that perhaps it is best that it came out in this fashion. I am not just interested in the immediate present. I am also thinking of the future. If you imagine that I could be calmed by a nice external appearance and ignore all other facts, you don't know me. And so I feel that it would [be] better for you to looks [sic] at things from more than just one angle. It so happens that I do care what will happen to you later and although I say nothing I betray my feelings sometimes.

Now drop this matter. You can always be assured of genuine friendship from me.

As Ever,
Brill

δ

In this letter, Brill spoke forcefully to Mabel, unapologetic about telling the truth as he sees it, thereby establishing his role as a benevolent and caring authority who has a certain view of her, obtained primarily through her psychoanalysis with him. Brill soon came to accept her relationship with Tony, as she reported in a letter to Leo Stein, c. January 1925: "Tony & I get along well & our incongruous match has been accepted (except by a few unfulfilled wishers who watch to see it dissolve). But <u>Brill</u> of all people likes Tony & says he's just right for me & a good protection!!!" (GLSC).

* * *

"Work!"

In the spring of 1924, the Lawrences returned to Taos and, despite the softening of hostilities from their sustained correspondence, the familiar tensions returned once they were back, fueled by jealousies, strong wills, and extreme emotions. Lawrence, in fact, often seemed moved to violence towards Mabel. As she described, after a particularly angry exchange, he admitted to her:

> "Well, I can't stand a certain way you walk ..."
> "Oh! Oh!" I interrupted, sobbing at him, "you want to *kill* me, that's what you want!"
> "No—o," he replied, in a hesitating voice. "Not exactly." (*LIT*, p. 192)

Soon after, the screenwriter Clarence Thompson, a mutual friend, warned her about Lawrence: "Mabel, do you know that that man is determined to *kill* you?" Frieda had apparently confided in Thompson, as he reported to Mabel: "She says he has *told* her he will destroy you ... She says she is *scared*" (*LIT*, p. 215). Under the strain of this unrelenting and potentially fatal connection to Lawrence, Mabel left Taos and returned to Finney Farm in the early fall of 1924.

During this period, Mabel arranged to meet with Brill. As she explained, "I was shaken and stricken ... In a final panic I hastened to New York to consult Dr. Brill, good old Brill":

> He said he had been waiting for the time to come when I must face—what? Well, I had been lucky. Luckier than anyone he'd ever known, to have gone on as long as I had ... without sublimating! Here I'd lived all these years in the primary urges and perceptions of youth ... There I was now, though, up against a need to—well, he called it *work*!
> ... I'd always scoffed at *work*! It always seemed to me the most pitiful escape, unless one had to, for economic reasons.
> "Well," said Brill, "you've *got* to work for your *living*!" I saw he meant I must work or die. (*LIT*, pp. 245–246)

Brill, with his characteristic certainty, prescribed work to soothe Mabel's distress, convinced this would sublimate her primitive urges.

He likely considered Mabel's immersion in the emotionally charged relationship with Lawrence as an expression of infantile and sexual longings. In *Basic Principles of Psychoanalysis* (1921), Brill states his view on the crucial importance of sublimation: "Every individual has been allowed by society to live through some of the pleasure principles, but he has been forced to adapt himself to the principles of reality. From our psychoanalytic knowledge we recognize this process as sublimation. Every activity or vocation not directed to sex in the broadest sense ... is a form of sublimation" (pp. 265–266). Brill considered Mabel as living too deeply according to the pleasure principle and in need of reorienting towards reality. Work was his solution for her.

Brill held himself to this same standard. Once he had "complained" to Freud about the weight of his responsibilities in furthering psychoanalysis in the United States and Freud replied: "Well, you are young; you should not complain, but act" (Brill, 1940, pp. 178–179). And, as explained by his close friend, the writer Theodore Dreiser, Brill viewed pain "as an incentive, an urge to life" while "he believed in action as the antidote to too much thought, the way of brooding and sorrow. Also, he wanted more labor, not less, for humanity, more toil, not less, more exertion" (1924, p. 457). This description captures Brill's convictions about action as the means to a more bearable and thus fulfilling life.

Brill espoused his long-held theories on the value of work in "What's Wrong With Cities?" and offered a very particular opinion concerning women: "After a woman has passed the age of forty-five or fifty and her children have grown up, she should have work to keep her well" (1931b, p. 50). In fact, Brill's identification of these specific years in a woman's life as a ripe time for work, implying the end of childbearing and entry into menopause, coincided perfectly with Mabel's beliefs about the productivity possible in the postmenopausal years, as first set forth in her poem "Change," discussed earlier. Mabel further developed these ideas in a later essay, *Change of Life* (1938), asserting that after menopause "sublimation is no longer an unsuccessful makeshift but is actually a way of life, life now more full and intense than before, creative in new ways unguessed during the child bearing [sic] period" (p. 4). Mabel's physical and hormonal states at this time made her exquisitely receptive to Brill's advice to sublimate.

Brill convinced Mabel of the urgency of continued analysis and encouraged her to resume treatment with him in New York. As she recalled: "He told me to return later on and we would deal with the problem together, and ... he made me realize it was necessary. Since I had already rented Finney Farm in Croton for the winter, I had only to go back to Taos to wait a month or two" (*LIT*, p. 246). Despite Lawrence's decisive role in her becoming undone and fleeing Taos, Mabel wrote to him about her consultation with Brill and he responded on September 14, 1924, with a knowing tone:

> I had your letter about Brill last night. I knew it was very much as he said: that there was a fatal disconnection, and that it was passing beyond your control. I am glad you are going to put yourself into a doctor's hands. Because you have now to submit to authority, and to a certain measure of control from outside. And except to an authority like a recognized doctor's, you would never have submitted.
>
> The thing to do is to try, try, try to discipline and control yourself. (p. 246)

Mabel replied to Lawrence, seeking his counsel and granting him a bit of authority as she considered his opinions along with Brill's:

> Now both you and Brill feel *I* have to do all the work this winter. With guidance I have to *do* the thing, whatever it is.
>
> Can you tell me *what* this thing literally is? Finding myself? ...
>
> *What kind* of control and discipline did you mean? *Would writing do* as a cure and a help? Shall I try to start a life-history or something? Save this letter if you think it would help Brill. It's so hard for me to formulate things, maybe it would aid him. (*LIT*, p. 251)

In her present struggles during a period that would prove crucially fruitful, Mabel looked for guidance from both Brill and Lawrence, men who exerted power and influence on her in vastly different ways.

While Brill is on holiday in London at this time, he writes his next letter to Mabel, offering his thoughts on a book she had sent him: Dhan Gopal Mukerji's *Caste and Outcast* (1923), an autobiographical account of growing up in India as a Brahmin and later living in the United States as an immigrant.

δ

Monday October 6, [c. 1924]

Dear Mabel,

 My vacation is almost at an end and I am very happy to return to the States as they say here ... I would have written to you before had you not sent me Caste & Outcaste [sic]. I had so many other things to do on board of ship that I just finished the book. The first part as you said is very interesting and as you wished it has broadened me. When I say it has broadened I don't mean that it has in any way converted me. It has given me much knowledge of Indian life which I never received in this form. The author is an intelligent person who knows what he is saying although I do not agree with his conclusions. In fact he gave me the impression of speaking to the gallery when he expresses such hopeful optimism for a mixture of East & West. This is a very long and cumbersome, or perhaps interesting, problem which I should like to discuss with you or with the author in your presence. The second part was a bit boring to me ... As for the Indian views of life and above all their "spiritual" outlooks I can say that we I mean people who go into the mind find nothing incongruous in them. It is simply a question of interpretation ...

 Well I could talk on and on but I must reserve it for later.

 With my kindest regards to you and Tony I am,

As Ever,
Brill

δ

It is intriguing to consider Mabel's motives in suggesting this book to Brill. He admitted "as you wished it has broadened me," thereby implying she explicitly appealed for openness to its ideas. *Caste and Outcast* introduced American audiences to Indian life and discussed differences between Eastern and Western spiritual views, an emphasis one can imagine Mabel embracing as she sought acceptance of her immersion in Native American life. One fascinating parallel stands out from the pages of Mukerji's book, where the author observed that, unlike Indians in their domestic life, Americans "had very little repose" and: "If Americans study how we create serenity in India ... they will be able to know serenity here in America" (p. 18). Repose and serenity were exactly what Mabel sought in her new life with Tony, although her own stubborn tendency towards activity often undermined her efforts.

When she returned to Brill in the winter of 1925, Mabel reported to Leo Stein, c. January 1925: "I am going to old Brill 3 times a week to see if I can learn to 'canalise' & get the habit of work—for my old age!" (GLSC). She also related in another letter to Stein from early 1925 that her resumed analysis strikingly improved her pained connection with her mother:

> One thing P.A. [i.e., psychoanalysis] did for me this winter was to enable me to acquire a pleasing relationship with my mother—which before—all my life had been something awful. Now we *like* each other & get a measure of comfort out of each other. This was very fundamental as doubtless you know & never reached till [sic] now. I am still working with Brill on another problem. Had dinner there the other night. (GLSC)

Occasionally, when Mabel was in New York, with or without Tony, she would have dinner with A. A. and Rose Brill at their home on the Upper West Side. This was not such an unusual occurrence at this time in psychoanalysis, as mentioned earlier.

* * *

This was the time in Mabel's life that generated the idea of her future voluminous memoirs, inspired by her renewed treatment with Brill, her correspondence with Lawrence, and her discovery of the powerful effects of writing. In a 1924 letter to Lawrence, she had described her revelation that when engaged in this work, she could feel purposeful and creative, particularly while addressing him:

> The other thing that releases me from this gummed-up state is *writing*. If I can overcome the terrible resistance and inertia that seizes me before I begin—if I can once get started and know I want to say something—it comes. Then I am off—in a good running pace. And *after* having done some writing, everything is different. The room I sit in seems beneficent, and the light bathes one in a mild peaceful glow. All the misery and tug and pull are gone. Then I can *do* anything. Easily ... Living isn't a mess and a struggle ... Also I can only

write *for* someone and you are positively the only audience I care to say anything to. (*LIT*, p. 250)

Mabel conquered her sluggishness and began a fruitful period of writing, although Lawrence did not long remain the sole or desired recipient of her manuscripts.

In *Notes Upon Awareness* (1939), an unpublished account of her psychoanalysis (as well as other treatments along the way), Mabel wrote about the impetus behind starting her memoirs. After referring to Lawrence's "disloyalty and treachery" and her subsequent turmoil in response to his personal attacks, she then described in detail the process she deliberately undertook to examine herself with unflinching candor, a passage quoted here at length for its compelling narrative:

> I could not stand this for long. To save myself I had to undertake a work, the work that Dr. Brill had counseled me to undertake the preceeding [sic] summer, for he had a great feeling about the saving grace of labor, which I had never had myself ... The work, the only work that suggested itself to me was somehow to find out what had made me, and whatever it was, <u>what</u> it had made me, to tell Lawrence about my whole life from the beginning so he would understand more completely, so he would stop calling me dangerous and destructive ... To give myself from the beginning to the end would be ... a subtle process of self-destruction and self-disintegration, more deadly than anything he could accomplish were he to take a hammer and beat my brains upon a stone. I knew before I started it that such a review as this done honestly might be suicidal; there might be no Mabel Dodge left when I got through ... I had this intuitive realization of the danger of such an examination but it seemed to me I had no choice left. What I was, false or mistaken or fabricated might perish under that eye I could examine it with, on the other hand unless I capitulated to the last chance of truth confronting me I would die—... and I could not die yet. I could not leave Tony who needed me ... He had told me that if anything happened to take me away from the earth he would follow me ... I had to stay for his sake. I had never known any unselfish feeling but this. It was my one and only maternal response.
>
> So I began the first book of Intimate Memories. So it was that Lawrence, working in me, succeeded in his intention to destroy me

as he had sworn to do. For observing that process that had built up the person called Mabel Dodge actually did unravel the fabric of the artificial creation. One can undo oneself. One can untie the knots in the heart, turn back the clock, and become as though one had never been. The leopard can, indeed, change his spots! (pp. 177–178a)

It is striking that embarking upon this courageous autobiographical project finds Mabel experiencing her "one and only maternal response" in relation to Tony, her resolve to remain living reinforced by her attachment to him. Actually giving birth to a child had not summoned her maternal flow. Several factors evocatively combined to allow Mabel to write so honestly in her search to bare herself: the encouragement and conviction of Brill, the passion of her reactions towards Lawrence who had helped her see, and this arising of a maternal feeling that perhaps she was able to direct partially towards herself during this risky endeavor. Her description of the dangers of examining one's past and of frank self-revelation certainly speaks to common fears of what the process of psychoanalysis might yield.

With her characteristic frankness combined with exhibitionism, Mabel shared early drafts of her memoirs with close confidants. In 1924 or 1925, Mabel had sent Carl Van Vechten five chapters of her first volume, *Background*, asking for his feedback: "I am writing these pages for my own pleasure. They cannot be printed, for too many names are included. But I am going to show them to two or three friends from time to time—people I can trust. Please don't show them or leave them lying about—it isn't fair to others for me to be careless with them … I'd like your opinion" (CVVC). Van Vechten replied with enthusiasm and generosity:

> Your book, of course, is remarkable: so full of your particular vitality and vividness; a document, too, but always imaginatively treated, with real selection. There is a suggestion of the method of Proust, and a reflection here and there of Gertrude Stein, but it is really all you, and nobody else but you could do it … And your grandmothers and the furniture! And your mother! There is not, as yet, enough about you … Some day, of course, it all must be published; perhaps some sooner, some later … I want to see more

as soon as it's ready! ... Probably it[']s going to be the best thing yet done in America.

In her c. January 1925 letter to Leo Stein, Mabel reported writing "a kind of honest autobiography ... It is not being written to print—it can't be—too much family and friends in it" (GLSC). Later that year, on October 7, she wrote to Gertrude Stein: "I have been working on an autobiography since last December ... It is not to be published but put away until a few people are dead! But I am going to let some people read it. Do you want to?" (GLSC). Lawrence described his powerful response to *Background* in a letter to Mabel dated April 12, 1926: "I should say it's the most serious 'confession' that ever came out of America, and perhaps the most heart-destroying revelation of the American life-process that ever has or ever will be produced ... My dear Mabel, one could shed skyfuls of tears except for the knowledge of the utter futility of shedding even one" (*LIT*, p. 266). From those she trusted, Mabel received strong validation of her style of writing and the candidness of her observations about herself and others.

In the same letter to Leo, c. January 1925, Mabel described the dissolution of her relationship with Lawrence: "He's too damn mean, that's the trouble. He has satisfied his sadism in a story called 'the woman who rode away' ... about a white woman whom he makes sacrifice herself voluntarily to the Indians who finally cut out her heart" (GLSC). "The Woman Who Rode Away" was printed in *The Dial* in the summer of 1925 for all to read. The fictional Mabel, who "had thought that this marriage, of all marriages, would be an adventure" (1928, p. 47), is killed by a Native American priest in order to release the lost power of men. Lawrence found a way to murder Mabel by literary means, without resorting to the violence he threatened. He still lived in Taos, and although he did not see Mabel during that summer, or ever again, they corresponded until several weeks before his death. After traveling to Mexico in the fall of 1925, Lawrence and Frieda moved to Italy in January 1926, remaining there until he died in March 1930.

CHAPTER NINE

Flirtations

Mabel's struggles between conformity and passion were notably obvious in two affairs during her marriage to Tony Luhan. In her first existing letter to Brill, she explains her payment of a new friend's psychotherapy bill in exchange for the handwritten manuscript of D. H. Lawrence's *Sons and Lovers*, a friend later revealed as one of her current romantic interests.

δ

April 24, 1925

Dear Dr. Brill,

I am giving you the mms [i.e., manuscript][1] of Sons & Lovers of D. H. Lawrence in return for your care of [rectangular piece cut out of paper here] & I am very glad to turn it to some creative use. It was given to me by Mr. & Mrs. Lawrence not openly in exchange for the ranch in New Mexico—but sometime after I gave Mrs. Lawrence the ranch she expressed the wish to give me the mms.

Ever yours,
Mabel Dodge Luhan

δ

Mabel had acquired this manuscript in 1924 from Frieda Lawrence in exchange for the 160-acre ranch in Valdez, north of Taos, that she had once purchased for her son, John Evans. Tormented by the unrelenting tensions in their relationship, Mabel had offered the Lawrences her ranch as enticement for them to stay in Taos, hoping the distance might improve their rapport. They accepted her proposal and eventually gave Mabel the handwritten manuscript of *Sons and Lovers* as payment for the deed to the land. Soon after, Mabel had a letter from Frieda suggesting it "was worth at least $50,000" (*LIT*, p. 228). However, in her biography of Frieda, Janet Byrne reported that, according to D. H. Lawrence in 1928, the manuscript was worth only $5,000 (1995, p. 300). It is interesting to note that Brill's family kept the manuscript until 1963, fifteen years after A. A. Brill's death, when they sold it to the University of California for $17,000 (Byrne, 1995, p. 378).

Everett Marcy, a young writer and object of Mabel's affection at this time, was the friend whose therapy was funded by Lawrence's manuscript. This was revealed by close examination of a later letter from Brill to Mabel dated May 25, 1930 that acknowledged receipt of the manuscript as payment for his treatment, with the name blacked out this time, rather than cut out as before.

Mabel had been on the East Coast in April 1925 and then traveled back to New Mexico by train, as indicated in Brill's next letter. He responds positively to her lost invitation for him and his family to visit.

δ

May 7, 1925

Dear Mabel,

I enjoyed reading your train letter and wish to tell you again that I expect to be your guest. I do not know exactly when we will start from here but we have the time tables [sic] and everything else, but I am only waiting to find out when school[2] ends.

I received a letter from Ida [Rauh] in response to mine. She protests that all she wanted was to keep you from making a false step in reference to our friend Lawrence. She evidently heard from him or communicated with him and she thinks that things would be on a much better basis, if you could keep yourself passive in this matter. At all events she will explain everything to you, she says …

As ever,
Brill

δ

Despite his intentions, Brill did not make the trip. According to his daughter, Gioia, "The whole family was going there for a visit one summer & I was promised my own horse but then one of my father's patients became suicidal or something so we never went" (personal communication, March 13, 1997).

Brill's next two letters mention a woman named Alice, perhaps Mabel's daughter-in-law, Alice Henderson, whom she likely had referred to Brill in her characteristic urging of others towards treatment.

δ

July 27, 1925

My dear Mabel,

I was away from here for about ten days and found your letters on my return. The only difficulty about the situation is I do not know whether I can take Alice by the first of September. I am flirting with the idea of taking a quick trip abroad for about three or four weeks. If I do that I will not be able to take her before the end of September. I am therefore not sending her the telegram you suggest. Simply tell her that I will let her know as soon as I can and that she should prepare to come beginning September first.

I thank you very much for the squaw with the snake. It is a nice symbolic picture[3] which as you say will be an interesting addition to my collection.

You have no idea how sorry I am that I could not see my way clear to spend some time at Taos, as I sincerely wanted.

With my kindest regards to Tony, I am,

Affectionately,
A.A.B.

δ

August 11, 1925

Dear Mabel,

When I got home yesterday I found your letter, and was so far too busy to go to the library and find some of the works, but I am enclosing a paper on the subject[4] which may serve your purpose ...

Concerning Alice, I would tell her to make arrangements to be in New York by the 25th of September.

Cordially yours,
Brill

δ

Although no further letters between Mabel and Brill exist until January 1926, she was in New York during November 1925, as revealed by her inclusion in Carl Van Vechten's daybooks from those years, which indicated that she saw Brill on at least one social occasion. It is not known if she consulted with him professionally at this time. During these days, Mabel was often in the company of Everett Marcy, with whom she was enjoying an intense flirtation that developed into an intimate involvement lasting about two years. On November 7, 1925, Van Vechten joined "Mabel Luhan at the Lido. She is at her most beguiling & dangerous. I think she wants me to have a 'thing' with the beau Everett Marcy." Ten days later, he reported: "Dinner with Mabel Luhan & Dr. Brill, at Frank's [Harlem restaurant]. Dr. Brill talks about Negroes. Later Everett Marcy comes in & takes Mabel to the movies. She acts so badly that I begin to know that she is having an affair with this callow youth. Dr. Brill says there is no doubt about it" (Kellner, 2003, p. 100). Given the changing nature of their analytic relationship, still maintained to a degree in their correspondence, it is intriguing to imagine the scene: Mabel, Brill, and Van Vechten dining together at a restaurant, followed by Mabel's dalliance with Marcy and Brill's confident pronouncement of her transgression. Marcy was seen with Mabel in New York as well as in California and Taos over the next two years. In spite of these frequent sightings, he does not appear in any of Mabel's memoirs (unlike most of her numerous friends and acquaintances, some of whom would have strongly preferred not to have been included).

Mabel apparently traveled back to Taos at the end of 1925 before returning to New York in January 1926, since in the following letter, Brill asked her or Tony to transport a mockingbird from New Mexico to him in New York. In this letter, Brill also referred to Mabel's current preoccupation with Orage, an English disciple of G. I. Gurdjieff, a mystic from Russia who founded the Institute for the Harmonious Development of Man in 1922 at Fontainebleau, France. Mabel had heard Gurdjieff and Orage speak in New York in the winter of 1924 and subsequently invited Orage to lead weekend groups at Finney Farm (Webb, 1980, pp. 301, 339). Gurdjieff's teachings appealed directly to Mabel's continual search for the essence of being, for the identity behind the mask, for freedom from the constraints of social expectations.

δ

January 8, 1926

Dear Mabel,

Just received your telegram. First, in reference to Everett: He has done much better of late and I feel that a lot can be done for him. He is interested and seems to react well. I could not keep him away from the crowd altogether, but I am satisfied that it does him no harm to go occasionally to Muriel [Draper][5] for tea. He has very few people that he can see, the association with Bobby [Robert Edmond Jones][6] did not turn out well. I suppose you know all about it. I would therefore suggest that we continue for a few months longer. I am glad to hear that you are coming here the beginning of February and I hope that you will not indulge in those wild schemes that I was told about after you left. I am referring to the $15,000. [sic] that you were supposed to have given to Orage. I don't like to interfere with your affairs but every once in a while I feel that you are going ariot. You may continue to be all the mad that you want.

A former patient of mine, Mrs. Marion S. Monaghan of Masilla Park, New Mexico, wants to send me a mocking bird [sic] which she has promised to do for the last seven or eight years. Now she has one ready to send me. She claims that she has a permit to send it out of the state but I am afraid that the bird will never get here alive, particularly as these birds cannot stand the cold and he will in all probabilities not survive the trip in the cold cars. Now if you will be kind enough to ask Tony to do me the favor, if you can't, and bring the bird to me in the event that Mrs. Monaghan will ship it to you just before you leave, I will be very thankful to you. You can send a wire to Mrs. Monaghan at the above address and she will have the bird in Taos a day before you are to leave for New York. She will also give you full instructions how to feed him over the journey and will send you the food etc., etc. Knowing my love for birds you will not hesitate to take that trouble.

Cordially yours,
Brill

δ

Orage was active in fund-raising for Gurdjieff and it appears Mabel did give Gurdjieff a donation of $15,000 through a disciple, Jean Toomer, another man with whom she was quite enamored. A letter from Gurdjieff dated February 1, 1926, thanked her for her donation. At this time, Mabel seemed in a whirl of impulsivity, with her attractions to Marcy and Toomer and her impassioned inspiration from Gurdjieff's offerings. Her marriage was seriously threatened, particularly by her feelings towards Toomer; Tony was very angry towards Mabel for her obvious involvement with the handsome disciple, and lashed out with threats of hitting her with a hammer and telling her own mother and son about the relationship (Rudnick, 1984, pp. 228–229).

Brill's request for Mrs. Monaghan's mockingbird reflected his long-standing interest in birds as pets, particularly those who mimic sound. In an undated, unpublished paper, *Ned: Our Starling*, Brill observed that his starling "learned from me to whistle 'Yankee Doodle,' and 'Where did you get that hat?' which he thereafter reproduced with the same intonations that I originally imparted to him" (SFA). In an essay about her treatment, *Psycho-Analysis with Dr. Brill* (1938), Mabel recalled his passion for birds: "This man is a bird, I remembered. He has features like a bird … and he loves birds very much" (p. 2). She described seeing Brill in his dining room, with his birds in their cages, appealing: "'Come on, Hansi! Sing! Come on, now,' and soon the finch would pipe up and trill his little song, and Dr. Brill would laugh and say: '<u>Again</u>. Come on now, Hansi! Sing'" (p. 9). For Brill, confident in delivering strong advice and having it be followed, one can only imagine his satisfaction in having a bird exactly imitate his voice.

* * *

Mabel returned to New York in January 1926, as indicated by an entry from Van Vechten's daybooks placing her and Tony there on January 28 (Kellner, 2003, p. 108). It is unknown if Mrs. Monaghan's bird accompanied them on their trip, or even if Mabel visited Brill during this time. They settled in at Finney Farm, where she remained for several months, immersed in the ideas of Gurdjieff. She wrote to D. H. Lawrence on April 3, 1926 to explain Gurdjieff's instructions for creating a self: "Observe Mabel … This Mabel has three modes or centres—instinctive, mental, and emotional … She *must* create a fourth one herself—the I … Become conscious now of your self, it is a new universe, a cosmos, the world of self-consciousness" (*LIT*, p. 263). Lawrence replied on April 12, 1926, warning: "In the end, if you Gurdjieff yourself to the very end, a dog that barks at you will be a dynamo sufficient to explode your universe" (*LIT*, p. 265). Over Lawrence's objections, Mabel continued to explore what Gurdjieff could offer. She was drawn to his idea that by increasing consciousness and self-observation, a person can create a new way of being in the world, liberated from conventional social demands, while living in greater balance. It is very likely that Brill would have been equally dismissive of Mabel's current experimentation, as he consistently objected to her impassioned engagement in any movements other than psychoanalysis.

Perhaps as a result of Mabel's captivation with Gurdjieff, more than a year passed before another surviving communication between her and Brill, beginning a pattern of less frequently documented contact that continued until the fall of 1935, when her memoir *European Experiences* was published and their correspondence then resumed with more regularity. In Brill's next letter, he addresses Everett Marcy's treatment.

δ

March 16, 1927

My dear Mabel,

The matter about Marcy is as follows:—When he wrote to me I asked him to come. When he got here, I gave him regular appointments, but he failed to keep his appointments, often coming late, etc. He was very unsettled, consequently I got tired and I told him to wait until he is settled enough to do regular work. I told him I would be very glad to see him from time to time just as he desired. I saw him about ten days ago, and I believe at the end of last week he called up for an appointment which I could not give him as I feel that it is absolutely useless for me to waste my time on him at the present time. He is in close contact with a lot of people, some of whom may not do him any good. I have neither the time nor the patience to give to people who are not seriously bent on working with me. So much for that ...

If Marcy will ask me to see him, I will be very glad to see him.

Very cordially yours,
Brill

δ

Even in the context of more relaxed approaches to confidentiality at this time, Brill's frankness about his impatience and frustration with Marcy is noteworthy. Perhaps he believed Mabel had a right to this privileged information since she was paying for Marcy's therapy. In an undated letter, Mabel wrote to Spud Johnson: "I had a disgruntled letter from Brill about Everett. Did you know he had dismissed him sometime ago? Said E. wouldn't work or keep his appointments & is very thick with some people who are not good for him." Earlier that year, Johnson had a different impression of Marcy's commitment to his analysis, reporting to Mabel on January 22, 1927 that Marcy "is going regularly to Brill," a fact he likely knew since the two lived together for a time in New York. Many years later, in 1940 or 1941, Marcy wrote to Mabel complaining about comments he had heard: "I burned quite a bit over the reported remarks—especially the ones about Brill and my being a 'hopeless case.'" One wonders if Marcy ever knew that Brill was more than willing to work with him if he could only devote time to his treatment.

Notes

1. Mabel used this abbreviation, "mms," for "manuscript," as well as "MMS," while Brill used "Mss" or "MSS."
2. Most likely New York University where he was teaching.
3. Current whereabouts unknown.
4. Never identified.
5. Once a popular salon hostess in London and married to the acclaimed American tenor Paul Draper (they were divorced in 1916), now living in New York where she was a writer.
6. Scenic designer.

CHAPTER TEN

Abreaction

Brill's next letter, in response to a lost one from Mabel, dates from over a year since his last existing communication. The "enclosure" she sent was almost certainly the order form for D. H. Lawrence's *Lady Chatterley's Lover* (1928); she had mailed one to Jelliffe on April 5, 1928, suggesting, "I think you will want to order one of these." As stated, the book would be published "unexpurgated" in a limited edition of 1000 with "500 copies for America at $10," with Lawrence in Italy listed as recipient of both order and payment. Lawrence had appealed to Mabel on March 12, 1928: "I shall send you a few of the little order-forms, and do please send them out for me … It is frankly and faithfully a phallic novel, but tender and delicate" (*LIT*, pp. 304–305).

δ

April 9, 1928

My dear Mabel,

    I am just in receipt of your few lines, with enclosure. I am very glad to know that you are alive, and also where you are. I heard all kinds of rumors about your whereabouts, but only recently, was I told that you are really alive and that you are still in Taos. There must have been something wrong in your conscious relationship to me. Let's hear about it.

We are all well, except that we are all getting older. I just saw Andrew [Dasburg] and I understand that Ida [Rauh] will be here soon. Andrew had a very successful exhibition. I believe every one of the paintings was sold, at a very good price.[1] I saw them and I liked them very much indeed. How is Tony?

I shall try to get a copy of Lawrence's last publication, but who is the American publisher?[2] Anyhow, I shall send a ten-dollar check to Lawrence and ask him to send me a copy.

Mrs. B.[rill] was delighted to hear that you had written to me. She asked a number of times, about you, and I said that you were mad at me.

As ever,
Brill

P.S. Remember me to Tony.

δ

In this letter, Brill invited Mabel to consider and communicate her feelings about her "conscious relationship" to him, as he sensed her silence had a reason and concluded she was angry with him. It is quite possible Mabel had sent Brill a recently issued copy of "The Ballad of a Bad Girl" at the end of 1927, had not heard back from him, and was miffed. This edition was printed in December 1927 by Spud Johnson on Japanese paper and illustrated with Lawrence's drawing, "The Bad Girl in the Pansy Bed." Mabel had mailed Jelliffe a copy of this published "Ballad" and received a reply dated January 5, 1928 that thanked her and sent "best holiday greetings to the bad little girl." If Brill never acknowledged the latest version of her poem, this probably caused her alleged anger.

As indicated by the beginning of Brill's next letter, Mabel took him up on his invitation to express her feelings towards him in a letter now lost, and he responds with a moving expression of his feelings for her, noticing her insecurity and reassuring her of his warmth and belief in her. In this expansive letter, Brill inquires about Tony's jealousy, likely caused by her recent passions for Marcy and Toomer, and mentions two novels featuring Mabel as a central character.

δ

May 3, 1928

Dear Mabel,

The only thing wrong about your letter that I see, is your closing sentence. You say "have a heart and sympathize with my weaknesses which are at the same time my strength." On the upper part of the same page you say "I know you like me to write openly, so I do it, etc." Still, it shows me that you are not altogether sure of yourself. Of course you know that I have always sympathized with you and consider you a unique woman. Unique in more than one way! It does not matter that you are doing all sorts of crazy things. ('This is not meant to be scientific.')

Ida and Andrew disappeared without saying goodbye to me, so I take for granted that they have made up, and felt so happy in their reunion that no outsider mattered. I am perfectly willing to help, and I see in Andrew perhaps more than you do ... The challenge to keep them together that you are throwing at me, will not take root with me. I do not believe that we can keep people together, and I do not try to do it, really.[3]

To go back to the most interesting part of the letter—that is yourself—you had better be careful about driving that car. All those unseen forces that you undoubtedly still believe in, will not always be at your side. I too, turned over a car once and it did not hurt me, but I do not believe in doing it again. So that [sic] try to control your death impulse by driving at a more moderate rate of speed.[4]

Why is Tony jealous? Is it the same old story or is there anything new? I cannot imagine you as a woman of forty-nine. You are so infantile, that in all probability you will be the same at seventy-nine. Naturally, thinking of your mother, who could marry at I do not remember what age,[5] and realizing that you have outpointed your mother so far, by about one thousand points, what can I expect.

Write me another letter and tell me what happened to Clarence [Thompson], to Everett, and to some of the others. Are they still complex instigators? Or have you really grown up?

I did not read Max Eastman's novel, "Venture." I shall get it and see whether he knows anything about you. I did see an illustrated edition of [Van Vechten's] "Peter Whiffle," with your illuminated face; but I was deterred from buying it. I think it was four dollars, or something, and as I have the other, I thought of asking you for one of your latest pictures, autographed, which will compensate me for not reading the book.

I hope that you are working hard on your memoirs. Do you expect to come to New York? I may come west.

Rose joins me in sending her love.

Affectionately,
Brill

δ

Eastman's *Venture* (1927) cast Mabel as the character Mary Kittridge who is a maternal figure for male revolutionaries (such as Eastman), offering them sexual, emotional, and financial comforts. He captured Mabel's restlessness: "She was always just entering upon some new spiritual experiment that involved a complete break with everything that had gone before. Either she was getting married, or she was getting divorced, or she was testing out unmarried love, or she was taking up sign-painting, or snake-dancing, or Hindu philosophy, or Hindu turbans" (p. 24). In another fictional portrayal, Mabel Dodge appeared as the salon hostess Edith Dale in Carl Van Vechten's *Peter Whiffle*, first published in 1922. Van Vechten described the atmosphere at her gatherings: "The crowds flocked to her place and she made them comfortable ... Arguments and discussions floated in the air, were caught and twisted and hauled and tied, until the white salon was no longer static. There were undercurrents of emotion and sex" (p. 122). The illustrated edition of *Peter Whiffle* mentioned in Brill's letter was published in 1927 by Alfred A. Knopf, with a photograph of Mabel in a turban, seated as if on a throne.

In this letter, Brill referred to his wife as "Rose" rather than Mrs. Brill as in the previous letters, likely indicating the increasing degree of familiarity between them that may have resulted from Mabel's visits on her trips to New York. As Brill's daughter remembered, "My mother liked Mabel & both had a good relationship." She also recalled, "I remember Mabel ringing the doorbell while we ate lunch (my father came home for lunch) & the maid setting an extra place for her ... She only dropped in for lunch after her analysis & when she visited NYC" (Bernheim, personal communications, July 2, 2000, March 13, 1997).

Brill sends Mabel his critique of *Lady Chatterley's Lover*.

δ

August 29, 1928

Dear Mabel,

I was very glad to get your letter and am very much interested in the new developments. I am very glad in many ways that Andrew has changed, as far as his relationships are concerned. From what I saw of Ida I was absolutely convinced that it was a hopeless situation, but Andrew, of course, would not listen to it. In fact, he became very irritable when I suggested it. As a matter of fact, only a few days ago [Grace Mott] Johnson[6] told me that Ida was getting a divorce.[7] I asked her whether she was sure of it, and she said that she had heard so.

By the way, have you read D. H.'s "Lady Chatterl[e]y's Lovers [sic]"? I read it with a great deal of interest. I think it is a very good book and I really feel that it was an abreaction on his part, to make it so pornographic in spots. Of course, you will say that it is just a frank expression of things. I maintain that he could have expressed himself in the same way without having recourse to some of the expressions that he uses. It would have made the book universally acceptable instead of limiting it to a small circle of readers. Of course, it is autobiographical; at least that is my feeling.

As usual, I could not make connections to get to Taos, but you can never tell when I will blow in there. And then I shall take some of those famous trips with Tony.

There is nothing new in my family. We are all well.

Affectionately,
AAB

δ

Brill's apparently pejorative use of the word "abreaction" in his commentary on Lawrence's novel is intriguing, given his urging Mabel to write her own autobiography in the spirit of abreaction. He seems to cast judgment on the "pornographic" elements of Lawrence's novel, suggesting the author should have curtailed his inclination to write freely about sexual matters. It is interesting to note that Brill had no such criticism of the same frankness in Mabel's memoirs. Her understanding of Brill's concept of abreaction was stated in a letter to Leo Stein from October 23, c. 1925, where she described the idea behind her writing: "It is an attempt to record experience as it happened—with no more or less content than the moment held. It is what the analysts call 'abreaction' in writing" (GLSC). Brill's suggestion that she write her memoirs was based not just in his belief in sublimation, as discussed earlier, but also on his understanding of Freud's theory of abreaction. He explained the process that Freud and Austrian physician Josef Breuer had together named the "Cathartic Method":

> Their idea was that if a patient can recall the unpleasant situation which gave origin to the symptom and live it over, so to say, he loses the symptom; that words are almost equivalent to the action, and that in going over some painful experience in the past there is what they called an *abreaction* ... in which the painful emotions associated with the experience were liberated and thus ceased to create physical disturbances. (1921, p. 7)

Mabel, in fact, had become a faithful disciple of Brill's beliefs, later admitting she experienced the kind of unburdening and liberation that such abreaction can bring, particularly in exposing the pain of her lonely childhood in *Background*.

Notes

1. Dasburg's one-man show at Frank K. M. Rehn Galleries in New York was held in the spring of 1928. His paintings generated $9,950 in sales (Coke, 1979, p. 79).
2. *Lady Chatterley's Lover* did not succeed in having an American publisher until September 1932 when Alfred A. Knopf, New York issued an "authorized abridged edition." The first three printings of the book were done privately in 1928 and 1929, in Italy and France.

3. In fact, Dasburg left Rauh soon after his exhibition at the Rehn Galleries and married actress Nancy Lane in December 1928.
4. Even Lawrence in Austria had learned about this habit of Mabel's, as he wrote to her on August 25, 1927 after receiving word from their mutual friend, the painter Dorothy Brett: "Heard from Brett to-day—she says you are learning to drive the Buick and stepping on the gas like ten heroines. Don't do it. Camminando si arriva. Stepping on the gas one goes over the edge, which is not an arrival" (*LIT*, p. 301).
5. Mabel's mother Sara had remarried twice: to Admiral Reeder after her husband's death in 1902; again after Reeder died in 1911 to a man named Monty, when she was likely in her mid-fifties.
6. Johnson and Dasburg were divorced in 1922.
7. Brill seems to have mistakenly believed Rauh and Dasburg were married. In fact, they never married. Rauh was divorced from Max Eastman in 1922.

CHAPTER ELEVEN

Another analysis

During the summer of 1928 in Taos, Mabel had received a visit from the Jungian psychoanalyst Frances Wickes, who convinced Mabel to return to New York and enter treatment with her: "She had spoken of mysterious separations that were growing between myself and the people of my world, and of a self-sufficiency she felt in Tony that he was building to compensate for lacks in me" (*FA*, p. 39). Frightened by Wickes's pronouncements, Mabel was further persuaded after two "dreadful dreams" the night the psychoanalyst left:

> In one there was a peach-tree growing in the patio of a convent place. A nun came to gather peaches and though they looked fair and ripe on the outside, they were brown within. That faded and I saw a lovely rose-bush with roses blooming on it. When I went up to it, the roses were withered and the petals blighted.
>
> When I woke up in the morning, I telegraphed Mrs. Wick[e]s I would come to her the first of October, and I wrote her of these dreams. If she had understood psycho-analysis deeply enough, she would have sent me to a specialist for a physical examination, for the dreams were true and tried to tell of organic changes that

could have been halted. But no one thought this was going on. (*FA*, pp. 39–40)

Now under the spell of Wickes, replacing her earlier captivation with Gurdjieff, Mabel traveled to New York at the end of 1928, staying until the last week of March 1929. Mabel's correspondence with her assistant Spud Johnson from this time confirms her whereabouts in New York, at One Fifth Avenue, and her analysis with Wickes. In one undated letter to Johnson, she related: "I have been very much in the work I came for—& I haven't seen many people ... But I am getting lots out of it. Wickes is grand." On January 17, 1929, she wrote: "I am getting so tierd [sic] of N.Y. & long to be home but will stick it out till [sic] April on acct. of Wickes who is wonderful." However, Mabel also recalled: "Like others before her, Mrs. Wick[e]s tried in every possible way to bring to the surface some evidence that I didn't really want Tony—but without success. It seems I did want him" (*FA*, p. 40).

During this analysis with Wickes, Mabel reported: "The roses dried and withered further, and the peaches moved to deeper decay during the six months she kept me on the rack, while Tony sat on Mt. Tamalpais passing the time and singing Indian songs for Marion" (*FA*, p. 40). "Marion" refers to Marian Shevky, the wife of the Turkish doctor Richard Shevky who had been dispatched to Taos by John Collier to determine the amount of syphilis in the Taos Pueblo. Mabel revealed Tony's affair with "Marion" (as she spelled her name) that developed while Mabel was away: "Marion grew dependent upon his strong, warm presence, grew to love him, and he loved her" (*FA*, p. 41). As mentioned earlier, Mabel's intense involvements with Everett Marcy and Jean Toomer had taken a toll on her marriage, likely resulting in Tony's retreat to his Native American world and his receptivity to another relationship. Devastated by this discovery, Mabel could nonetheless admit a kind of justice in it, as Tony's affair "evened up accounts, for I had leaned away from him to try and subjugate one and another" (*FA*, p. 41).

When Tony eventually joined Mabel in New York in March, she observed: "I saw he was different ... and I asked him about it, he told me a good deal ... No one had taken my place, no one ever would; still, he loved Marion" (*FA*, p. 41). Although Wickes urged Mabel to continue analysis, Mabel soon returned to New Mexico with Tony, as indicated in a letter to Van Vechten dated March 20, 1929, where she announced her departure that week. On April 9, 1929, she wrote to Van

Vechten from Taos, thanking him for his attentions while she was in New York and expressing relief at being home: "We are so happy to be back here!" (CVVC). Although Brill had inquired in a previous letter about Mabel's plans to visit New York, Mabel chose not to see him during her extended stay, most certainly because she was in treatment with another analyst.

During the summer of 1929, Mabel realized that the analysis with Wickes had missed the signs of a physical disease. Concerned about her symptoms, she returned to her hometown of Buffalo to be examined, resulting in a hysterectomy and several weeks in the hospital (*Doctors*, p. 40). In fact, after the surgery, she admitted to her son, John Evans: "I should have had an operation last year instead of psycho-analysis, I believe" (*FA*, p. 49). This trip to Buffalo exposed the strain in her relationship with John, who had moved there from Taos in 1925 with his wife, Alice, to get away from his difficult relationship with Mabel and to be nearer his maternal grandmother. Now a banker in the family tradition, John visited her in the hospital each day:

> Having me down for once, he launched into me ... I had seen so very little of him, but there was a strange antagonism between us always which dated back to his birth. Every afternoon he delivered some bitter piece of his opinion of me and as he went out the door, leaving me in my weak state with tears pouring down my face, he would raise his hand and say, with a peculiar smile, "Be seeing you." (*Doctors*, p. 41)

However, once she was well enough to leave the hospital, Mabel was invited to stay with John and Alice for a few days before her return to Taos. There she witnessed a scene frighteningly close to Mabel's own rejection of her son: when John returned from work one day, his daughter Nancy grabbed his hand and he said to her, "Oh, get away from me" (*Doctors*, p. 42). This is a striking reminder of the transmission of such treatment through the generations, as it recalls Mabel's instructions to her husband Karl about her newborn son: "Take it away ... I don't want it here" (*EE*, p. 52).

* * *

Over a year since his last letter, Brill writes to Mabel in response to a lost communication from her. She had sent him an article that appeared in both the *Santa Fe New Mexican* and the *Taos Valley News* from October 1929 about La Posta, a building she had built and was now trying to sell. The headline read: "Unique Mabel Luhan Place Can Be Bought For Only $80,000 at Taos" (in Luhan scrapbook, *Misc. Vol. I*).[1]

δ

November 9, 1929

Dear Mabel,

Like a voice from the desert when I looked at the hand-writing on this peculiar-looking envelope, I mean the peculiar design with the symbolic Los Gallos.[2] I said to myself, is it possible that Mable [sic] thought of me again; and behold when I opened it I found your symbolic scribbles around La Posta.

It reads very interestingly and one is tempted to buy this "remarkably artistical and distinctive place" for the nominal sum of $80,000. It would be lovely to live in that environment, but alas, I am tied to Manhattan Island.

Anyhow, it is mean of you to send me this thing without writing anything about yourself, and about the results of your mystic affair [i.e., with Jean Toomer]. Are you coming to New York this winter? If you do, do not wait until you leave to let me know of your presence. I excused you the last time because I always excuse you, but I shan't do it again.

With my cordial greetings to Tony and to all my other friends with whom you are coming in contact, I am,

As Ever,
Brill

δ

Brill seems miffed that Mabel was not in touch during her last stay in New York. His next letter provides more information about his feelings, as he refers to lost letters from Mabel about her "last analysis" with someone whose work he clearly does not endorse. He once more appeals to her to visit New York, although his efforts were unsuccessful, as she and Tony traveled to Carmel, California in February 1930, where they remained until at least May.

δ

January 20, 1930

Dear Mabel,

I was in the most feverish state since I last wrote to you and I am still more or less in it. However, first I wish to thank you for your letters which allowed me to take up the threads broken off sometime ago. I was very interested in all you said and there is no use of making any comments about your last analysis. I, as you know, do not believe in conscious introspection, and if you do not do enough of it as you complain, I take it as a good sign.

However, you are not the type of person to let matters alone, you are bound to do something and try everything. I do not believe that in your case it is very dangerous. It is somewhat disturbing, but you know that my definition of an outlet is an absorbing interest. It need not give us pleasure, most of our outlets are not pleasurable.[3]

We were very pleased with the photographs of you and Tony,[4] both of you look fine. To me those photographs express a great deal of your mental status, a description of which will be deferred to a later date ...

I hope that you will see your way clear to come East. I saw Maurice and he seemed to be in fine shape. He is as paternal as ever to Vera [Sterne].[5] There are a great many other things that I would like to talk to you about, writing is so unsatisfactory ... What did you think of [Hans] Prinzhorn? I like his works very much.[6]

Affectionately,
A. A. Brill

δ

The German psychiatrist Prinzhorn had recently visited Mabel in Taos, as he acknowledged in a letter to her from Frankfurt, dated November 30, 1929: "I still stay in my mind in Taos and that country." He wanted to return, as he wrote to her on May 11, 1930, to "join your circle at Taos." It is a testament to Mabel's curiosity and appeal that she attracted to her Taos home such prominent figures in psychoanalysis as Prinzhorn and, later, the psychoanalyst Sándor Radó.

Notes

1. La Posta failed to sell. In 1936, Mabel donated the building to the town of Taos, when it became La Posta Community Hospital.

2. The name of Mabel's adobe estate in Taos, for the Mexican ceramic chickens mounted on the roof. The envelope from her stationery featured a red and white drawing of a chicken surrounded by a circle of type announcing "Los Gallos Taos New Mexico" (see Illustration 10).
3. Brill's definition is reproduced almost verbatim in his *Psychoanalytic Psychiatry* (1946): "Outlets ... are not always pleasurable ... Many people find their work not particularly pleasurable. Yet it provides an absorbing interest and hence a useful outlet" (p. 127).
4. Most likely the two photographs from 1929 in the Luhan archives, showing each seated on a horse.
5. Sterne first met Vera Segal at the Elizabeth Duncan School when she was fifteen years old. They were married on her eighteenth birthday in 1923, when Sterne was forty-five.
6. Brill would have likely read Prinzhorn's most recent book in the original German, *Psychotherapie: Voraussetzungen—Wesen—Grenzen, ein Versuch zur Klärung der Grundlagen* (1929), translated by A. Eiloart in 1932 and published as *Psychotherapy: Its Nature—Its Assumptions—Its Limitations, a Search for Essentials*.

CHAPTER TWELVE

Lorenzo

Brill's next letter to Mabel, again replying to a lost one from her, refers to the manuscript of Lawrence's *Sons and Lovers* she had sent him on April 24, 1925 as payment for his treatment of Everett Marcy. Brill also mentions for the first time his daughter, Gioia, and her upcoming marriage at age nineteen to Philip Bernheim.

δ

May 25, 1930

My dear Mabel,

Was pleased to hear from you, and very interested in what you said. You seem to be hazy about the Mss, so I will tell you what the facts are. You offered it to me in lieu of paying for [name blocked out with blue ink, but reads: Everett Marcy][.] There was no question of giving it to me as a pledge. As you know you didn't have to do that. But you gave it to me as payment for the treatment. I have your note which you have written to the Philadelphia dealer[1] telling him that the MSS belonged to me, and it was upon this note that he surrendered it to me. Now, as a matter of fact at the time you offered it to me you also told me that about $2000 was offered by the Phila[delphia] book dealer ... Since Lawrence died I have been approached by two people who somehow knew of my having this manuscript. They claimed to represent the best dealers in New York, and the best offer was $600. I told them I do not care to sell it, which is true.

The only news here is that our daughter, Gioia, will marry[2] next Wednesday. Occasionally I hear from Buffalo patients of John [Evans]. They don't know that I know him, and he doesn't know they are coming to me. Everything they say about him and his wife seems very satisfactory.

Mrs. B. joins me in greeting you and Tony.

Cordially yours,
[A.A.B.]

δ

Brill was likely reporting on news of John Evans because his relationship with Alice was a concern for Mabel, perhaps heightened by observations during her stay in Buffalo after her hysterectomy. When John's marriage began to falter, he appealed to his mother on December 15, 1930: "I don't like the feeling that you are so far away ... Why does anyone love me—I cannot give myself to anyone. I do not want anyone to know that you know about this, as it would only make for unpleasantness ... I count on you, tho'." Despite their recurrent tensions, John did reach out to Mabel for help. (Alice and John divorced in 1932.)

In her next letter to Brill, Mabel announces the completion of *Lorenzo in Taos*, an autobiographical account of her relationship with Lawrence, told in the form of a book-length letter to Robinson Jeffers, the famous poet whom she wanted to lure to Taos. At the time she first met Jeffers, earlier in 1930, he lived in Carmel, California with his wife, Una. Having failed dramatically in her attempt to establish Lawrence as the voice of Taos, Mabel asked Jeffers to take his place: "Well, Jeffers, that is all I have to tell you about Lawrence in Taos. I called him there, but he did not do what I called him to do. He did another thing. Perhaps you are the one who will, after all, do what I wanted him to do: give a voice to this speechless land" (*LIT*, p. 255). Central to the publication of *Lorenzo in Taos* was obtaining permission to publish Lawrence's letters, as Mabel had included almost 100 of his (as well as over twenty of Frieda's) letters to her. She had finished this memoir only shortly before Lawrence died on March 2, 1930. But when Frieda read the manuscript, she objected to its depiction of herself and Lawrence, withheld permission to publish the letters, and requested that Mabel rewrite her book (Byrne, 1995, p. 346). Mabel and Brill exchanged thoughts on this setback.

δ

Sept[ember] 14 [1930] Taos.

Dear Brill,

Thomas Seltzer[3] wired me last week asking for "Sons & Lovers" mms—has a good buyer, he said. I wired you have it & will sell. Do let me know outcome! I wrote a pretty good book about Lorenzo. But Frieda is such a fool she won't let me publish the letters. Though the publishers all say it would run up sale of books & mms.

Love,
Mabel L.

δ

September 19, 1930

Dear Mabel,

Your letters are always interesting and I regret very much that I did not answer them before. I was out of town. It is too bad that all the interesting things that you are writing cannot be published. I hope that some way will be found whereby they can come to light before you are dead, because at that time I shall be dead too and look what I'll miss.

Concerning the manuscript I do not think I care to sell it. I had it for so many years and I like the idea of having it. Seltzer came to see me and made me an offer but I just do not feel like selling it …

Do you expect to come to New York?

As ever,
[A.A.B.]

δ

Had *Lorenzo in Taos* not been published in his lifetime, Brill would indeed have missed a lot, as Mabel included many references to him. In June 1931, Frieda Lawrence finally granted permission to print D. H. Lawrence's and her letters, thereby allowing Mabel to proceed with publication. Frieda had just arrived in Taos after spending tiring days in New York negotiating unpaid royalties, copyrights, and contracts. Mabel and Frieda had not seen each other for seven years and, at the time of this reunion, Mabel already had a publishing contract with Knopf. All she needed was Frieda's permission. Apparently exhausted from her New York ordeal and warmly engaged by their meeting, Frieda consented this time to Mabel's plea but requested that she dedicate *Lorenzo in Taos* to Tony Luhan instead of Robinson Jeffers (Byrne, 1995, pp. 343–346). Although Mabel retained the format, in which she addresses Jeffers throughout, she added a dedication "To Tony and all Indians" before her preface: "Dear Jeffers—This book tries to show you how we felt and acted some years ago" (p. 9). In 1932, *Lorenzo in Taos* was published, claiming on its book jacket to be "as thrilling as any novel and, in the opinion of many, the best portrait we are likely ever to get of that strange genius, D. H. Lawrence" (Luhan scrapbook, *Lawrence, Vol. II*).

Brill writes to Mabel about his reading of *Lorenzo in Taos*.

δ

February 27, 1932

My dear Mabel,

"Lorenzo" came to me a few days before I was taken sick, and I began to read it, when on the 4th of this month, I was suddenly taken sick with a bad appendix and had to be operated on. I am still in the hospital. As soon as I was able, I continued with "Lorenzo" until I finished it. I consider it a very interesting and human document, and I congratulate you on having produced not only a good contribution to human relations, but an excellent literary production. I was naturally interested in the references to me, some of which I probably analyzed differently than you would, but none of them in any way offended me. They all amused me. When I shall be myself again, I will write and have it out with you on a few points.

Meanwhile, I thank you for sending me these echoes from the past, and send you and Tony my very best wishes.

As ever,
Brill

δ

In *Lorenzo in Taos*—after quoting from Lawrence's letter to her on January 27, 1922, before they had even met: "You want to send Brill to hell, and all the analytic therapeutic lot ... No, *never* adapt yourself. Kick Brill in the guts if he tries to come it over you" (*LIT*, p. 28)—Mabel reported on her early experiences with psychoanalysis in 1916 and 1917:

> But you know, Jeffers, one cannot hand oneself out to just anyone. I had never met anyone that could understand all I had to give ... I had been in a psychic jam once or twice and had been eased out by Dr. Jelliffe and again by Dr. Brill. But, heavens! With these analysts one has to be so careful, one has to weigh everything lest one give them more than they can swallow and they turn and rend one for it! Unless one fits oneself into their systems and formulas so they can pigeon-hole one into a type or a case, they grow puzzled or angry or sad. I knew Walter Lippmann[4] was right when he told me I was "a sport" and unclassifiable, but psychoanalysts do not seem to admit exceptional people. One has, then, to be continually assuaging them and measuring down to them out of sheer, kindheartedness. When I think of the time I have spent assuaging analysts at twenty dollars an hour! (p. 71)

Despite this somewhat dismissive summary of her work with psychoanalysts, Mabel did not cease her reliance on Brill for guidance and clarity, through their correspondence and visits.

Writing in *Lorenzo in Taos* from the distance of the passing years, Mabel asserted: "Somehow Lawrence was right, and the analysts were not. Although he never 'adapted' and never fitted into the environment, though he suffered and made anyone who came near him suffer ... Lawrence was right" (p. 26). She concluded: "Lawrence died because he was what is called a neurotic, and because he scorned to learn the mundane mastery that may insure a long, smooth life if the living impulse is emasculated and overcome" (p. 26). Mabel's pronouncement is certainly intriguing, as she apparently attributed Lawrence's early death to his refusal to submit to societal norms, in much the same way that Mabel herself balked when Brill challenged her to adapt to city life. Her tender tone betrays her identification with these wilder aspects of Lawrence, the ones that were set against conforming, to sublimating more primitive impulses. Although Mabel chose to return to Brill for psychoanalysis a number of times over the following years, her lifelong torment remained the war between two extremes: submission to cultural expectations, including sublimation and adaptation, and the embrace of more elemental and passionate urges.

As promised, Brill writes again to Mabel about *Lorenzo in Taos* and comments on the third volume of her memoirs, *Movers and Shakers*, not yet published, in which the second half deals predominantly with her relationship with Maurice Sterne.

δ

April 12, 1932 [see Illustration 13]

Dear Mabel,

I was very glad to hear from you, and I am very intrigued about the volume of 1915–1917, l'affaire Maurice. But, alas, alack! by the time it will be ready, I shall probably not be interested in it!

As for LORENZO, as I said to you before, I believe it is a great book. My feeling is that the reviewers who are not even slightly conversant with your life would not be so interested, but I am sure that those who know you personally, would be fascinated by it. But, aside from the personal element, I would say that literarily it is a great success. As for arguments, it would take so long to argue about these matters, that I would rather not start. Some day when we meet again, and have plenty of time, we shall discuss matters.

With my kindest wishes to you and Tony, in which Mrs. Brill joins me, I am,

Affectionately yours,
Brill

δ

The reviewers seized upon *Lorenzo in Taos* as a somewhat bizarre or twisted venture by Mabel into an unusual kind of biography, or, more accurately, autobiography. One perplexed critic in *The New York Times Book Review* (February 28, 1932) called it "in the last analysis, a puzzling book ... more of a revelation of Mrs. Luhan than of Lawrence." And Aldous Huxley, in London's *Sunday Reference* (August 6, 1933), was baffled and angered: "Psychoanalysts ... are men of science—more or less; but many of their patients go to them as they would go to sorcerers—in the hope of being shown some short cut to well-being. A deplorable feature of contemporary life is the fact that many intelligent and highly cultivated people have taken to a kind of high-class pseudo-philosophical hocus-pocus" (both in Luhan, *LIT: Reviews*).

In contrast to the often bewildered and irritated tone in many press reviews of *Lorenzo in Taos*, Mabel received direct praise from her friends. Even Maurice Sterne wrote on March 10, c. 1932, "Everyone is talking about your book with enthusiasm and interest. I expect to read it soon" (Luhan scrapbook, *Lawrence*). Una Jeffers professed her admiration in a letter dated February 4, 1932:

> Robin joins me completely in enthusiasm about "Lorenzo in Taos."
> Your book came yesterday and I have already read it through again and repeat again it[']s a grand book: Its fresh, vibrating, rushing <u>instancy</u> ... its sincerity and complete lack of pose and affectation quite aside from the interesting material—and the lyrical quality of natural scenery and the clear characterizations of everybody!!! (Luhan scrapbook, *Lawrence*)

Mabel would have taken pleasure in knowing that across the ocean an avid reader of Lawrence's work, H.D., was captivated by her latest memoir. In Vienna, where H.D. was staying for her psychoanalysis with Freud, *Lorenzo in Taos* kept her up late into the night reading. H.D.'s lover Bryher had ordered Mabel's book for her, writing from London on May 20, 1933: "I had the Taos book sent out as the old dame was analysed partially by Brill and then went mad ... such a dreadful jumble, one should be very careful NOT to break off pa [i.e., psychoanalysis] in the middle." H.D. replied on May 23, 1933: "Anyhow I stayed up too late reading Taos. It is marvellous ... I never laughed so much in my life ... Did she actually go 'crazy,' or only F-blue [Gurdjieff's Institute at Fontainebleau] for a while?????? Nothing I have read has amused me so, she is a wonderful recorder" (Friedman, 2002, pp. 300, 313–314).

Notes

1. Identity unknown.
2. Brill had also let Freud know about Gioia's marital plans, apparently in a lost letter which Freud answered on April 6, 1930: "Now, as for the surprising news of Gioja's [sic] engagement, it is occupying my thoughts in more ways than one. In the first place, I have never been able to fulfill my duty as her godfather and would be very pleased if you and Mrs. Brill could show me a way to participate from here in the upcoming wedding celebration" (SFA). It is unknown what role, if any, Freud played in this ceremony.
3. Lawrence's publisher in New York until the mid-1920s.
4. American author, editor, and journalist, who was a good friend of Mabel's during her New York years.

CHAPTER THIRTEEN

Intimate Memories

The first book of Mabel's four-volume autobiography, *Intimate Memories: Background*, was published in 1933 by Harcourt, Brace. Although her original plan had been to wait until some people had died before bringing out her memoirs (as she had indicated years earlier to both Gertrude and Leo Stein), she clearly abandoned this idea and forged ahead. Perhaps she was influenced by Lawrence's advice, offered in a letter from April 19, 1926 after he had read her manuscripts: "Collect your MS and keep them all in a safe. Don't show them to anybody else, just now ... Then, after a few years, take out your MSS again, and do what you wish with them" (*LIT*, p. 268). However, Lawrence had also cried out in a letter that same year: "Why oh why didn't you change the names! My dear Mabel, call in all the copies, keep them under lock and key, and then carefully, scrupulously change the names: at least do that: before you let one page go out of your hands again" (*LIT*, p. 266).

Mabel did not change any names and was most worried about the effect of publication on her mother. In *Family Affairs*, Mabel wrote about pressure from her publisher, Alfred Harcourt:

> But I couldn't face publishing it. The thought of those revelations, that had cost me so much to write and would hurt the family so much to read, sent hot flashes all over me whenever I considered it for a moment. Still, one part of me was tempted. Harcourt was very skil[l]ful. He told me it was a lovely book and that it wouldn't hurt anyone.
>
> "But my mother!" I replied. "And my aunt Georgie!"
>
> He kept on writing and urging me, and the more I thought of it, the more I wanted to publish it and follow up Lorenzo in Taos, that had been so hated and so admired, with another book, and see what people would think of it.
>
> The thought of my mother was, finally, the only consideration that held me back—the thought of her anger, really. And since, more and more lately, we had all been forced to think of her in connection with her money and what she could do to us when she didn't like what we were doing,[1] I had to consider this and even write of it to Harcourt and tell him that if she didn't like the book, she might disinherit me. But he replied that he thought it would make her proud of her daughter, for he felt sure it would be one of the two or three outstanding books of the year. (pp. 287–288)

After deciding to move forward with publication, Mabel received a letter from her mother: "I don't want you to put anything about me and my affairs in that book of yours. Why don't you write about all those crazy people in Florence. If you do I'll write the publisher I won't have it and that he's not to sell it" (FA, p. 326). The book, however, was already in press, and Mabel's mother did not follow through on her threat.

When *Background* was published, Mabel sent her mother a copy: "I ... was waiting for a blow-up, but it didn't come. After quite a while, she acknowledged it, only saying: 'Monty [her husband] is at the book ...' And later, when she got to it, her only comment was: 'I don't see why you had to write about your Uncle Carlos like that'" (FA, p. 401). With the kind of openness that characterized the entire volume, Mabel had described the lonely, dull life led by her handsome Uncle Carlos (the Mediterranean husband of Aunt Georgie, the youngest sister of Mabel's mother), and then revealed: "He would take me into his arms and kiss me ... And he would whisper, '*Cherie, cherie, tu es si douce,*'... My first kisses in this world were from Uncle Carlos's perfumed Latin lips, and no other man of my own race has ever in any way shown me this kind of love" (p. 142). This comment underscoring "race" is certainly compelling given the radical leap, years after these kisses, of Mabel's marriage to Tony Luhan.

In Brill's next letter, he praises *Background* and encourages Mabel to continue publishing her memoirs without overdue concern for the short-term consequences.

δ

March 29, 1933

My dear Mabel,

Just finished the "Background" of your "Intimate Memories," and I hope that the others will be following soon.

Your "Lorenzo in Taos" I read when I was convalescing in the hospital, and although I was very interested and saw glimpses of yourself in it which were particularly interesting, it was nothing like your "Intimate Memories." Here you are at your best. I am sure, however, that you are only giving the world glimpses of yourself. Nevertheless, I feel that it would be wrong for you to follow your original scheme and wait until you are dead and buried before your other memories are open to the world. You could surely give them out with a little concealement [sic] and a little glossing, which certainly would be much better than nothing. I say "nothing" because, after all, I will never read them if you do not give them out and many other people who are most interested in you will be equally deprived of them. Last, but not least, you, yourself, will miss a lot.

After all, what do we care what happens after we die? As Victor Hugo said "After death, there is nothing but equalling nothings."[2] So, please Mabel, hurry up and strike the iron when it is still blazing. Your volume is interesting and fascinating, and one of the best books of mental and emotional evolution that has come to my attention.

As ever,
Brill

δ

Although Brill was right about the intense interest of many people in Mabel's memoirs, others were hurt so badly by the publication that they never spoke to her again, particularly after reading the later volumes. Maurice Sterne, for example, wrote to Mabel on July 1, 1933 about *Background*, praising it as "a fine work and consistent with the Mabel I knew ... both a small model and mould of the future woman Mabel" (Luhan scrapbook, *Intimate Memories and Letters*). But he was later deeply offended by her portrayal of him in her third memoir, *Movers and Shakers*. Nonetheless, Brill's unequivocal and forceful acclaim for the first volume of Mabel's autobiography was generally reflected in comments by others and in highly favorable reception by the press.

The New York Times (March 26, 1933) praised Mabel's writing as a "frank art that is admirable from beginning to end" and proclaimed "[T]he book has the importance of a chronicle of revolt, for it is manifestly the minute reappraisal of a background." *The New Republic* (May 10, 1933) considered *Background* worthy of high merit: "Here is the beginning of a life work as significant in its own right as any one of a chosen number of French eighteenth century memoirs" (both in Luhan, *Background: Reviews*). Book sales matched the enthusiastic reviews and Harcourt's earlier reassuring prediction: *Background* was judged a best seller by *The New York Times* in April 1933. The American public's thirst for exposing the true inner life under a muffled and well-ordered outward presentation is reflected in the commercial success of Mabel's refreshingly honest book, filled with candid observations.

Not all reviewers, however, sang Mabel's praises. The *Buffalo Courier Express* (March 16, 1933) was certain that *Background* "is sure to create something of a sensation in local society, for these memories are not only intimate, but in some instances brutally frank." As for Mabel's treatment of her subjects: "[S]he has not hesitated to drag them out and hold them up to view with a merciless disregard for the sensitive relations of friendships and even close family ties that is rather shocking" (Luhan, *Background: Reviews*). Mabel's reluctance to publish her memoirs while anyone was still alive was certainly well-founded. She risked friendships and family trying to achieve her longing for public approval and a kind of fame.

On March 26, 1933, within days of Brill's previous letter to her, Mabel wrote an essay, *My Attitude in the Writing of Autobiography*,—published in an abridged version by *The New York World-Telegram* on April 19, 1933 under the title, "Mrs. Luhan's Life Story Aims to Illuminate Psychology of Children: Lawrence Protégé Tells the Motives Which Led to Her Much Discussed 'Intimate Memories: Background'"—that remains unpublished in its unedited form. Here Mabel explained that she wrote her memoirs free from the influence of an anticipated audience, and that she had initially planned not to publish these volumes until she was dead—an arrangement akin to confidentiality in psychoanalysis where revelations are protected from public exposure. Consistent with Brill's teachings (although not acknowledging him as a source), Mabel set out to "try and write down, myself, my whole life from first to last, so that I could understand it better, so that I could become more conscious and more free" (p. 2), a reference to Brill's commitment to abreaction and belief in the liberating effects of writing and making personal history conscious.

In this essay, Mabel credited D. H. Lawrence with the initial idea of putting words to her experiences, resulting in "a surprising realization": "I had never written things down before. I had talked them over, or mused upon them … Now, when I wrote down some sequences of facts for Lawrence, I was thrilled to find how <u>reasonable</u> and <u>logical</u> life seemed" (p. 2). Thus emboldened, Mabel embarked on her autobiography project with "one clear determination":

> I would, from the very beginning, look upon myself as an object in space like other objects apart from me; I would try to see myself as clearly as I saw all the others moving and being about me. I would make a great effort not to identify myself, in sympathy and interest, more with Mabel than with Mary or Martha, but I would regard her as a victim of circumstances, of heredity and environment, as the others were. (p. 3)

Drawing upon her knowledge of Jung's teachings, Mabel continued to explain her mission:

> Dr. Carl Jung tells us everyone has a "persona" carefully built up to face the world with, a kind of social facade or outer shell that hides or protects the real self …
>
> Now almost all autobiographies have been the histories of the "persona" only; of the ingenious, mechanical, masquerading self. The most real, as well as the most rare, autobiography, is the one that consciously describes the activities of the "persona," and at the same time tells the true reactions, thoughts, and feelings beneath the mask that it is. That is the terribly difficult thing I tried to do in

> my autobiography; difficult because there is nothing harder in the world than to really get on to oneself ...
>
> To determine then to, so to speak, unmask one's "persona" in an effort to obtain the true history of an individual, necessitated a stoical attitude that, painful as it was to maintain, <u>could</u> result in as much reality as was there to tell about; along with the freedom of expression that came from being able to ignore the public, the criticism of other people, or the desire for their admiration. (pp. 3–4)

This last passage, with its value placed on free expression, seems to flow directly from Mabel's own immersion in psychoanalysis, not just from her own treatments with Jelliffe and Brill—during which she revealed her private thoughts, recorded and discussed her dreams, and found a secure place away from public scrutiny where she could practice being herself—but also from her readings in psychoanalysis and her desire to educate herself. It seems impossible that she could have written *Background* without the illuminating experience of psychoanalysis.

Background was published as the product of Mabel's persistent, even unrelenting, efforts to understand herself and her childhood experiences. Despite her reservations about publication, she could also feel "What a relief, in autobiography, to be oneself!" (p. 6). By breaking her own previous silence about her childhood, she hoped to inspire others not to grasp onto theirs too firmly. Mabel ends her essay with a moving plea towards openness and against secrets, a passage that also ends her published article in *The New York World-Telegram*:

> But there was a reason why I finally agreed to let it go [to be published]. It was the hope that, in showing up the dark places in my own childhood, I could perhaps help some children today. Of course there is a vast difference in the understanding of child psychology since the years of the eighties and nineties. Yet I myself know plenty of misunderstood children, and besides them, I am sure there are many grown-ups who, to this day, carry in their deepest souls horrid little recollections of small acts which they shudder to remember ...
>
> Well, if this book "Background" can help even three or four parents to understand the queer, lonely, intense, inner lives of their children, and can make a few grown-ups, with guilty, intimate childhood memories, realize theirs was a common and almost

universal experience, then I have done a right thing in publishing it, no matter what anyone says! (pp. 7–8)

Publishing these early memories was certainly personally liberating for Mabel, as she revealed in *Family Affairs*:

> "Background," then, delivered me from my hatred for my mother. You can't hate what you are sorry for, you can't hate others when you understand that they can't help what they do and say.
>
> For these last years, then, I have been free of those terrible, unexpressed resentments and depressions that I had had to endure whenever I was with her, feelings that were physical and that came, either like serpents coiling and uncoiling in madness in the vagina, or like an iron hand clamped inwardly upon the contents of my belly, so that heart, stomach and liver were squeezed temporarily dead. (p. 3)

Brill would certainly have subscribed to this belief that Mabel's physical symptoms eased and vanished after the cathartic process of abreaction through writing about her mother.

Soon after the publication of *Background*, Mabel's mother died, on May 23, 1933. Muriel Draper wrote to Mabel on June 20, 1933, praising the memoir ("I have wept over it ... Mabel darling, it is such a valuable thing to do"), and offering: "Carl [Van Vechten] tells me your mother died. It must have released you; she has been so long in you like the coiled spring of a watch that didn't tell time" (Luhan scrapbook, *Intimate Memories and Letters*). Mabel described the sequenced effects of her mother's death. Initially, she felt very little until she boarded the plane for New York and saw Tony watching: "He kept his eyes upon us, was still looking, until he faded out of view. That made my tears come. He always, always touched the live spot in me—just he and no one else!" (*FA*, p. 446). Then she arrived in New York and visited her mother's body:

> I leaned towards her ... and all of a sudden I heard myself saying, inside me: "Forgive me, Mother, that you couldn't love me!"—and the voice shook me and made me cry. I cried with my hands over my eyes, to shut out the sight of such an aloof, sweet creature as she was, as she still was, more aloof than ever, as it seemed, and so alone from first to last ...

I felt glad I had cried for my mother. I had not liked her much. (*FA*, pp. 451–452)

It is striking that Mabel seemed to forgive her mother for being unable to love her own daughter, an insight likely born from her final understanding of the challenges her mother faced—a lonely life with an unstable husband—as well as Mabel's own grasp of the qualities in herself that made her hard to love.

After her mother's funeral, Mabel had lunch with "dear old Brill" at his home in New York: "Brill and I had a long, laughing talk. We really like each other ... I touched upon my books, which he had already read, and whether it had really hurt my mother very much; but he said: 'No. I think it tickled her, and satisfied her hate for your father ... After all, she triumphed'" (*FA*, p. 474). Brill's reassurance about her mother's feelings must have been quite meaningful to Mabel, perhaps even empowering her to plan for further publication of her memoirs despite her hesitation to print potentially hurtful passages about those still living.

Until this lunch meeting in 1933, it is unclear if Brill and Mabel had seen each other since 1926 when they had met in New York. Although Gioia Bernheim did recall in a letter (personal communication, March 13, 1997) that Mabel spent some time at her parents' house between 1930 and 1934—"Mabel probably was low in cash & wanted a place to stay when my family put her up for the winter. She would always find ways to do what she wanted"—no other sources place her in New York, except for her mother's funeral, until April 1934. An article in the *Chicago Herald Examiner* on April 20, 1934, reported: "Mabel Luhan is still in New York at the moment ... being very gay and going to parties with those whom many could consider too high-brow to be fun" (Luhan scrapbook, *Taos*). On April 26, 1934, Mabel wrote to Van Vechten that she was leaving New York for Taos. It is certainly possible Mabel may have seen Brill during her visit, but no letters between them exist from this time.

Months after her mother's death, Mabel's own maternal skills were challenged when in 1934 she wrote her son an unwelcome, regrettably lost, letter. After his divorce from Alice, John Evans had married the novelist Claire Spencer on December 5, 1933, and Mabel unfortunately continued to offer advice and criticism of his parenting. John's reply was fiery and furious, stating that her "life with Tony has become a farce and a wreck," accusing her of jealousy and meddling in his life, and pleading with her to "clear out of my life, once and for all":

> I am writing to tell you, and for the last time, that I AM LIVING MY LIFE AS I WANT TO LIVE IT, and shall continue to do so, THANK GOD, until I die ...
>
> YOU, lecturing to ME on children and child-love! YOU, the perfect Mother, her whole life laid on the sacrificial altar of child-love, (!) are telling ME? MY GOD ...
>
> There is more love in the little finger of my hand for each one of my children than you ever had for me.

John's attack of Mabel for her utter lack of sacrifice as a parent runs chillingly parallel to Mabel's similar complaints about her mother.

* * *

Winter in Taos

In Brill's last letter to Mabel about *Background*, he had appealed to her to "hurry up and strike the iron when it is still blazing" and expressed hope that more autobiographies would soon appear in print. Likely spurred on by his encouragement, as well as praise from friends and the press, Mabel published two books with Harcourt, Brace two years later in 1935. *Winter in Taos*, a memoir outside of her *Intimate Memories* series, is a masterfully written narrative of a winter day from beginning to end. This book is markedly different from her other autobiographical volumes, with its focus on nature and domestic details rather than on personalities and conflicts. Mabel's descriptions of interior and exterior worlds are evocative and sensuous, vivid in their language and contrasts. She writes about the effect of winter on her mood:

> Something like a shiver went over me at the thought of the winter thickening still more, covering us, clamping us down, until I remembered what I learned long ago, but always forget and have to learn anew each year: that if one gives up and lets it come down over one, if one sinks into the season and is a part of it, there is peace in this submission. Only in resistence [sic] there is melancholy and panic. (p. 102)

Mabel's acceptance of the rhythms of the seasons is in great contrast to her earlier, but still recurring, consuming strivings to control her environment.

This inspired treatment of the entwined cycles of nature and human experience earned her praise from writers and critics. American author Thornton Wilder wrote to Mabel that *Winter in Taos* "... was as good all through as it was in the chapters you showed me in Taos. It has such serene poise at the heart of it ... I am very fond of it." Maurice Sterne commented in a letter on April 21, 1935: "I didn't think that you could be so objective—could observe sympathetically—I always felt that you were too much interested in what is going on inside of Mabel—that was bound to interfere with perceiving what is going on outside of Mabel" (both in Luhan scrapbook, *Winter in Taos*). The *New York Herald Tribune* (March 31, 1935) considered the memoir "entertaining reading" and *The New York Times* (April 7, 1935) deemed: "Its best parts are all ears and eyes, nose and palate" (in Luhan, *Winter in Taos: Reviews*). *Winter in Taos* established Mabel as a highly skilled observer of her surroundings.

* * *

European memories

The second volume of her memoirs, *European Experiences*, also published in 1935, covered the years she spent in Europe as Mabel Dodge. On September 30, 1935, Mabel wrote to Leo Stein from St. Joseph's Sanatorium in Albuquerque about her experience of publication:

> Here I am flattened out ... They say it is the result of Flu—but I doubt I had that—I feel it is more likely the pain & strain of bringing out the last book "European Experiences"—for every time I do bring out one of my books I suffer an eclipse: my heart falters & grows faint & I give up. Actually it is no easy thing to break the veils that one disguised one's trivialities with, one's ignorances & puerile sufferings ... The trouble is one betrays everyone's persona as soon as one betrays one's own, & probably one has no right to tear off these masks. (GLSC)

In spite of her doubts, Mabel had forged ahead again, perhaps in the belief that bringing painful truth to light is more valuable in the long run than the immediate reactions of others.

In Mabel's next letter to Brill, written more than two years since their last existing piece of correspondence, she describes her physical and emotional distress after publishing *European Experiences* and complains about not being understood by the press. She also relates her bizarre lunch with Sándor Radó, a psychoanalyst who had been part of Ferenczi's circle in Budapest, and had become the director of training at the Berlin Psychoanalytic Institute in 1922. Brill had invited Radó to come from Berlin to be the first director of the newly established New York Psychoanalytic Institute in 1931, and Radó had accepted. (The New York Psychoanalytic Society, founded by Brill in 1911, had become recognized as an Institute in 1931 by the American Psychoanalytic Association.)

δ

Oct[ober] 22 [1935]

Dear Brill,

When this last book came out I sent several copies to friends but I haven't heard from some of them whether they got it or not. You were one. Did you get it? … Only a few people, critics, seem to know what I am trying to do in these books! They use such words as "unintentional" & "unconscious"! This gripes me! They don't seem to see one can become objective about one's subjective past & observing oneself like a laboratory specimen, describe its behavior for use in tabulation! Anyway, I bet you get me. Don't you?

Just now I am in one of those fearful periods where I can't work, can't respond, seem empty & unknowing. These always pass but it has gone on too long this time. I published "Winter in Taos" last spring, rewrote "European Ex[periences]" & published it this fall, rewrote & edited "Makers & Shakers"[3] the volume about New York 1911–1914 this summer, but for real writing I haven't done any for months & am lonesome for that full flowing feeling! I used to get <u>started</u> by you when I was near enough but now it's too far away, & I am rather hard up so I have to roam around, go thro' the motions of living & hope for the best, but it's a bad depressing phase. I don't have those awful depressions I used to have before analysis, only colorless grey oldish states of being!

I was rather intrigued by your Dr. Rado. He acted. I mean I couldn't fathom the little man so I supposed he was clowning in some way. Then Maurice [Sterne] acted up thro' his embar[r]assment & self[-]consciousness & irritated me. So the lunch party wasn't very successful, & to admit the truth, dragged so I had a message delivered to me from the kitchen that they had telephoned me from the Indian school[4] they wanted me out there. So I left the party & dashed out! Fortunately I had the presence of mind to drive out to the school where I saw the schoolteacher, for my party all got into their car & followed me out there! I by that time was on my way back <u>here</u> where I met them leaving again, they not having found me, returning <u>here</u> where they ran into <u>Tony</u> who had staid [sic] away until he thought they were gone for he didn't want to see Maurice! Maurice was by then looking dark & mad & hurt. Ah me! These things are so hard to manage well. Tell me, is Dr. Rado a wonderful analyst or just a little boy? He acted so simple & had the oddest ideas. He said our buildings of adobe had no <u>edges</u>, all were <u>round</u> because of fear of pain. He said he could analyze all the ingredients in any food he ate, & we had some little cookies made of flour, egg & vanilla & powdered with sugar. Not difficult to fathom! But he analyzed these with the utmost seriousness. I liked Mrs. [Emmy] Rado the best, so cheerful, well balanced & unimaginative but slightly hard boiled thro' her lack of imaginative apprehension![5]

Why don't you come out here & give me a whiff of analysis to start me off? Are you well, happy, busy, all the family too?

Love,
Mabel

δ

The reviews that Mabel specifically quoted to Brill were from the *New York Herald Tribune* (September 20, 1935)—"The most unfortunately risible chapter, pure burlesque, though unintentionally so, would be spoiled by condensing it"—and the *Chicago Daily News* (October 2, 1935)—"Unconsciously, Mrs. Luhan becomes her own Boswell." In addition, *The New York Times Book Review* (October 20, 1935) observed: "It is astonishing that any book as frank as Mrs. Luhan's should also be so dull ... it is an extremely disappointing affair." In contrast to these disparaging reviews, at least one critic found some delight in her new autobiography: *The New York World-Telegram* (September 19, 1935) noted that "Mabel crossed out some of the most intimate passages, but left enough hot stuff in her book to give us all a good time" (all in Luhan, *European Experiences: Reviews*).

Mabel's cumulative response to the reviews of her memoir was an emotional collapse, a reversion to a familiar and airless place of depression. In her letter to Brill, she seemed to take some refuge in the knowledge that he understood her at these times, a powerful sustaining of her therapeutic connection with him. She would have done well to recall her own newspaper column from 1917, "Mabel Dodge Talks About the In-Between Times," where she described the same emptiness she now felt. In contrast to the "best times" when "you are *focused, one-pointed*; all your energy pouring out in one direction" and "accomplishing, and creating," there are the other times:

> I have always called them the intervals: those darkened times when all the tempo of life dwindles down to a faint, slow beat ...
>
> You look back sadly to the height from which you have descended! How far away! You look forward to a dark, blank wall! ... You feel no strength for climbing. You can only sit still; but "blessed is he who *hath the strength to sit still* and the *wisdom to keep silence* [sic]" at these times.
>
> For, don't you see these are the recuperative pauses? You are surely, silently drawing yourself together out of the boundless silence around you. You gather and gather energy, power, life—it fills you like water fills a glass.

Mabel knew then that "So *much happens* in the interval!" and, had she been able to draw upon her own resources, she could have reassured herself by remembering her very own words: "Try and feel yourself just accumulating strength day by day—night by night—and one morning you will lift your head and find your sky above you—and you on your way again—putting something through!" (Luhan scrapbook, *Misc. Vol. I*). This kind of faith in reinvigoration is what she was seeking from Brill.

In his next letter, assuming the tone of a pep talk, Brill speaks directly to Mabel's despair about the critical reception of her memoir, employing a more intimate and personal approach than in his preceding letters. For the first time, Brill uses the word "love" in his parting sentence, warmly reassuring her of his views and feelings.

δ

October 26, 1935

Dear Mabel,

First, I never got your book. Consequently, I did not read it because somehow I felt that if you had written a book you should send me a copy. However, I read some of the notices, and I said to myself, "That is the way with the newer generation." "Times change, and we with them" is an old saying. For that reason I think it was a good move to give out these books at the present time because there are still a great many who are fascinated by what you say. I have heard many such statements.

I feel very badly that I am not near you now to pull you out of this grey period. I imagine that I know exactly how to do it when I am with you. Your exhibitionism has probably been more or less shocked because of some of the critics and your libido, as it were, withdraws from the conflict! But Mabel, you can put it all over them! You always looked them straight in the face and told them to go to Hell, and you should continue to do so. I am sure that sooner or later you will have gathered sufficient libido to overcome such little pricks of your narcissism. After all, you have done remarkably well, and you deserve a small period of libidinal stagnation. Don't be surprised, however, if some day I am out there in Taos! I have had no vacation, and if I were not tied up with giving courses, etc., I would come right out.[6]

Concerning Monsieur Rado, Mabel you are great! Your characterization of him is perfect. The reason that I did not answer the letter that you sent after you met him was because you said that he did not claim to be a real Freudian. Had I answered your letter, I would have said that he was a G— D— liar to give you that impression, and that he did that for some political reason. I invited him to come here because I never thought that he was anything but a Freudian.[7] He is a good lecturer, and as he had been so occupied in the Berlin Psychoanalytic Institute, I thought that he would be a good man for our own institute, which I started about four years ago. He has done very well as a teacher, but he has always been known as a politician etc., etc. From your description of him I note that he did not fool you much. I believe, however, that you are wrong about his wife when you say she is unimaginative. You have not seen enough of her.

Your description of the luncheon is wonderful! I just roared with laughter when I read it. I could visualize Maurice with his wounded narcissism in the presence of Madame Rado, with whom he is supposed to have or have had an affair. (Mable [sic], this is not for publication. I am giving you public gossip.) I would have given anything to have seen him meet Tony. You should have known that the only reason why Maurice wanted to bring them to you was to show off, and you had to spoil it all by being called away from the luncheon.

Things are not very different here than they have been. I am just as busy as I have always been and I am still enjoying my work, except the lack of time with which I am always obsessed. There are so many things that I would like to do and I cannot do them. My children, of course, are grown up. Gioia has been married now five years. She married a boy friend [sic] as soon as she graduated from high school. They attended college together[8] and graduated in June 1934. Since that time they have been living here and are seemingly getting along well.[9] Edmund is a senior in Harvard. He is specializing in biology and is doing well. Both of them are a little neurotic, but not very badly so.

There are a great many things that I should like to tell you, but I shall have to wait until we meet. I am always delighted to receive letters from you. They are so refreshing that I can always imagine that you are talking to me. You see I love you just as much as I ever did and I am convinced that your other friends feel the same.

As ever,
Brill

δ

Perhaps emboldened by Brill's letter, and by what she considered to be inaccurate reviews, Mabel was moved to write a letter to the *New York Herald Tribune* challenging its reviewer's opinion. The newspaper replied in print on November 3, 1935:

Mabel Dodge Luhan writes us to protest against our having said that some of her effects, in "European Memories," were unintentional ... "Can't you concede that one may examine one's subjective past and write about it objectively? Anyway, believe it or not, that is the method by which these intimate memories are written ..."

We feel a little embarrassed about answering ... If Mrs. Luhan insists that she meant her book to convey what it does convey, we can't very well contradict her ... But—er—well—a book necessarily conveys a good deal about the person writing it as well as the subject ... We mean, it is a revelation of Mrs. Luhan in the present as much as in the past. (in *European Experiences: Reviews*)

Even though she could wilt from negative responses to her candid pursuit of a kind of objective truth in her memoir writing, Mabel maintained an ardent devotion to the value of unmasking as a way of liberating both herself and others.

In her next letter to Brill, Mabel reports that she is now working on a new book, in which the main character, Gaza, senses homosexual leanings in the man she desires. Her novel, *Water of Life* (c. 1938), reached 390 pages and remains unpublished.

δ

Nov[ember] 4 [1935]

Dear old Brill,

Your nice letter here. Thank you. I feel better but still diminished. I think you are right. I feel my work is good & has its importance so the critics hurt my feelings! But if I can get to work I will be alright. I am <u>trying</u> to do a novel on homosexuality! That ought to hold them.

Love,
Mabel

δ

Unfortunately, the storm about *European Experiences* was not over, as now Mabel was experiencing the backlash from friends whose feelings she had hurt. On October 22, 1935, she had written to Leo Stein about her dilemma in publishing these memoirs, which featured him and Gertrude in a chapter entitled "The Steins": "You may not like it. I am horrid in it as I <u>was</u> then ... Gertrude may want to sue me ... Several people who are in it & to whom I sent it haven't written so I fear they are hurt. Muriel Draper, for instance ... Horrors! Yet what to do? Either not do it or really do it, it seems to me" (GLSC). Leo replied on November 3, 1935:

> As for your book, there are brilliantly vivid pictures in it and interesting tales, but for the question that you specially pose there is a good deal to be said against you. You said in a former letter "one betrays everyone's persona as soon as one betrays one's own." Let us admit this as permissible. The trouble is that in writing like this, you do so much more than this—ever so much more than this.

Stein believed Mabel was doing harm in writing her way about others and also asserted that Mabel's account of his and Gertrude's relationship "is false in every particular."

In her next communication with Brill, Mabel included a typed copy of this letter from Leo Stein, and Brill quickly responded.

δ

Nov[ember] 30 [1935]

Dear Brill,

I am sending you this copy of Leo's letter to read because I think it will interest you. It is a very interesting letter in itself. Please return it in enclosed envelope.

Did Harcourt send you another copy of "European Ex[periences]"? I wrote them to do so. They sent one the first time to 15 W. 70th St! It should be there! Let me know if one way or the other, you have a copy! I want you to have one.

Ever yours,
Mabel L.

δ

December 5, 1935

Dear Mabel,

I have not as yet received any book, and I will say that it would have been impossible for me not to receive any had Harcourt sent it.

I was very interested in Leo's letter, and I was not at all surprised at his attitude. You will have to be fully prepared for just such and even more violent reactions from people whom you have or will discuss in the future.

If you could say that "so and so" is a genius and a wonderful person you would have no such reactions, but if you tell the truth, as you say it, he or she will not be satisfied. I would suggest that you collect all these protests in another volume as sort of a postscript to your works.

Cordially,
Brill

δ

Brill's measured response to the negative comments about *European Experiences* must have been heartening for Mabel. He embraced the conflict, even suggesting that she publish the written objections to honor her turmoil around speaking the truth as she saw it. Brill's ideas likely inspired her organization of the scrapbooks she created for each of her published memoirs: the first section generally features reviews, both positive and negative, pasted onto the pages; flipping over the scrapbook and starting from what was once the back, Mabel included typed copies of both positive and negative letters about that particular memoir.

Among the letters in the scrapbook for *European Experiences* is one from Edwin Dodge asking "Why did you have to do those Intimate Memories?" and another from Nina Bull who, in anticipation, became very nervous after reading Mabel's latest volume: "Now by way of removing my own 'façade': —I find that all attempts to see your purpose clearly and objectively are decidedly distorted by a fear of what you are going to say about me in your next books … It is the half-truths that you publish, Mabel, that are so damning! Publishing can become a vice, just as reticence can. It can become a mania" (all in Luhan scrapbook, *European Experiences*). Bull appealed directly to Mabel for restraint in her published observations.

This scrapbook also contains a letter from Carl Van Vechten, c. fall 1935, in response to Mabel's letter from October 4, 1935: "Did you get my new book? Not a word out of you … Nor from Muriel. I hope to goodness I didn't hurt her feelings. I tried not to & edited & pared it down." Van Vechten's reply addressed the question of truth in her writing of *European Experiences* and praised instead *Winter in Taos*, published the same year:

> Of course I[']m not "mad." It didn't seem very important to me to write you about the book because I don't like it and I didn't see any sense of telling you that! You seem to belittle every character in it, including yourself ... and the characters I know, I would hardly recognize from your dealing with them, but maybe that's the way you see it and feel it and maybe you are right. I suppose "truth" can always be no more than one's own point of view ... Permit me to prefer (and love) Winter in Taos. (in Luhan scrapbook, *European Experiences*)

Van Vechten had written to Gertrude Stein on September 23, 1935: "Has Harcourt sent you Mabel Luhan's European Experiences? & have you see[n] how Mabel writes (at length) about you & Alice? I think you better had. It will amuse you or something!" He appealed again on October 14, 1935: "Please write me when you read Mabel's book!" (Burns, 1986, pp. 446, 448). When Stein finally read *European Experiences*, she replied: "We did get Mabel's book ... and Alice deep in it reads me choice pieces, and they are pretty choice, but where are you in it, I hoped you would be in it it seems Muriel [Draper] is so mad she went back from Chicago although she was headed for Taos, a good time is always to be had by all" (Burns, 1986, p. 460). In fact, Draper had pleaded with Mabel on April 16, 1935: "I do hope there is nothing in the 'European Volume' to hurt the Drapers' feelings ... I would hate to have them hurt by an attitude of the past congealed in the written word." Mabel reportedly reassured Draper that she would not include anything unkind, as revealed in a c. 1936 letter to Mabel from Nina Bull: "I've just heard that you told Muriel Draper you wouldn[']t put anything in it about her that would be embarrassing—& I don[']t doubt you intended not to—but she is simply furious—& honestly I would be too if you wrote like that about me." While in a quandary about writing of the past with brutal honesty and judgment of not only herself but others, Mabel apparently decided to ignore the bonds of friendship in her editing and publishing decisions. Her passion for self-revelation and her hope for its harsh yet beneficial effects may have blinded her to the sensitivities of others. In the end, over both her own and others' objections, Mabel valued telling her own story the way she believed was most true to herself. She even reasoned that public exposure could be preferable for those who desired privacy and wanted to hide behind their masks: her actions might force truths that, in her mind, others were unwilling to face. To many friends' dismay, however, she never seemed to understand the permanent consequences of her actions on some of her relationships.

At the end of 1935, Mabel sent a copy of *Winter in Taos* to Brill. Since no feelings were hurt and reviewers were positive, Mabel had not been plagued with doubts or in need of reassurance after its publication.

δ

December 13, 1935

Dear Mabel,

> I got the book and I am reading it with great pleasure and avidity. I am enjoying it immensely. I think it is a fine book and I like your style, etc. ever so much. More anon!
>
> Affectionately,
A. A. Brill

δ

Notes

1. Mabel's mother had cut off John Evans's allowance when he divorced his wife Alice in 1932.
2. Brill (1947b) cited this quotation more accurately: "But, if 'after death there is nothing but equal nothings' as Victor Hugo puts it, they nevertheless still live in our memories" (p. 203). This quotation from Hugo's *Les Misérables* appears as "Beyond the tomb are only equal nothings" in Wilbour's translation (1931, p. 27).
3. Mabel's original title for *Movers and Shakers*.
4. Likely one on the Taos Pueblo.
5. On October 28, 1935, Emmy Radó wrote to Mabel about this lunch: "I was sorry about the luncheon too. Maurice was quite tense, he had been hurt the day before by Tony … Tony did not seem to be pleased by seeing him; and so Maurice was not in the right mood in Taos." She reported: "My husband cannot forgive himself, for not having made himself understood by you."

6. Brill was then teaching psychoanalysis at the College of Physicians and Surgeons, Columbia University, as well as New York University and the New York Psychiatric Institute.
7. Although for years he considered Freud a hero, having been deeply drawn to him after hearing him lecture in 1913 at the University of Vienna, Radó became gradually more and more critical of him and disdainful of what he saw as Freud's self-importance (Hale, 1995, pp. 34–35).
8. University of Wisconsin (Bernheim, personal communication, July 2, 2000).
9. In fact, they remained married for seventy years until Philip died in 2000.

CHAPTER FOURTEEN

New York memories

In Brill's next letter to Mabel, written months before the publication of her new memoir, *Movers and Shakers*, he makes his first written invitation for her to stay with him in New York—an offer, as mentioned earlier, not unprecedented for psychoanalysts at this time. He also asks her to welcome a friend of his to Taos, Isador Coriat, a Boston psychoanalyst who was among the first in America to view literature and art through the lens of psychoanalysis.

δ

June 30, 1936

My dear Mabel,

Two events have happened in my family! My daughter, Gioia, gave birth to a son about a week ago, and I have the proud added title of "grandfather."[1] Secondly, my son, Edmund, graduated from Harvard[2] and I was in Cambridge to see him go through the motions; and that is why this letter. I met an old friend of mine there, Dr. Coriat of Boston. Among other things he told me that he expects to take his vacation in Taos. I told him that I would write to you and that you would be very glad to meet him. Coriat is one of the pioneers in psychopathology ... Should he come there, I am sure you will find him interesting and I will appreciate any favours that you might show him.

I am on my way to Europe. I am going to sail on the 8th of July for about a month.

I am sure you are busy on your next book, which will contain all the letters that you got permission to reproduce. The other night I met Vera [Sterne] on the street ... and she told me that Maurice was in New York for a while, and thereupon she proceeded to tell me about the memorable visit. It was interesting, but not very enlightening. Em[m]y Rado told me some time ago that you were anxious to come to New York, but that you could not afford to do so. If you ever wish to do that, Mabel, I will be very glad to house you. We have plenty of room and you will be free to do whatever you darn please!

With my kindest greetings to you and Tony, in which Mrs. Brill joins me, I am,

As ever,
Brill

δ

Mabel's reply describes the arduous process of getting permissions from all those whose letters she planned to include in her new memoir, such as Hutchins Hapgood, Maurice Sterne, Marsden Hartley, Andrew Dasburg, and Leo Stein, as well as one letter each from Jelliffe and Brill.

δ

August 3 [1936]

Dearest Brill,

You may be getting home soon so this is an answer to your letter of early July. Dr. Coriat never appeared—at least not at my garden gate, so I couldn't be nice to him as you asked. I would have been, for your sake.

The proofs (damn!) of "Movers & Shakers" come this week—the book comes out Sept[.] 24—& a copy will go to you. I am so <u>bored</u> with it! Bored at myself, at that period, which I tried to pin down on the pages like an entomological [sic] specimen! Also bored at all the work I had to do getting permissions, & coaxing coy correspondents to say yes, editing most of the meanness & malice & wit out of it so as not to hurt peoples' [sic] feeling[s] too much (poor Maurice! I don't know what he's going to do!) Yet of course in those days I was very negative & most of my reactions were critical in a most negative way. In fact I was running in reverse most of the time. All my opinions were colored, & such as they were then I put them down. I am not at all like her any more. I am pretty well regulated now & know fairly well how to keep my balance. So well, indeed, that I shall not open & read any of my press clippings on this book! Carl Van Vechten, Muriel Draper & others don't speak to me at all since my last book!

Love,
Mabel

δ

Brill next writes to Mabel, offering continuing support for her efforts to present the past in a true light, no matter what the fallout. He also restates his wish to visit her in Taos, which he eventually did in June 1937.

δ

September 15, 1936

Dear Mabel,

After I returned from abroad, I had to go away for another few weeks, which accounts for my not answering your letter before. I also received a letter from Coriat, in which he told me that he had to change his plans and did not go to Taos. I am very grateful to you just the same.

I am very interested in your new production and I am sure I will read it with a great deal of interest. I do not blame you for being bored with it. One is always more or less bored with anything that one has had to toil over, particularly if it concerns feelings and views which one can no longer sponsor.

I am naturally very interested in your summation of your erstwhile reactions. I remember distinctly some of the situations and

I frankly agree with you about your attitude and manner of that time. Do not forget, Mabel, no matter how just you would be, everybody dislikes seeing himself in an obscured, narcissistic light, and that would particularly hold for such individuals as Maurice. You have undertaken something which the world wants, but which is more or less dangerous, but I am very glad that you are doing it. In the end it is bound to reflect credit on you.

You know I am a grandfather—I have a grandson of about three months, and I anticipate great things from him, but I would love to have a chance to spend a few weeks in Taos and just talk to you; and although I have said it before, I will say it again—that you should not be surprised if someday you find me there.

With love,
Brill

δ

In her next letter to Brill, where she only mentions *Movers and Shakers* at the very end, Mabel requests financial help for La Posta Community Hospital from both him and his good friend Sam Lewisohn, a financier, philanthropist, and art patron who lived in New York.

δ

Sept[ember] 24 [1936]

Dear Brill,

Here we are with a hospital building. The community is very poor & yet we have to equip the whole place somehow. If you could know what it would mean to poor mothers to have a <u>dry</u> place to have their babies instead of under leaking roofs, & for <u>all</u> of us, if we get pneumonia, appendicitis or such things <u>not</u> to have to motor 100 miles, you would realize how much everyone here needs it. But it is very hard to get a town built! We <u>have</u> to go begging. So <u>can you</u> help us? I am writing Sam Lewisohn—maybe he will ... And we are <u>crazy</u>! We want to <u>open</u> it in November! Help! Can you think of anyone else I know in the east to ask & <u>will you ask for me</u> & raise something? When you come, then, you will have a nice place to go & be sick in if you have to!

Love,
Mabel

"Movers & Shakers" out in October. Horrors!
Why don't you telephone Sam & <u>make</u> him help?

δ

Movers and Shakers, the third volume of *Intimate Memories*, was published by Harcourt, Brace in the fall of 1936. The memoir begins in 1912 with Mabel Dodge's return to New York from Italy, and her settling in at 23 Fifth Avenue where she held her famous salons. It covers the time of her analysis with both Jelliffe and Brill, and ends with her marriage to Maurice Sterne and her departure for New Mexico to join him there. Mabel was keenly aware of how badly she treated Sterne in her memoir. He was deeply offended, as he related in his own memoir that he "was terribly upset" about "her cruel portrait of me" (*S&L*, p. 235).

Mabel's stated plan in her previous letter to Brill not to read any reviews of her book was certainly self-preserving; they would likely have destabilized her, no matter how balanced she believed herself to be. The critics ranged widely and wildly in their comments. The *New York Mirror* (November 19, 1936) insisted: "There is little of real worth ... Me, me, me is the song she sings ... Skip it." *The New York Times* (November 19, 1936) offered a more positive, although guarded, view: "It has been accurately said that egoists make the best autobiographers, and since few writers as self-centered as Mrs. Luhan have ever found time from themselves to write at any length, her books, as revelations of self, belong almost alone. The picture of herself is, of course, the most fascinating and the most complete that she has to offer." The reviewer at *The New York Times Book Review* (November 22, 1936) predicted: "When Mabel Dodge Luhan announced that she was about to write some intimate memories her friends and former friends must have braced themselves, for when Mrs. Luhan says intimate that is more or less what she means." Clifton Fadiman in *The New Yorker* (November 21, 1936) asked: "What lady would I most dread being cast upon a desert island with? I have often pondered the question ... momentarily the heavy favorite is Mabel Dodge Luhan." Practically alone in his unequivocal praise, Floyd Dell, in the *New York Herald Tribune Books* (November 22, 1936), expressed his delight in Mabel's "gift of portraiture": "Were people ever so naïve, so eager, so silly and so charming, so cruel and so sweet, so intelligent and so absurd, as these in her books?" (all in Luhan, *Movers and Shakers: Reviews*). Dell's review came the closest to capturing the spirit that Mabel intended for her exposure of herself and others.

Almost two months after Mabel's pleading letter, Brill replies that he has a copy of *Movers and Shakers*. Featured on the front cover were photographs of the journalist (and her former lover) John Reed, Lincoln Steffens, and Walter Lippmann; on the back, Maurice Sterne, Hutchins Hapgood, and the scenic designer Robert Edmond Jones with Mabel Dodge Luhan on the binding side. Both covers promised "Intimate Memories of the Salon at 23 Fifth Avenue ... and After" (in Luhan scrapbook, *Movers and Shakers*).

δ

November 17, 1936

Dear Mabel,

I did not answer your last letter because I had no chance to talk to Sam. Finally, I talked to him, and he promised that he would send you some money. As for me, I can send you a little and I will do so, but I hoped that I would be able to find someone who has more money than that so as to send you a substantial sum. Maybe I will succeed.

I just received your book. It looks very promising, but I have not yet read any of it. The blurb intrigues one, particularly one who knew the crowd. I am very glad that the book has come out now. I am convinced that ten years from today there will be very few people who will really appreciate it. Be that as it may, I am sure before I even look at it that it will make a hit. At any rate, that is my wish.

Affectionately,
Brill

δ

Nov[ember] 21 [1936]

Dear Brill,

Thanks for your letter—hope you like the book when you read it & hope the public <u>buy</u> it! Just now I am entirely given up to the hospital—getting it opened before cold weather ...

Love,
Mabel

δ

In the following letter, Brill writes to Mabel about *Movers and Shakers*. Although he had quipped to her in his letter of April 12, 1932 that "alas, alack! by the time it will be ready, I shall probably not be interested in it!," he was clearly enthusiastic.

δ

December 21, 1936

Dear Mabel,

Now that I have read your book, I can tell you that I enjoyed it very much. It was fascinating to me to re-live and re-visit a number of very familiar and interesting scenes. I have recommended it to a number of people and those who have read it speak very well of it. Some of them were a bit shocked which, of course, is to be expected, and the only persons who objected were a few who are friendly to Maurice. I naturally defended you and I shall continue to do so. As a matter of fact, I know that you could have said much more than you did.

I am sending you a small check as a contribution to your hospital, and I hope that Sam kept his promise to me and sent you something.[3]

Wishing you a Happy Christmas and a Fine and Prosperous New Year, I am,

Affectionately,
Brill

δ

Certainly, those loyal to Sterne had good reason to be offended by the memoir's unflattering portrayal of him. Mabel blamed him for her loneliness, published his love letters, and mocked him: "'Darling!' he breathed hotly into my ear. 'Darling! I *love* you!' How many times had he practiced *that* in his life? *Darling*. How I hated the word!" After his "strong, rather bland hands" touched her body during lovemaking, she was "worn out by the dreary vicissitudes of evolution" (*M&S*, pp. 368, 377–378). She displayed her capacity for cruel detachment from Sterne after he was pulled from the water in Provincetown, nearly drowned: "The body of Maurice, as it lay swollen and shapeless over a barrel with its discolored face and swinging arms, had lost its charm … Where once he thrilled and mesmerized by his fire or his beauty, he only repels." She admitted her own lack of true interest in him even during their marriage vows: "I made the responses in a cold, tight voice, wishing it were over" (*M&S*, pp. 403, 525). As Brill suggested in his letter, Mabel could have revealed much more, referring perhaps to Sterne's syphilis. Even if this omission showed some restraint on her part, Mabel's portrayal of her lover and then husband was merciless in its exposure of him, and, by extension, of herself.

In *Movers and Shakers*, Mabel discussed her experiences with psychoanalysis, devoting a chapter each to "Dr. Jelliffe" and "Dr. Brill," evaluating her treatment from the viewpoint of twenty years later. It is noteworthy that Brill made no mention in his previous letter of the chapter about him, although the meaning of this is unknown. In contrast, Jelliffe wrote Mabel on November 16, 1936 after reading sections of her new memoir: "Just a line to ... congratulate you on your last child. It is amazingly lusty and thus far full of joy and life ... I have but glanced at the 'Makers & Shakers' [*sic*], dipped into 'my' chapter and just skimmed that on Dr. Brill."

In this chapter on Jelliffe, Mabel provided details of her work with him and assessed its effectiveness. When she started her analysis in January 1916, she wrote: "I enjoyed my visits three times a week to Jelliffe's office." Mabel believed at this early point that "Psychoanalysis was apparently a kind of tattletaleing. I was able to tell, not only everything about myself, but all about Maurice. I grew calm and self-sufficient, and felt superior to him" (p. 439). The initial glow of the liberating aspects of self-revelation to a supposedly non-judging other was quite powerful for her. Mabel embraced the power of naming: "I longed to draw others into the new world where I found myself: a world where things fitted into a set of definitions and terms that I had never even dreamt of. It simplified all problems to name them. There was the Electra complex, and the Oedipus complex and there was the Libido" (p. 440). In her continual search for understanding, she was convinced at this time of the therapeutic action of identifying fears and preoccupations.

Emboldened by her experience with analysis, Mabel then sought to convert others to her new beliefs, particularly Sterne. Ultimately failing to urge him into treatment, she approached from another angle, inviting Jelliffe to observe Sterne directly during a weekend visit to Croton, hoping he would witness firsthand Sterne's flirtatious manner with other women. But when Mabel later met with Jelliffe to compare notes, she was confronted with the discrepancy between her views and those of her analyst. Jelliffe could not agree with Mabel's judgment of Sterne's behavior and instead offered his own analysis:

> "If he [Sterne] intended anything else, it was unconscious. Possibly your interpretation of it is colored by your own unconscious," he continued, looking at me searchingly. "You know we are always projecting ourselves. Often what we think we find in others is nothing but our own hidden life. What we need is the power to see in ourselves the traits and motives we imagine we detect in others! So long as we are merely subjective all our criticism is but self-criticism." (p. 443)

Mabel considered Jelliffe's perspective: "Heavens! I thought. I must track down *the Maurice* in me now! Was the real Maurice quite other than I had pictured him to myself? Heavens!!" She then concluded: "These were interesting, fascinating, new ideas. Unfortunately, they remained in the realm of ideas only and produced no change in my nature" (p. 443). It seems that once Jelliffe challenged Mabel to look deeper into her own unconscious, the appeal of that pursuit of understanding was diminished for her.

Eventually, Mabel came to believe that Jelliffe, whom she now saw as "commanding, quizzical, sure of himself, and not to be moved," had his own agenda with regard to her tumultuous relationship with Sterne: "Dr. Jelliffe, I realized, had been trying to pry us apart ... for he felt that my subjective feeling for Maurice made me sick." Jelliffe reportedly reassured her: "I do not want anything for you that you do not want for yourself. This is *your* affair. You yourself have that in you which will decide what is best. Your judgment, not mine, will solve your problem" (pp. 444, 456–457). Up against what Mabel perceived as Jelliffe's dogmatism, she remained stuck, unable to find perspective on her own tortured behavior patterns with Sterne.

Mabel ended her analysis with Jelliffe after six months, explaining: "When the amusing speculations had gone on for a few months, they finally ceased to amuse, and the old fatigue and depression came back" (p. 467). She concluded: "I am afraid I did not learn much about myself with Jelliffe, but ... I enjoyed my outings in his office" (p. 454). At this point, Mabel seemed to regard psychoanalysis as more of an intellectual game than an undertaking that challenged closely held views of the self.

In contrast was her appraisal of Brill:

> The "analysis" with Dr. Brill was very different from what I was accustomed to! ...
>
> I liked Brill immensely from the very first. One could have confidence in him, for his integrity was apparent at once, but it took me quite a while to learn that I could not continue my interesting speculations with him. I would begin hopefully:
>
> "Do you believe a manic-depressive can cure herself? Jelliffe—"
>
> "That's enough," he would interrupt. "You are not here for conversation." (*M&S*, pp. 505–506)

Mabel's reference to "manic-depressive"—her first and only in her memoirs—may indicate her acquaintance with Brill's earlier description of manic depression: "Sometimes the patient is excited, exhilarated, restless, manic, and sometimes he is melancholy, retarded in thought and action; depressed. Suddenly a wave of excitement lasting a few days, weeks, or months, usually two to six months, will come over the patient: the emotions run up and gradually down and remain normal for a period" (1921, p. 222). All these symptoms would certainly have seemed familiar to Mabel.

In her treatment with Brill, when Mabel tried to engage him with questions, "He told me not to try to be clever but to tell him a dream!" (p. 507). Mabel noted the difference between her two analysts: "Brill was all for action, whereas Jelliffe was speculative and considered the play of the psyche and the mind a good outlet in itself. Brill believed in externalizing things. Apparently nothing counted unless it was painted, written down, or formulated into some life-pattern composed of persons and their movements" (p. 506). Brill's emphasis was on action and results; he lacked tolerance for wonderings and pressing preoccupations.

The following passage in *Movers and Shakers* reveals Mabel's sensitivity to Brill's feelings during one point in her analysis:

> No, I had to be careful and not hurt him, I thought. I liked him very much, for he was so real and substantial. At times one could see his eyes alter in expression while he sat peering at one behind his specs ... After a moment ... he would generally announce something devastating but intense that would make one jump—although he tried

not to bring himself and his opinions too much into the affair. He wished to leave it all to the one before him. He figured that his job was to bring the horse to water. All the real effort must be mine. (p. 511)

At this time, Mabel reported that she was no longer depressed and approached Brill: "When I tentatively attempted to say I thought I might stop coming to him since I felt so much better, he sternly replied, with an angry gleam in his glasses: 'Don't be ridiculous! You have scarcely begun your analysis yet!' So I did not dare to discontinue my visits." Mabel, however, soon came to resent that Brill "called all my mysticism a fantasy life and frowned upon it severely. He became arbitrary and dogmatic." She concluded her chapter: "All the analysts ... become dogmatic at some point, and each one feels he must fit one into his own pattern." She assumed that Brill "did not like me to have interests outside of his own tastes, or at least I drew that conclusion. For instance, he had not much use for my radical friends" (pp. 511–512). It is interesting to note that, despite Brill's apparent dismissal of some of her friends, in his letters to her over the years he continually inquired about them and at times even treated them.

One of their shared connections was Andrew Dasburg, Mabel's longtime friend and a former patient of Brill's. It was, in fact, her 1918 invitation to Taos that first brought Dasburg to New Mexico, a place he visited yearly until he moved there in 1933. After months of symptoms that puzzled doctors, Dasburg had recently been diagnosed with Addison's disease. In her next letter, Mabel appeals to Brill out of concern for Dasburg, yet also suggests the possibility he may be unconsciously developing his symptoms to avoid yet another serious romantic relationship.

δ

March 4, 1937

Dear Brill:

Andrew Dasburg is very ill and under the care of Dr. [Richard] Lovelace in Albuquerque. It occurs to me that from your long experience of Andrew's extremely neurotic make-up you may be of great service in helping the Lovelace Clinic to determine the diagnosis of his case.

He apparently has all the symptoms of Addison's disease and he also responds to the treatment for Addison's disease. However, last year, he seemed to be producing a case of diabetes and had all of the symptoms of it; but this cleared up and was obviously what is called false diabetes. I do not know whether as yet physicians recognize a neurotic illness called "false Addison's disease", but with a make-up such as Andrew's is, it would not surprise me at all to find that he is unconsciously producing the symptoms of a sickness of which he may never have heard, simply because it allows him to make a complete escape from responsibility, effort, and marital relationship. I have known him so long, just as you have, that I have been able to watch him produce a different type of neurosis upon each occasion when he was unconsciously building up an escape from a wife. As you know, he has done this successfully already three times and possibly may now be engaged upon his fourth attempt.

It is ingenius [sic], if it really is the case that this is a false Addison's disease, for his unconscious to fall upon the adrenal and lymphatic system to project the picture ... If Dr. Lovelace sees fit to mail this letter on to you, please reply directly to him ... and give him the benefit of your psychiatric opinion.

Sincerely yours,
[Mabel]

δ

It is not known whether Brill ever communicated with Dr. Lovelace. One can only speculate how Brill may have responded to Mabel's strong belief in psychosomatic ailments, a conviction that likely stemmed from her exposure to Jelliffe's ideas, as she described: "Dr. Jelliffe told me his fascinating theories on disease and his belief that nearly all bodily illness is a failure of the spirit expressing itself at the physical level ... Tumors, cancers and so on, appeared to him to be manifestations in the flesh of one's unsublimated hatreds for people outside oneself whom one regarded as parasites and whom one was unable to successfully deal with" (*M&S*, p. 20). Mabel certainly presumed that Dasburg's symptoms were psychosomatic in origin.

Notes

1. Thomas Owen Bernheim was born on June 19, 1936, according to a note written by Edmund Brill (SFA).
2. Edmund Brill graduated from Harvard with a B.A. in biology and remained there to earn two graduate degrees in biology, an M.A. in 1937 and a Ph.D. in 1941.
3. Lewisohn had already mailed Mabel a $50 check, included in a letter to her dated December 17, 1936.

CHAPTER FIFTEEN

Brill in Taos

In the summer of 1937, after many promised and unrealized plans, Brill finally traveled to Taos to stay with Mabel. Although no correspondence exists to document the visit, an unidentified newspaper clipping described "Mabel Lujan's Party for Psychoanalyst":

> Mrs. Mabel Dodge Lujan is entertaining with a party at her "big house" in Taos Tuesday night to introduce Dr. Abraham Arden Brill, noted psychoanalyst, author and lecturer on psychoanalysis and ps[y]chosexual sciences at Columbia university [*sic*]. Dr. Brill is her house guest from New York.
>
> Several Santa Feans have been invited and are planning to attend. (in Luhan scrapbook, *Misc. Vol. II*)

At this time, Mabel had begun work on a manuscript entitled *On Human Relations: A Personal Interpretation* (1938), a description of the psychoanalytic method that she dedicated to Brill: "From whom I gathered whatever I know about psycho-analysis but not holding him responsible for my interpretations."

In the following letter written after Brill left Taos, Mabel acknowledges mailing him a copy of this "P.A. mms" and announces editorial changes she made "without waiting" plus an addition she would like his secretary, Laura Buck, to insert. Here she gathers phrases from different sources to support her conviction that the superego's influence on choices can offer comfort in times of suffering. She also mentions the novelist Myron Brinig, whom she first met and befriended during his 1934 visit to Taos.

δ

July 3 [1937]

Dear Dr. Brill,

I forgot to thank you for the 2 pieces Miss Buck sent me—Phoenix & yours.[1] They came 9 days after you left ...

I put some more about fire in the P.A. mms[2] without waiting. By the way I sent you a copy of that by air mail yesterday to keep for yourself ... Please let me know if & when you get it.

Also I have a line I want Miss Buck to insert in the part about jealousy being from a feeling of ego displacement & that <u>all suffering is ego-suffering</u>. I want added: "and the only cure for ego-suffering comes from the superego."[3] I mean it has appeared in my experience that all <u>ego-anodyne</u>[4] is from the superior renunciation & submission to reality, imposed by the superego. We have in our memory such lines (that come from our projection) as: "And He shall wipe away all tears,"[5] and Buddha's: "Il faut se soumettre,"[6] and "not my will but thine be done,"[7] and many others that come from experiencing the solace of giving up ego pleasures & claims in favor of the higher mandate within us. Evedently [sic] all religious experience derives from the activity of the superego. Gurdjieff called it "the 4th centre" & said we are only developping [sic] it—that in most people it is only a potential. It is strange that in some people we like we find <u>none</u> of it. Myron [Brinig] really has no superego (he has just sold his new book to M.G.M. for $75000 though!)[8] Tony has quite a lot of it.

I had a letter Friday from Edward Greenbaum[9] saying he & family will soon be here. I am so glad, & will give them an indian [sic] dance. He sent me a very small bill, small for what he had done it seems to me but large for me to pay right now! $300. The same way you did. I feel I owe you & Rose so much—an everlasting obligation. Never mind—if—I only sell my P.A. mms I am going to pay everyone what I owe. All well & happy here. I finally got jealous of Marian Shevky because Tony & she really are crazy over each other, & I got a trifle acid & she left for Albuquerque for a few days till [sic] she finds a friend to stay here in the little house[10] with her. She said she was very lonely & left. I told Tony for goodness sake to live with her & get over it next winter while I am in N.Y.!

Love,
M.

δ

In Mabel's next letter to Brill, she reports Dasburg's recent improvement in health (perhaps she no longer doubts his diagnosis of Addison's disease), as indicated by his ability to paint a mural for the Colorado Springs Fine Arts Center in 1937. Mabel had written Dasburg an exuberant letter, c. 1937, about this work, praising him for triumphing over his illness and noting his "marvelous faculty that only a man, of all living creatures, possesses, the faculty of transformation, in Brill's language of sublimation" (Coke, 1979, p. 98). In her letter to Brill, Mabel also complains about an unstable Russian woman, Alexandra Fechin, the ex-wife of the Russian painter Nicolai Fechin, who was obsessed beyond reason with Mabel's assistant Spud Johnson. Mabel enclosed a copy of Alexandra's threatening letter to her, dated August 6, 1937. An excerpt gives a flavor of the danger: "This letter will serve as a notice of warning to you ... IF ANY INJURY PHISICAL [sic] OR PSYCHICAL ... COMES TO SPUD JOHNSON WHILE SPUD STAYS ON YOUR PREMISES, BE I DEAD OR ALIVE, YOU WILL BE BROUGHT BEFORE AUTHORITIES."

δ

August 8 [1937]

Dear Brill,

    Please wire me if this letter sounds dangerous enough for me to "take steps."

    This is a russian [sic] woman who has been implacably persuing [sic] Spud Johnson for 4 years although he hates her. He does not care for any women ...

    Everyone knows she is really crazy but I think her paranoia may have reached a dangerous point & she might shoot or something!

Should she be "certified"? Please wire. All well here & having a nice summer.

Andrew has improved ever since he saw you. The letter he sent you was unfortunately in Marina's hands & too much consciousness of her had to be in it. I did not see it.

Hope you got my long epistle sent after you left!

Love,
Mabel

δ

Brill replies immediately:

δ

August 11, 1937

My dear Mabel,

I found your letter when I got home and read it with a great deal of interest. I will comment on it more fully in the future. I am so darn busy and it is so dastardly hot that one does not like to sit down and think.

I have not received any letter from Dasburg as yet.

Just sent you a wire concerning Spud's case. The letter sounds paranoid, and as I told you, show it to some authorities for your own protection. As a rule, Russians talk a lot and threaten and do not do things, but as this sounds paranoid and as I do not know her, I think it is best to give it over to the police or district attorney or whoever the functionary in your town happens to be, so as to protect yourself.

Will write you more fully in the future.

Love,
Brill

δ

Mabel next writes to Brill about her lively time in Taos with their mutual friends from Beverly Hills, the editor Carl Hovey and his wife, the screenwriter Sonya Levien. Brill had visited them after his stay with Mabel in early July 1937, and Sonya had written to Mabel on July 16, 1937: "It was thrilling to meet A. A. again! He spent the weekend with us at the beach, and was even more sane and supporting than I remembered him. He said you gave him the most marvellous time! He was full of it—and you!"

δ

Saturday, Aug[ust] 28 [1937]

Dearest Brill,

The [Carl and Sonya] Hoveys & ourselves have had a heavenly 10 days. This is to tell you they are returning next summer, & they will try & arrange their visit with yours to be here the same time. We will have lots of fun & renew old days. We all have our families, but we are all surrounded otherwise by newer friends & it is nice to keep the old days alive, don't you think? I like continuity.

Sonya will be writing you. Andrew is slumping. Terribly anti-social, cut off & self-centred.

I showed Mrs. Fechin's letter to the district atty & the district judge. They both replied she is crazy & should be certified ...

Two weeks ago "someone" poisoned my favorite spaniel, & the week before my white riding horse was poisoned, singled out among all the other horses. I had ridden him for 14 years!

I feel it is dangerous but what can be done? Spud still on the place. Sonya & Carl liked him so much. Here we are in autumn already! Is it cool there? Feeling fine & healthy.

Love,
Mabel

δ

Weeks after returning to New York from his trip west, Brill replies more fully to Mabel's intervening correspondence. He begins and ends this next letter mentioning psychic suicide, a topic currently of great interest to him. In his article, "The Concept of Psychic Suicide" (1939b), Brill defined it as a self-inflicted death purely by psychological means: "I am convinced that the same forces which lead to ordinary suicide can impel some people to die without the need of resorting to any physical agency. Somehow, some people can make up their minds to die, and just die" (p. 246). Brill seems to suggest that Mabel constructs a world of distress around her. He lists the recent events that may be contributing to her current despair, including completion of the final volume of her memoirs, *Edge of Taos Desert*, and the public and painful deterioration of her relationship with John Collier. Since Collier had become the head of the Bureau of Indian Affairs, his relationship with Mabel and Tony Luhan had shown increasing strain. Mabel was angry that he seemed to ignore the local Indian problems in Taos now that he was an important figure in Washington, and when she had an opportunity to criticize him in the press, both local and national, she did just that (Rudnick, 1984, pp. 264–265).

δ

September 2, 1937

My dear Mabel,

In the first place, I wish to apologize for not writing before. Since I returned to this hellish cauldron I have had no energy to sit down and talk in a friendly way to anyone ... I read your first letter with a great deal of interest ... You do not imagine for a moment that I had no cause for talking to you about psychic suicide. I knew perfectly well; your complaints and your letters indicated that. The foundation of the hospital, your fight with your old friend, John C.[ollier], the completion of your works—all these represented a consummation of a task which was almost titanic.[11] I might say that your works, including the one that is coming out, represented your whole life's work, and like the sensitive creature that you are, you were ready to give up.

Since I was there, you are different and you are going to continue. Remember, that nobody ever realizes his or her wishes completely. The realization of one drags another in its wake. The disturbance that you still show, which makes me feel a bit apprehensive, is the feeling of the hostilities that surround you. The Russian woman does not amount to anything ... The chances are that she will never bother you again. Somehow, I cannot make myself to believe that John C., who was always so attached to you, turned out to be a vindictive villain. He undoubtedly disagreed with you, and should I hear his side, he would probably have ample justification for his feelings. But, I am sure that he still loves you.[12]

Please do not connect the poisoning of your spaniel and your white riding horse with John and the hostile Indians. I naturally could not deny that some stupid, vindictive person did poison these animals, but is it not also possible that these quadrupeds might coincidentally pass away at this time, that their demise was due to different causes. Above all, do not surround yourself by an anal-sadistic[13] halo of unconsciously attracting punishment. I think that this is still an emanation of the death instinct or your erstwhile effort at psychic suicide.

I was very happy to hear that the Hoveys were there. From the tone of your letter I can see that they have left a very fine impression with you. I do not mean an impression of themselves because you have known them well yourself, but I mean a healthy impression. As you say, we do not make many friends as we advance in years, and the old ones are most valuable because they stand for something that inspires confidence. As I told you, I always liked Sonya. I did not know Carl so well; and the last time I was with her, I felt that my feelings about her were not mistaken. It will be nice if we can arrange to be there together. I certainly will try to do it.

By the way, I never received those two pictures which I bought. Tony sent me some other things, the drum which I bought in the pueblo, but not the pictures. I wonder did he send them? ...

With my love to you all, I am,
Brill

δ

Brill's supportive interpretations of Mabel's feelings and behavior in this letter must have been reassuring to her; she considered going to New York to consult with him about becoming a novelist, likely proposed earlier in a letter to Sonya Levien, as revealed in Sonya's September 12, 1937 reply: "I realize the difficulty you are having in making the transfer [from autobiography to fiction] ... I think a visit with Brill is a wonderful idea. Some day I'm going to do it also. Go to New York for a couple of months and have some sessions with him." With Mabel inclined to resume therapy, Sonya further encouraged her, on September 23, 1937: "I envy you going to Brill. Don't renig [sic] on that! It will be a fine change ... My love to the Brills. How I wish I were going with you—and going through it myself. I need his guidance so much." Carl Hovey also supported Mabel's return to Brill, writing to her on September 14, 1937:

> It is awfully interesting that you are going to New York and will see Brill. Without having an inkling that novel writing was in your

mind I remarked to Sonya at Taos that I thought the time had come for you to go into that form ... As for Brill, I wish I could see him once in six months and have every member of the family do the same. He throws you into focus, again gives you a fresh view of essentials.

It is fascinating to discover the overlapping of friendships and analytic relationships, with Mabel, Sonya Levien, and Carl Hovey all welcoming Brill as a guest in their homes and then longing for his guidance in decision-making and emotional life.

Likely responding to a lost letter from Mabel, Brill replies with a direct invitation for her to stay at his house while she is in New York. His wife, Rose, also writes to Mabel at the same time: "I have learned with much delight that you contemplate coming to N.Y. for a worthwhile spell, and we are pleased to offer you the hospitality and comfort that our home affords."

δ

September 15, 1937

Dear Mabel,

I certainly think it would do you a lot of good to come here, and I expect you to live with us. I told Mrs. B. about it, and she was very pleased and said she would write to you. We thought that you might bring Tony with you. However, with or without Tony, you will be very welcome, and I am sure that you need it. So much for that!

Do not be excited because I used the word, "anal-sadistic"; you are like so many other people who should know better—that terms only describe certain qualities which we all have, which at times are exaggerated. There is nothing to be ashamed of, and if you did not have that particular quality, you would not have done a damn thing. However, we shall discuss all that later ...

I hope that by this time you have heard from Rose.

As ever,
Brill

P.S. The postman just brought me your new book [i.e., *Edge of Taos Desert*]. I am looking forward to reading it with a great deal of pleasure and interest.

δ

Edge of Taos Desert: An Escape to Reality, the fourth volume of Mabel's *Intimate Memories*, was published in 1937 by Harcourt, Brace and Company. It begins with her last night in New York in 1917, when she proclaimed to herself, "I feel like a Change," and ends in Taos with Tony's coming to her teepee at night, marking Mabel's embrace of a forever-altered existence: "My life broke in two right then, and I entered into the second half, a new world that replaced all the ways I had known with others" (p. 6). The reviewers were divided about this new volume: *The New York Times Book Review* (September 19, 1937) found "real beauty in these pages" that chronicle "one urban, cosmopolitan, hyper-civilized woman's discovery and adjustment" (p. 3) to the pace and spirit of life in Taos, while *The New Yorker*'s Clifton Fadiman mocked the plot and its author, beginning with his subtitle, "A PASSION-FRAUGHT STORY OF TWO LOVERS WHO FOUND EACH OTHER IN THE WIDE-OPEN SPACES OF THE GREAT SOUTHWEST ... REAL INDIANS FOR THE KIDDIES!" (September 18, 1937, p. 96).

Still trying to determine whether she will return to New York for consultation with Brill, Mabel sends him a telegram.

δ

September 17, 1937

... BUT HOW ABOUT ME HAVE YOU RECEIVED MY THREE LETTERS AM I EXPECTED FOR WORK WITH YOU LATE OCTOBER LOVE = MABEL.

δ

In the following letter from Brill, in response to a lost communication from Mabel apparently stating her intention to resume analysis, he continues his appeal to her to travel to New York, but discourages her from seeking treatment with anyone but himself.

δ

October 11, 1937 [see Illustration 18]

Dear Mabel,

I read your letter with much interest. I can understand your feelings perfectly, and I would not care to urge you to come to New York in spite of the fact that coming here would not mean that you would necessarily be changed to the extent that you think. Remember, the whole idea about analysis was yours. It was not my suggestion. The only thing that worries me is that you should have so much fear of it. It would seem from the way you behave that the subtitle of your last book is more like the way I put it twenty years ago than the way you put it.[14] As a matter of fact, I do not think that you need analysis. My feeling is that whatever you wish to do you could work out yourself. I think, also, that it would be dangerous for you to to [sic] talk to anyone who does not know you as well as I do. When I talked to you about psychic suicide, it was because I was impelled to do so by your general behavior, and I feel that it has done a lot of good.

For the rest, if you wish to come, I will do everything to make it pleasant for you, but since you dislike New York as much as you say, it is a question whether you should really run away or discover that it is only a haystack in the moonlight instead of a ghost. I love you just as much as I did before ...

Affectionately,
Brill

δ

Brill's direct expression of love for Mabel must have been vastly comforting for her as she struggled with a range of feelings. He also pointedly reminded her of how deeply he knows her, urging her to trust his guidance. Although Mabel remained committed to the idea of returning to New York for treatment, as she explains in her next letter to Brill, her plans are interrupted by the marital crisis of a friend, the famous conductor Leopold Stokowski. Although in the middle of a divorce from Evangeline, his wife of eleven years, he was seeking a location for them and their two daughters during the holidays. She also refers to another divorce, that of her close friend Walter Lippmann.

δ

Nov[ember] 7 [1937]

Dear Brill,

It looks now as though I had better wait until after Xmas for my visit to you. This is not an evasion for I want to come but the Stokowskis are getting a divorce & at the same time they want a neutral meeting place at Xmas for the children. She is Tony's friend & he is mine & they have been coming to us for some years & when they asked me this I felt I should do all I can to help. So I have given them a house for the holidays & we will have a tree, & eat together & that will help them. They both love the children very much. After that I should be free to go east. I am not writing and feel I need a jog from you to get me going but I feel fine though of course restless.

Were you surprised at Walter & Faye Lippmann's divorce? I was—& especially at her bitterness in her complaint after all these years. Personally I believe Walter is a little mad because he is so extremely Rational. I consider that rationalism carried to such an extreme is as much an insanity as any other extreme, & the repression of any possibility ... Did you see a picture of him recently in Time? He looked as mad as a hatter![15] His irritability must have increased until Faye couldn't stand it ... Well, he always cared more for his neurosis than for her or anything else. What an irony that Reason should drive a man mad! But I believe that is the case here. Do you agree? I'l[l] surely come later. Please explain to Rose. I am disappointed. I <u>might</u> take a month now. How would that be?

Love,
Mabel

δ

Although in Brill's next letter he playfully suggests that he will travel to Taos before Mabel journeys to New York, she did succeed in making the trip in January 1938. He writes to her candidly and at length about Grace Mott Johnson, Andrew Dasburg's former wife and Brill's current patient, whose life had become so unraveled that Brill intervened financially to support their twenty-six-year-old son, Alfred. It is striking that Brill so directly stepped in to help the son of his two patients—an involvement with considerable impact, as Alfred later wrote to Rose Brill after her husband's death: "I have always felt that Dr. Brill was a second father to me. No other older person has filled a similar place in my life" (SFA).

δ

November 13, 1937

Dear Mabel,

I did not care to write to you before because I did not care to influence you one way or the other, but I was quite sure that the issue would be as is. Don't forget that I am not urging you to come to New York and I can see the reasons for your hesitation. Maybe it would be better not to come, but remember my offer always stands. I have an idea, however, that Mrs. Brill and I will see you in Taos before we will see you in New York.

I had a letter from Sonya and she told me what a wonderful time she had there and is urging me to go there next summer when she and Carl will be there with the children. We may be able to meet there.

What you tell me about the Stokowskis is interesting, but let me tell you something about Johnson. I saw her on and off, and noticed that for the last few years she was becoming more and more paranoid. She became involved with the negro question, lived at the colored Y.W.C.A. in Harlem, spent all her money on negroes ... She got mixed up with a certain African prince and attributed all kinds of ideas and feelings to his influence. She used to come and tell me about it, but I could do nothing. You know her. Any disagreement with her scheme evoked all kinds of explosions, and I could do nothing at all. Her financial condition became more and more precarious. She could not pay for Alfred [Dasburg], Jr., so I took it upon myself to pay his tuition fees at M.I.T., and I am glad to say that he graduated[16] and has a very good position ... However, about 5–6 weeks ago I was telephoned ... by the Y.W.C.A. that Johnson was acting peculiarly so that it was necessary to have an attendant with her. I had her sent to a hospital and visited her there. She was very confused, more or less delusional ... She seems to be getting along quite well. Whether she will ever recover is a question. I have my doubts. If you talk to anyone about it, I think it might be advisable not to tell all the details. Andrew undoubtedly knows it from Alfred, whom I advised in this matter.

Your dissertation about Walter is very interesting, but I have seen so little of him during the last 15–20 years that I really cannot tell what happened. The rumors here are that he is madly in love with the [Helen Byrne] Armstrong woman, who is going to get a divorce and marry him.[17] I know that he is visiting Sam and Margaret [Lewisohn] regularly. They are very friendly with him. Mabel, c[']est la vie!

I got a letter from Marina [Dasburg] in which she tells me that they expect to come East.[18] Frankly, I cannot make any headway about the diagnosis ... However, when I see him, I will tell you more about it.

As ever,
[A.A.B.]

δ

In her next letter to Brill, Mabel enclosed a catalogue from the 1937 exhibition at the Los Angeles Public Library entitled "The Manuscripts of D. H. Lawrence: A Descriptive Catalogue," where an incomplete manuscript of *Sons and Lovers* had apparently fetched a notable price. As discussed earlier, in 1925 Mabel had given Brill a complete handwritten manuscript of *Sons and Lovers* as payment for his treatment of Everett Marcy.

δ

[before December 10, 1937]

Dear Brill,

Please note price[19] of the incomplete mms—& also description of it. You surely have the real one. Why not do something about it?

M.D.L.

δ

In November 1937, the *New Mexico Quarterly* reported: "We understand that ... Mabel Dodge Lujan has gone to New York to be re-psychoanalyzed" (Luhan scrapbook, *Misc. Vol. II*). However, from the date of Brill's next letter, as well as later newspaper accounts, it seems she did not leave Taos until January. It is moving to read his reference to their partnership as "we," an acknowledgment of their creating together a way towards her increased vitality and health.

δ

December 10, 1937

Dear Mabel,

I am very sorry to hear that you are not feeling well, and at the same time (ambivalence) I am glad that you are coming.

I was quite sure that you needed New York treatment and I am sure that once you get here, we will get you out of all your difficulties.

There are so many things that I should like to write about, but I am so darn busy that I haven't time to dictate.

Concerning the manuscript, as I told you, I gave it to Mrs. B. and whenever I try to talk to her about it, she becomes irritable, so I have said nothing to her since you wrote to me. I will broach the subject in due time. Incidentally, she said she would write to you when I told her that you decided to come, so you will probably hear from her soon.[20]

Affectionately,
Brill

δ

Notes

1. Likely one paper on the topic of the phoenix (an image of great meaning to D. H. Lawrence) and the other one by Brill, very possibly—given his upcoming reference to "psychic suicide" in his September 2, 1937 letter to Mabel—a reprint of his paper on this topic presented at the 14th International Psycho-Analytical Congress, Marienbad, August 5, 1936 (Brill, 1939b, p. 246).
2. Mabel's writing about fire in *On Human Relations* most likely refers to her first chapter where she proposes: "The idea of fire seems to be at the bottom of all the religions from the past ... How shall we learn to emulate the phoenix that rises from its ashes? How can we die and rise again?" She believes psychoanalysis provides a means to such an end by bringing light to previously dark places and suggests that one of "the principal motives of psycho-analysis is to ... liberate the fire" (pp. 4, 6). It is not known which of these passages Mabel added after Brill's visit.
3. This sentence does not appear in the typescript in the Luhan archives.
4. The origin of this phrase is unknown.
5. "God shall wipe away all tears from their eyes" (Revelation 21:4).
6. "It is necessary to submit oneself," a phrase Mabel ascribes to the Buddha, but with no known source for her attribution.
7. "Not my will, but thine, be done" (the Gospel According to Saint Luke, 22:42).
8. Brinig's 1937 novel *The Sisters* was made into a movie of the same name by MGM in 1938, starring Errol Flynn and Bette Davis.

9. A New York lawyer married to the sculptor Dorothea Schwarcz and father of two sons, Daniel and David.
10. A term Mabel used to refer to the guest house where D. H. and Frieda Lawrence lived for two months when they first visited her in Taos (*LIT*, p. 105).
11. Mabel may have shared Brill's letter with Sonya Levien, who wrote to her on September 12, 1937 about reading *Winter in Taos*: "All the beauty, sensitiveness and extraordinary difference of your life, burst upon me freshly. You write so vividly! Your pictures are so alive! Brill is right. Your accomplishments are titanic."
12. In fact, after Mabel died in 1962 and Tony in 1963, Collier wrote affectionately about them in his memoirs: "I want to record that in their separate and their joined lives there has been beauty, generosity, naiveté, human goodness, and a luminousness whose dying sundown gleam is around them still" (1963, p. 106).
13. Brill describes this term: "We call this second phase of ego organization *anal-sadistic* because at this age, when the child has difficulties learning to control his bowel movements, he is also very aggressive and destructive" (1946, p. 189).
14. By referring to the subtitle, *An Escape to Reality*, Brill is likely recalling both the passage in his letter from the spring of 1924—"I strenuously objected to Maurice and to Tony. In both cases I felt that you were descending to a lower level in your *flight from reality*" (emphasis added)—and, even more, to his undocumented interpretation in 1917 when she moved to New Mexico, as mentioned in *The Statue of Liberty*: Mabel may have been referencing Brill's viewpoint when she proclaimed that psychoanalysis had "demolished" other approaches to understanding "by proving they were *escapes from reality*, merely holding out a promise of flight from the pain of living in the here and now" (1947, pp. 66–67; emphasis added).
15. Lippmann was featured in a photograph in *Time* (November 1, 1937), perched on the arm of a chair smiling down at Faye (p. 32).
16. Alfred Dasburg received a B.S. in electrical engineering from M.I.T. in June 1936.
17. Lippmann was wildly involved with Helen Byrne Armstrong, the wife of his close friend Hamilton Fish Armstrong, editor of the journal *Foreign Affairs*. They married on March 26, 1938.
18. They moved to her family home in Bryn Mawr, Pennsylvania.
19. Unknown.
20. No such letter exists from Rose to Mabel.

CHAPTER SIXTEEN

Psychoanalysis again in New York

Mabel returned to New York in January 1938 and likely stayed some of the time with Brill, accompanied perhaps by Tony, who had also been invited, until she found a more permanent residence. A letter from Jelliffe to Mabel dated February 23, 1938 was addressed to her "c/o Dr. A. A. Brill, 15 West 70th Street" and indicated they met during this time: "It was nice of you to come to see me." The *Santa Fe New Mexican* (March 9, 1938) reported that Mabel was "in New York with her husband, Tony Lujan of Taos pueblo this month. Mr. and Mrs. Lujan have been visiting Dr. A. A. Brill, the noted psychoanalyst, whom they entertained in Taos last summer." Gioia Bernheim remembered their presence at dinner:

> Mabel & Tony used to come to NYC regularly & my parents always gave a formal dinner party for them. Tony wore a tux but his hair & decorations were Indian style. He also brought his Tom Tom & played & sang after dessert. He never joined in any conversation during the evening & Mabel seemed to ignore him. The other guests would be prominent people selected to please Mabel. (personal communication, November 31, 1996)

Although Bernheim also stated that Mabel "never stayed with us when Tony was present" (personal communication, March 13, 1997), it is still possible they were guests at Brill's home. In fact, an article from *The Denver Post* (June 5, 1938) placed Mabel there: "We found her a guest in the home of Dr. A. A. Brill, the New York psychoanalyst" (Luhan scrapbook, *Misc. Vol. II*). It is certainly unusual for a former or current patient to sleep at her analyst's home, equally stunning that Mabel's location was revealed so openly in the press.

Mabel's presence in New York generated much intrigue. On February 24, 1938, the *New York Post* announced "Mabel Dodge Is Back, Looking for City Studio":

> With her Indian husband, Antonio Luhan, the picturesque author expects in future to divide her time between their hilltop home in Taos, N.M. and a New York apartment with a room in it big enough to hold a crowd ...
>
> "I want to come back and do something for young people if I can," Mrs. Luhan said this morning. "Maybe if I opened a place here something might come of it, something that would be helpful. Many young people who are trying to think for themselves seem to me to be very restless.["] (*Misc. Vol. II*)

An article in *The Washington Post* (March 5, 1938) placed Mabel and Tony in New York at the start of March and stated her intention "to establish a part-time salon" in her belief that "the present generation cannot solve its problems because it is 'always rushing somewhere.' The solution, she says, would be to sit in the sun in the desert—or for that matter any place—and think" (*Misc. Vol. II*).

By the beginning of March 1938, Mabel had rented an apartment in New York, according to *The New York World-Telegram* (March 5, 1938): "The energetic Mabel Dodge Luhan, who has taken a flat in New York, plans to settle down here for several months at least ... She gave a large cocktail party reception just a week ago, but to everyone's disappointment Tony Luhan and the Indian drums which he plays so expertly were missing" (*Misc. Vol. II*).

During this extended time in New York, Mabel reentered treatment with Brill as planned— "I am not writing and feel I need a jog from you to get me going," she had stated in her November 7, 1937 letter—to help unblock her creativity. In *On Human Relations*, she acknowledged the benefit of resuming an analysis: "But when the new problems of life arise, as they will, certainly he will want to discuss them with the analyst if he finds he cannot solve them alone. Then he will return, perhaps only for a few days, or for a month or two, and he will discover what is obstructing him" (p. 97).

Mabel's return to psychoanalysis was noted both privately and publicly. Thornton Wilder reported to Stein and Toklas on March 27, 1938: "In New York I had lunch with Mabel. She is now being analyzed by Dr. Brill" (Burns & Dydo, 1996, p. 213). Sonya Levien wrote to Mabel in New York on February 13, 1938: "It must give you a fine feeling to be working with Brill again. His very nearness gives me a sense of sanity and reassurance. I envy you." A reporter for the *Cleveland Plain Dealer* attended a party in New York held in Mabel's honor and revealed on March 13, 1938: "Mrs. Luhan has been in town recently, without her Indian husband ... Mrs. Luhan, I hear, is undergoing a course of analysis and hopes to become a fiction writer after this long spell as a rememberer" (*Misc. Vol. II*).

In the spring of 1938, Mabel wrote to Una Jeffers that she was now "excavated" and "extroverted" by Brill, thus freed up to work and newly available for interactions with people (Rudnick, 1984, p. 298). While in New York, she generated ideas about writing projects and stirred up public interest in her upcoming work. The headlines of her native *Buffalo Courier Express* on April 3, 1938 announced: "Mabel Dodge Luhan Next To Write Conversation Pieces." When the reporter asked about her next book, she replied:

> "No more books for the present. I have a new idea. In fact, when I first came to New York, a month ago I visited a friend of mine, Dr. A. A. Brill, who introduced psycho-analysis into this country. I wanted him to tell me how to get out of the pattern of writing autobiography. For weeks and years every time I sat down to write it was about myself and my memories. Now I want to write about other people. And I shall call the work Conversation Pieces. If you continue too long in one field, you lose flexibility. And that is what I want to regain."
>
> Conversation Pieces, it would seem, are to be about famous individuals. Not what they do, for everyone knows that. But how they appear over a luncheon table. What they eat, what they say, and how they think. (*Misc. Vol. II*)

Mabel wrote a minimum of three Conversation Pieces featuring Vincent Bendix of the manufacturing and engineering Bendix Corporation, architect William Lescaze, also journalist and editor Roy Howard. As Spud Johnson reported in the *New Mexico Sentinel* (May 22, 1938), Mabel abandoned this project after her interviewees objected to how much they had unwittingly revealed about themselves during lunch: "But while they so pleasantly ate, they forgot I was remembering them! Most of the people I interviewed were horrified to find that I remembered positively everything they said—and as a result they blue-pencilled all the interesting bits and I got discouraged and gave up the idea" (*Misc. Vol. II*). Not even one of these portaits was published in the magazine *Cosmopolitan*, as originally planned.

The next two letters concern Mabel's friend, Mabel Brooks, an artist in New York. Although the connection between Brill, Mabel, and Brooks is not known, it seems likely that Mabel was referring Brooks to Brill for analysis.

δ

March 23 [1938]

Dear Brill,

I don't want to resume relations with Mabel Brooks but it might be kind if you would have your secretary write her a note—quoting the enclosed letter[1] because it affords her an opportunity & an outlet ...

Ever,
M.D.L.

δ

March 26, 1938

Dear Mabel,

When I talked to you on the phone, I had not rea[d] the letter that you sent me in reference to Mabel Bro[oks] ...

I do not like to do as you suggest. The fact is that I do not want to have any deeper relations with [her] than I already have, but I feel that it would do good [if] you would send her a note and tell her whatever you [letter cut off here] ...

Cordially,
[A.A.B.]

δ

Brill turned Mabel's request around, asking instead that she contact Brooks herself.

In Mabel's next letter to Brill, she describes a meeting between her friend Myron Brinig and Theodore Dreiser. She also mentions the writer Carman Barnes.

δ

Thursday [before April 8, 1938] [see Illustration 19]

Dear Brill,

Last night Myron had a terrific literary hero-worship transference to Mr. Dreiser. We all went home in the same taxi—dropped Carman at 825 5th Ave, dropped me here, then Myron took <u>him</u> home. I was nearly asleep when the telephone rang at 1.30 & he said "I <u>had</u> to call you & tell you what a <u>great</u> man I think Dreiser is. He is so <u>rich</u>, so <u>warm</u>, so <u>real</u>. He is as big as his work. I feel so happy to have met a <u>great</u> man at last" & more of the same. I was pleased because he needs to have a little hero-worship. He does model his books <u>somewhat</u> on Dreiser's, I believe. I never thought of it before.

Also Dreiser should be glad to be appreciated by the serious younger men, don't you think so?

I thought it a fine lively evening altogether.

Love,
Mabel

P.S. A wire from Tony says to stay here thro' April.

δ

Brill's next reply refers to Mabel's essay, *Psycho-Analysis with Dr. Brill* (1938), an account of her treatment likely written and perhaps completed during this visit to New York.

δ

April 8, 1938

Dear Mabel,

I was very interested in the aftermath of the dinner and it might do Myron some good to worship Dreiser. I believe your theory is correct. Well, Dreiser does appreciate it when people look up to him, as far as I know. When he was living in New York before, he always had Thursday evenings when all those youngsters would come and have drinks and sandwiches, etc. That went on for a few years; he rivaled you in that matter. For years he has been more or less indifferent.

I hope you change the title of that paper on psychoanalysis with Brill.

I see no reason why you should not stay here if Tony feels that way, and last but not least, if you feel that way.

Affectionately,
Brill

δ

April 11, 1938

Dear Mabel,

Dreiser is now in Mt. Kisco, N.Y. (Hampstead Road), and I doubt whether you can get him to come to New York. At any rate, you had better write him yourself.

I am returning the letters ...[2]

As ever,
[A.A.B.]

δ

Mabel wrote Dreiser the same day, pleading with him to join in her quest to "do something for young people," and he replied on April 19: "It was so nice of you to wish to introduce Carman Barnes and Myron ... to me and I enjoyed that evening and your letter of the 11th. In it you ask me <u>don't I want to help young people</u>? Yes. And in a number of ways I have tried—whether successfully or not—has not always been clear. What—in particular—would you have me do?" It is unknown if Dreiser and Mabel ever joined forces for this cause, but she did establish with Barnes the kind of mentoring relationship she hoped to have with younger people. Barnes had written to her on April 5, 1938 that "meeting you seems like a revelation—a flash of something I am always searching for—but never find," and Mabel then referred her to Brill for psychoanalysis.

Mabel's *Psycho-Analysis with Dr. Brill* is a ten-page typescript that has remained unpublished until its inclusion in this volume as an appendix. It is a rare historical document offering a view into an ongoing analytic relationship, both a narrative account of two sessions from this period of her analysis as well as a personal endorsement of the process and impact of psychoanalysis. It begins with Mabel's announcement to Brill: "I want to work on a problem of work … I don't want to do autobiography any more … I just want to write. When I write I am alive—when I don't I am nothing … Here I am back in New York with you and I don't know what to do with myself most of the time. I feel bored, frightened … I have no <u>self</u>" (pp. 1, 3). They make an appointment for the following day, which Brill begins with a request for one of her dreams. This leads to her musings about the analytic process:

> How describe the peculiar and infinitely variable course of a psychoanalytic ordeal? For ordeal it is and must be since all change is painful, and all organic growth means change …
>
> Does anyone suppose there is no pain involved when a tree drives its roots deeper, and expands its girth? Well, a psychoanalytic experience is as mysterious, as solemn, as organic as such a growth … What a good gardener the psycho-analyst has to be if he would bring to life the arrested growth. (pp. 4–5)

Conveyed here is Mabel's genuine understanding of the inevitable suffering and toil of psychoanalysis, as well as her grasp of the facilitating role the analyst plays in initiating new development.

Mabel then describes Brill's approach to his work: "He has an infinite faith in life, in its richness, its variety, its ingenuity. He has sat for many years before many people … and he has often seen the amazing miracle take place before him, often, the miracle of a person's discovery that all the answers are within himself, unsuspected for long yet forever ready" (p. 5). In contrast to the dogmatism she had ascribed to him in *Movers and Shakers,* Mabel now observes: "A man like Brill never concerns himself with what solution the patient will find. He does not care what the patient's answer to life is so long as he does answer, that he lives again" (p. 5). This view is certainly different from the opinions he forcefully expressed in earlier letters to Mabel, such as on March 18, 1919: "Now don't you think that you ought to have some regard for the future and give up all that ridiculous mystical Indian business. Everybody thinks you are crazy." Mabel's current evaluation of Brill's faith in a person's discovering his own answers is likely more accurate at this later time in his career, when he is more established in his practice and more senior in his reputation.

Mabel next writes passionately about the indescribably unique course of analysis: "And what this science called 'Psychoanalysis' consists of—this method of knowing oneself, this curious dream system—and its attendant associative process, how is it possible to tell, except by going through it?" She advocates a personal analysis for each psychoanalyst, believing that afterwards, in his own practice, the analyst "will never be dogmatic, he will not try to lead his patient in any arbitrary way, or determine what the result shall be. He will sit before his patient and with a certain humility and respect he will watch for the god to rise and lead the man" (p. 7). Mabel's appreciation for the incomparable experience of submitting oneself to analysis before practicing it is noteworthy in its clarity and prescience, anticipating future psychoanalytic institutes' requirements of psychoanalysis for each candidate. Early pioneering analysts like Freud and Brill did not undergo their own treatments. Her description of the analyst's attitude in approaching his work also anticipates Brill's own later account: "They [psychoanalysts] sit behind each patient for an hour at a time and listen attentively and passively to everything that he expresses—often to things uncomplimentary to themselves. I wonder if an outsider can really appreciate the patience, forbearance and self-denial that such practice demands" (1942, p. 548).

During this analysis with Brill in the spring of 1938, Mabel reports in her essay that "slowly the inhibited feeling for life began to rise again. That again there seemed to me to be wonderful people in the world and amazing things to tell about them; that color came back into life as the life in me moved once more." She observes that Brill "must have known what he was doing, and what he refrained from saying, but he only seemed to watch and to repeat over and over: 'What did you dream?' and 'What does that suggest to you?'" (p. 9). Mabel clearly seems to believe in the healing process of searching inside herself for resources.

In Brill's following letter to Mabel about *Psycho-Analysis with Dr. Brill*, he forcefully objects to her labeling their current sessions as psychoanalysis, and to her reporting of their lunches afterwards: "After such an hour as is sometimes very hard to face through Dr. Brill would get up and say: 'Well—let's go home and have some lunch,' and we would go around the corner to the house, and in the dining room there would be a good meal ready and friends smiling, and the birds there in their cages against the wall" (p. 9).

δ

April 14, 1938 [see Illustration 20]

Dear Mabel,

I cannot quite understand why you gave me another copy of this "Psychoanalysis with Dr. Brill". The copy that you gave me before is marked #4. It is exactly the same as #3 that you left yesterday. Now, please let me repeat what I said. The title is very bad. A psychoanalyst does not act that way and does not go for luncheon with his patients. It is misleading in every way, and not only is it wrong, but I am sure I should be criticized by the psychoanalysts, and perhaps by the Academy of Medicine. Some might think that I was being advertised. And, naturally, I would have to disavow this whole thing if it should come to a show-down. I, therefore, suggest that you either change it or call it something else. In changing it, you could say that you were analyzed by me before, and many years later on a visit you called on me and at the same time spoke about these matters—but it is not psychoanalysis. Psychoanalysis, you know, takes a long time, and is conducted in an entirely different way than we are doing now.

I am sure you could make a good paper out of it if you would form it a little differently, but I cannot approve of its present form. Will tell you about it more when I see you on Friday.[3]

As ever,
[A.A.B.]

δ

Brill was obviously concerned about condemnation by the New York Academy of Medicine, founded by physicians in 1847 to provide local medical professionals with an association to speak for them on issues of healthcare and public health policy, as well as to maintain standards of quality in medical care. His objections are intriguing given the open and public relationship he had with Mabel: dining with her; inviting her to stay at his home; and visiting her in Taos. Brill seemed acutely aware of how his actions might be misinterpreted by the medical or psychoanalytic establishment in New York, and he warned Mabel about exposing him in this way. Although he wrote that "a psychoanalyst does not act that way," he *is* a psychoanalyst and he apparently *did* act that way, resuming her analytic treatment and their lunches together. Brill's attempt to edit Mabel's description of her analysis with him is fascinating in itself, since their apparent collaboration resulted in her neither changing the title nor deleting mention of their shared meals. Mabel hoped that *Psycho-Analysis with Dr. Brill* would be published, and she soon sent copies to Harry Burton, editor of *Cosmopolitan*, as well as to her agent Edith Haggard at Curtis Brown, Ltd. For Brill's career, it is probably fortunate that the essay never appeared in print.

* * *

Before returning to Taos in May, Mabel attended a New York party given by Vincent Bendix for the unveiling of a clay bust of Carman Barnes by Nison Tregor, a young Russian sculptor whose works she admired and perhaps collected.[4] The *New York Daily News* on May 3, 1938 reported the story of that evening with the headline, "Mabel Luhan Lops Off Carmen [sic] Barnes' Curls": "The sculpture was duly admired by all the guests except Mabel. Mabel, an artist who can always be expected to do the unexpected, carefully examined the bust and then went over and pinched off the soft clay which formed the long curly bob ... Mabel finally persuaded Mr. Tregore [sic] and Carmen [sic] to leave it that way" (*Misc. Vol. II*). In fact, when Barnes received the final marble sculpture, she wrote Mabel on June 6, 1938: "I am awfully glad you took off the hair. It looks fine." Mabel, once again, had left her indelible mark.

Notes

1. Lost.
2. It is uncertain which letters Brill was returning to Mabel. If from Dreiser, they are lost, as only one letter exists in the Luhan archives, from a later date of April 19, 1938.
3. Since April 14, 1938 was a Thursday, Brill is likely referring to the following day. In New York at this time, there were several daily mail deliveries, so letters often arrived the same day they were mailed.
4. An article from this time mentioned that in her New York apartment Mabel was "surrounded by the works of a young Russian sculptor, Nison Tregor, whom she is sponsoring" (*Buffalo Courier Express*, April 3, 1938, *Misc. Vol. II*).

CHAPTER SEVENTEEN

Back in Taos

After her arrival in Taos, Spud Johnson wrote a lively article in the *New Mexico Sentinel* (May 22, 1938) about Mabel's extended and transformative visit to New York:

> Having left home during January in a more or less anti-social mood which she had nursed for a year, Mabel Dodge Luhan has returned to Taos after a New York whirl, completely "socialized."
> Slightly thinner, with a new, urban manner, she is starting things humming in Taos to a new and faster rhythm ... the Big House is being opened, swept, dusted, repaired—and it begins to look like a real social season in Mabeltown this summer.
> "Everything suddenly opened up," she said ... of her metamorphosis. "As soon as I got to New York, it was as though someone had pressed a button. I began to see hundreds of people and was on the go from morning to night every day for months ..."
> "Dr. Brill and his wife [are coming to Taos] on their way back from a ysychiatric [*sic*] convention in San Francisco. And of course Robin and Una Jeffers and the twins will arrive soon from Carmel. Carl Hovey and Sonia Levine [i.e., Sonya Levien] will come whenever they can get away from Hollywood." (*Misc. Vol. II*)

Mabel's New York trip, including her latest treatment with Brill, clearly left her energized and stimulated, eager to welcome many visitors for the summer months in Taos.

In her first letter to Brill since returning to Taos, Mabel asks directly whether Carman Barnes—who had written to her on May 16, 1938: "I am still seeing Dr. Brill. He is very sensible"—has remained in treatment with him. She also refers to Brill's upcoming visit, much anticipated by herself and Sonya Levien, who, in a February 13, 1938 letter to Mabel, had written about her plans to be in Taos at the same time as Brill: "Aside from the very good reason that we adore you and Tony and Taos—it will be a wonderful chance to get Dr. Brill to take Serge [her son] in hand—for at least an hour a day." Unfortunately, Sonya's commitments in Hollywood prevented both the trip and having her son in the unusual arrangement of daily treatment with the vacationing Brill. In her closing, Mabel refers to her essay about menopause.

δ

May 8 [1938]

Dearest Dr. Brill,

I miss you like anything, just having you there at 88 [Central Park West]!

Where is Marina [Dasburg]'s letter I asked you to read & forward to Dr. [Ashley] Pond?

How is Carman? Did she stick?

I am mailing you the little old-fashioned silk box Frieda [Lawrence]'s mother[1] made for Lawrence's postcards & they must be kept in it. We are looking forward <u>so much</u> to your visit.

I have written a pretty good article called "Change of Life"—

Love to you & Rose ...,
Mabel

δ

May 11, 1938

Dear Mabel,

#1.: The letter that you gave me (Marina's letter) I, myself, sent from the post office in Asbury Park, N.J., on Friday evening ... That was the Friday that you took luncheon with us.

I saw Carmen [sic] once more and there is really nothing to be done at the present time except that I was willing to discuss her affairs with Mr. B. [i.e., Vincent Bendix]. She left me with the idea that he would call me up. So far, he has not, and naturally I cannot ask him to come. Please make no effort to have him come, etc., if he does not wish to.

So far, we have not received Frieda's silk box, but will write you as soon as it comes.

I am glad that you are busy and hope to see you soon. Rose joins me in affectionate greetings.

As ever,
Brill

δ

As Brill indicated, Barnes did not remain in therapy for long. She wrote Mabel nine months later, on February 8, 1939, recalling her sessions and expressing her outrage at the cost of treatment and perhaps something about Brill himself:

> Brill dismissed me, you know. Now Mabel! I think he is very interesting, but I feel HE needs psycho-analyzing, not me! Of course they say you never know when you are crazy, but then I am not crazy enough to be psycho-analyzed to the tune of three or four thousand dollars ... Brill didn't tell me anything except to go to the country, work, marry Ben, have three children. All of which I intend to do, and am doing.

These directives reported by Barnes are quite familiar, recalling the times Brill gave Mabel the same didactic advice. Note that Brill once again relaxed confidentiality and discussed a patient's treatment with someone outside the therapy, offering in addition to speak with "Mr. B." about Barnes's "affairs."

Mabel's 1938 essay, *Change of Life*, is an expansion of ideas initially expressed in her published poem, "Change." It remains unpublished, despite her hopes that it would appear in *Cosmopolitan*. This prose piece calls upon women to resist the view of post-menopausal years as barren and devoid of vitality: "Who was it that first told women that it is all over after the menopause ... ? For how many centuries have women felt it was proper to feel sad and submissive because they could no longer bear children?" (pp. 1–2). Now that "the eager insistent flesh no longer tyrannises [sic] over the total creature," Mabel encourages women to explore their newly possible creativity and energy: "Woman must arise, self-kindled, and burn, and shed her fire upon the earth" (pp. 4, 6). Her activist approach to dismantling traditional views of menopause is striking for its time and rousing in its passion. Inspired by her own words, she gathered creative lives around her in Taos and continued her quest to engage with the dynamism of new ideas and spirited personalities.

Mabel also hoped *Cosmopolitan* would publish excerpts from her unfinished psychoanalytic treatise, *On Human Relations*, that she planned later to expand into a book. On May 15, 1938, she wrote editor Harry Burton to describe her approach to writing about psychoanalysis—"I have tried to use colloquial language and to avoid the language of the specialist. I have tried to put myself in the place of those people who shy away from psycho-analysis for one reason or another and to attempt to demolish those reasons"—and to ask about his interest in publishing her work: "I have got to try and make some money this year and I am not conditioning myself to writing for mags. just for the fun of it." He responded enthusiastically on May 18, 1938—"And now for the first of the psychoanalysis articles!"—but was concerned about her style and appealed to Mabel on May 27, 1938 to revise: "I have never seen a more cogent piece of work in my life. I am convinced, however, that this form of essay would never reach Cosmopolitan's audience the way the dialogue form (which you used in the original Brill profile) would do." He reminded her they had initially discussed a series of articles "exhibiting a patient, who knows nothing about psychoanalysis, starting through the routine, and having the dialogue between him and the analyst unfold the whole process step by step, so that, as the patient undergoes the analysis, the reader practically does, too." Burton asked her to inform him of her decision.

Mabel also sent her manuscript of *On Human Relations* to her agent Edith Haggard at Curtis Brown, explaining in a letter on June 1, 1938 that she had written the account of psychoanalysis for Burton, but hoped that her "popularized version of this science" would appear as a book: "Also could you try and sell this 'Psycho-Analysis For Beginners' to a publisher?" Haggard informed Mabel on June 13 that she had sent the manuscript to Alan Collins, head of their New York office, "who will get in touch with Bennett Cerf," co-founder of Random House.

Carl Hovey had also read Mabel's manuscript, praising it highly in a letter to her on June 8, 1938: "You have done it splendidly, with great sympathy, tolerance—and forthright realism." The next day, he wrote again, more critically: "When you use the vital language of your own personal experience ... it is shot through with excitement and discovery. But when you use labels and write like Brill, as you sometimes do, anybody might have written it." Mabel's strength, Hovey and Burton point out, derives from her talent for writing straightforward dialogue that illuminates psychoanalytic technique and concepts. When she resorts to more jargon-filled prose, her achievement is less unique, less powerful.

Mabel must have mailed Burton a letter, now lost, indicating she was unwilling to rewrite her manuscript in dialogue form. He sent her a telegram c. June 16, 1938, still hoping for publication in *Cosmopolitan*: "IT STANDS UP MAGNIFICENTLY AND YOU ARE TO BE WARMLY CONGRATULATED I AM NOW GOING OVER IT AGAIN TO SEE IF I CAN FIND ANY WAY TO ADAPT SOME OF IT TO OUR NEEDS."

Mabel now had to wait to hear from both Burton and Haggard to learn the fate of *On Human Relations*.

* * *

Brill in Taos again

Brill and his wife, Rose, visited Mabel and Tony in Taos in the early summer of 1938, his second time as her guest. In her account of the Jeffers's stay that summer, *Una and Robin in Taos* (1938), Mabel featured Brill leading an animated discussion, quoted here at length:

> Dr. Brill was in a holiday mood on his way back from the meeting of the medical association in San Francisco. The very first day he sat in the center of a little group of admirers in the living room at the Big House ...
>
> He was glowing with kindness, his chin beard twitched up and down and his eyelids fell half over his eyes, which darted here and there like sly fish. He saw every fleeting expression on every face about him, every movement of each person as well as each restraint of movement ...
>
> He was talking to us about fulfillment. Fulfillment for a man, he said, lies in the sexual act itself but not so for a woman.

> "What fulfills a woman then?" Una asked ...
> "Maternity," replied Brill succinctly.
> Una looked, silently, her disagreement.
> "Certainly," he laughed. "Man is constituted for sowing his seed. Woman for receiving it, cherishing and nourishing it. Life intends this to be so and it is so ..."
> He grinned around at us all. He himself seemed content with this arrangement ... There was something singularly compelling in the dynamic little man that geared up the mechanism of social intercourse and made things move faster even on the deep summer day. No one was languid or weary or sore [sic] distressed in his company! Rose Brill, in the background, gave small reassuring smiles and nods instinctively trying to tone down ... his occasionally startling language. She had acquired a technique, through their years of companionship that attempted to deprecate and condone his freedom while at the same time she completely accepted his hypothesis and this split her somewhat and gave her countenance a certain mixed expression. (pp. 1–2)

One must wonder about Rose's private responses to her husband's pronouncements about women and fulfillment. A psychiatrist herself, who had worked for some time at the New York State Hospital, Rose apparently retired early to raise their children while Brill labored intensively in practicing and teaching psychoanalysis. We can only imagine Mabel's own reactions to Brill's insistence that motherhood was the primary fulfillment for a woman; her own problematic and alienating experience as a mother to her son was certainly the source of much pain, as was the isolating and formative experience of herself being the daughter of another self-involved, withholding mother.

Brill was the star at a party hosted by Mabel during his visit. Weeks later, on July 3, 1938, Spud Johnson wrote an article for the *New Mexico Sentinel* describing the festivities, entitled "Spud Goes To A Party; Taos Village Enjoys Big Four-Star Week-End As Celebrities Gather At Mabel Luhan's Home":

> Mabel Luhan gave one of her big parties, to which almost everybody in the valley was invited, and there were all the celebrities:
> Robinson Jeffers, mysterious, hawk-eyed, California poet; here for his usual summer month with his family.

> Dr. A. A. Brill, American's Freud and Jung rolled into one rosy ball of a man; Mrs. Luhan's houseguest ...
>
> Dr. Brill ... was all out-going. Short and plump, with a glow on his good-humored Jewish face, he was warmly friendly to old and new acquaintance alike. You felt that his keen mind and wide experience at once catalogued you—inexhorably, but with sympathy and understanding ...
>
> Shocking Taos dowagers with his easy, natural references to sexual matters or influences, he nevertheless seemed to offend no one, so obviously good-natured, wise and tolerant were his remarks. And his jollity was accentuated by the almost vaudeville-stage German-Yiddish accent, which he has never completely lost, despite his many years' residence in New York. (*Misc. Vol. II*)

Mabel explained her inclusive guest list—"Everybody in the village had heard of Dr. Brill and were crazy to look upon him"—and the entertainment: "Of course I had the Indian boys there to dance and Dr. Brill was thrilled with their fresh gai[e]ty, their dark glow and flash, their instant impetuous precision, and their delight in motion" (*URT*, p. 14).

One of Mabel's guests asked Brill to speak about the dancing he had just witnessed:

> So Dr. Brill stood in the centre of that simple gathering, beaming around at all of them and began:
>
> "Now I did not see anything erotic in this Indian dancing ..." (My God! I thought!) but he went on in the most characteristic manner to say that in the past it was the fashion to affirm: "I think, therefore I am" but that he preferred to say, "I move therefore I am," for motion is life and dancing is still more life. He told us he had an old friend in New York—a busy man of over eighty, and this old man insisted on going to night clubs and he loved to dance ... The old man's family were quite nervous about their relative and often consulted Dr. Brill about him. Wasn't it terrible, they asked, he insists on going to those places and <u>dancing</u>! "I said I don't see why,["] but they said, what if something should <u>happen</u>? He might <u>die</u> there, <u>dancing</u>! And I always answered: [']'Well, wouldn't that be fine? Don't you think it's better for a man to die dancing, than to die in his bed? <u>I</u> think that's a man's death!"

Everyone in the room was won by this—they burst out laughing and clapping, even the spinsters. (*URT*, pp. 14–15)

Clearly, Brill's energizing presence in Taos was a source of deep pleasure for those in conversation with him—Una had observed: "I didn't expect to like him. But he's so kind, isn't he?" (*URT*, p. 6)—and his departure created a tangible absence, as Mabel described: "The Brills did not stay long, only a few days, ... and when they left we very definitely missed them. He animated the environment, he was stimulating in different ways, ... in an affective manner that seemed to release us all into deeper emotions and responses for he was so brimming with kindliness and affection himself that with him one emerged from one's cold cave of introspection" (*URT*, p. 15).

In her first letter to Brill since he left Taos, Mabel asks for his psychoanalytic understanding of a tragic accident in the Taos pueblo to her son's close friend, Eliseo Concha. Mabel also inquires about Brill's contact with Bennett Cerf in her ongoing effort to publish *On Human Relations* (see Illustration 21).

δ

June 24 [1938]

Dear Dr. Brill,

We all missed you very much as soon as you left. Especially Una Jeffers bemoaned your loss for she had a great transference to you. Even Robin who is so indifferent said: "Too bad he had to go. He is so interesting & besides that, so kind."

This letter is to tell you about something that happened 2 days ago in the pueblo to my favorite indian [*sic*]. He is Eliseo & John Evans' boy friend & blood brother since childhood. He is named Eliseo Concha. Well, he is a very good carpenter ... Two days ago, then, I got a telephone message calling me out to the Indian Hospital. Eliseo had had an accident to an eye so I went out & he was in bed. His brother was with him. He had had an accident to his right eye from a stick years ago, & their mother has been nearly blind since they were babies, from trachoma. When I saw Eliseo lying there I said: "What happened? Why do all you Conchas have trouble with your eyes?" Eliseo said: "I guess it was fixed that way long ago. I was lying on my back under a building & hammering a joist & my hammer slipped & the nail shot sideways right into my eye ..." What do you think? Is it from a tremendous mother fixation or identification? Or do you know of any races who attempt to compensate for a parent's loss by giving themselves? It does seem very queer. And it is very sad. Eliseo is very handsome & a grand worker. While I sat by him he said:

"This morning after breakfast I went to kiss my little girl goodby[e] & when my eyes fell on her face the thought came to me: 'I must not go down to work today.' But I thought that foolish ... I did not want to listen & I went & at 10.15 it happened. That is the first time I did not <u>listen</u>. All my life I have <u>listened</u> ... Now this time I didn't listen & see what I got."

Did you telephone Bennett Cerf? I <u>do</u> want to sell my book! Harry Burton sent me another long telegram last night. He says he is still trying to see how to make <u>his</u> public understand it. He said "after 3 readings it still stands up magnificently & will be considered one of the grand books of the times." But he is very <u>flattering</u> & likes me so it doesn't count!

Love to you all,
Mabel

<u>Answer</u>.

δ

In her next letter to Brill, Mabel is eager for him to view the photographs in Robert Hobart Davis's *Man Makes His Own Mask*. Davis, an editor and photographer, had published 160 copies of this highly praised volume in 1932, priced at $100 and featuring 118 arresting portraits of contemporary men, including Theodore Dreiser, D. H. Lawrence, and Carl Van Vechten.

δ

Saturday [after June 24, 1938]

Dear Dr. Brill,

An additional item re Elizeo [sic]. Tony reminded me that his grandfather, his mother's father, lost his left eye also ... What <u>does</u> this family eye fatality mean to you?

Re this famous book of Bob Davis' photographs ("Man makes his own mask"), be sure & look it through, & it will interest you because he says he can get the essential man when he photographs him. Be sure & return the book carefully as it is Mr. Davis' own copy & is very expensive. I want you to see it.

Is Bennet[t Cerf] going to publish my book? I have done all the corrections & additions & it is being re-typed now ...

Yrs,
M.D.L.

δ

Brill's response to Mabel cautions her against counting too heavily on Harry Burton for publication. He also mentions the corrections "we" made, likely referring to his many edits and comments that appear in the margins of Mabel's typescript of *Notes Upon Awareness: Addressed to Krishnamurti*, a greatly expanded (261 more pages) version of *On Human Relations* written to Jiddu Krishnamurti, the popular Indian philosopher and spiritual teacher, in the form of letters meant for him.

δ

June 28, 1938

My dear Mabel,

I just received your letter. I, too, was very sorry to leave as quickly as I did, but c'est la vie!

My feeling for the Jeffers is about the same as their feeling for me. I liked Una very much. I believe that the description of her in the introduction to his forthcoming book[2] is very characteristic—in fact, perfect. I was very interested in the whole family. I need not tell you that I am an admirer of Robin. Since I got back, I have been reading for a second time some of his poetry, and I feel that I appreciate it better than I did before knowing the man.

When I returned home, there was a message that Bennett had called me up ... When I called back, I was told that he would be away for two weeks. There is nothing to do but wait, then. I have an idea that he wanted to talk to me about a work of Freud's, and as I heard from Freud about it,[3] I have no doubt at all that he will call me as soon as he comes back, and then I shall talk to him.

What you write about Eliseo is very interesting. Nothing new. Even civilized whites show the very same thing. In fact, the insurance companies will tell you that certain accidents run in families. I heard one of the insurance company doctors read a paper on the subject, and he mentioned the fact that in some families injuries to the eye are as common as certain constitutional diseases in other families. I have seen a number of cases of the same kind. [Alfred] Adler[4] reported similar cases in the early part of his Freudian life. One could dismiss the whole thing and say it was an accident, but from what Eliseo, himself, told you, you can see it is more than that. It is undoubtedly a mother identification, stimulated by some castration fear or punishment. There must have been something that made him hear the voice saying, "I must not go down and work today." Of course, what Eliseo called "listening" we say is reflection. Primitive people project to the outer world what we have long considered something due to a process of reflection, based on conscious and unconscious mentation.

I believe that this Harry Burton is just bluffing you, but it is possible that if he would read the book as we corrected it, he might change his mind.

My trip home was uneventful ...

I can assure you that I enjoyed my short visit with you. I was interested in everything and I know that we all had a very pleasant time.

With my very best to all of you, I am,

Affectionately,
Brill

δ

Notes

1. Baroness Anna Elise Lydia von Richthofen-Marquier.
2. *The Selected Poetry of Robinson Jeffers* (1938) included a foreword in which Jeffers depicts Una as being "more like a woman in a Scotch ballad, passionate, untamed and rather heroic—or like a falcon—than like any ordinary person" (p. xv).
3. If this indicates communication by letter, then it is not located. In a June 7, 1938 letter to Mabel (see Illustration 21), Cerf had written: "Please ... tell Dr. Brill that if he doesn't translate for Random House the new book that Dr. Freud is said to be writing about the Bible, I will

make his life absolutely intolerable for him." This book is most likely *Moses and Monotheism,* published in 1939 in both German and English and translated not by Brill for Random House but by Katherine Jones for Knopf.

4. Viennese physician and psychoanalyst who became a follower of Freud in 1902.

CHAPTER EIGHTEEN

The Jeffers affair

In her next letter to Brill, Mabel encloses the completed 100-page typescript of *On Human Relations* in her continued pursuit of its publication. She also mentions Myron Brinig's 1938 novel, *May Flavin*, which *Time* magazine pronounced as "written in a style as choked as the author's emotions" (June 27, 1938, p. 59), and announces that her current writing project features her in dramatic conflict with Brinig, mirroring the mutual distaste and anger that now characterized their friendship. A few days later, she writes again, asking Brill to send her an autographed photograph of himself.

δ

July 1 [1938]

Dear Dr. Brill,

This is the corrected copy of that MMS. There are many improvements I owe to you. I hope you like the new title too. Do you? I am giving you this copy and send[ing] two to my Curtis Brown agent. If it suits you to do so, will you please lend this one to Harry Burton to read—asking him to return it to you—because he really seems to like this effort …

I hope you telephone Bob Davis' secretary Miss [Marian] Price, to lend you his book "Man makes his own mask." She telephoned Miss [Laura] Buck to let her know when you wanted to borrow it. Lots of our friends are in it! Study them! ...

Myron [Brinig] got a lot of bad notices of his book & now seems to have disappeared. No one knows where he is. I still yearn (not yen) over him! I am now working on a half[-]finished novel called "Water of Life" that has him & me in it, only the end is much sublimated & <u>an improvement upon real life!</u> The beginning is all craving for power, irresponsible life, & sexual expression, & the end is fulfillment for a woman thro' maternity, & death for the man after a volcanic eruption (when, luckily, he had completed coitus with the woman on top of the mountain!) How's that for using your teaching? Heigho!

Love from all of us,
Mabel

δ

[before July 5, 1938]

Dear Dr. Brill,

We are getting a few people[,] well known, to send us signed photographs <u>Greeting Our Taos Theatre</u>. As your face is now known to every inhabitant, won't you send us one, please? We are getting quite an interesting collection to hang in the lobby ... They are all of people who have visited Taos.

Please.

Ever,
Mabel

Love to dear Rose.

δ

In the following letter, Mabel acknowledges receiving photographs Brill had taken on his recent visit to Taos. As she recalled: "Dr. Brill photographed everybody as was his custom in the country. The man never moved without his Lieca [i.e., Leica] kodak [sic] hung on his shoulder and he took us all several times" (*URT*, p. 13). It is likely these pictures are the ones in the Luhan archives, some labelled "by A. A. Brill": four photographs of Los Gallos (see Illustrations 23 and 24), two of the town of Taos, one of Mabel on horseback, dated 1938 (see Illustration 22), and one of Tony standing outside. In the spirit of the common overlap of friendships and psychoanalysis, Mabel also sent Brill a June 28, 1938 letter from Carman Barnes: "I called Dr. Brill before leaving New York, but he was still out of town ... Everything has changed for me <u>inwardly</u> since you left; not because of Dr. B. though, although he undoubtedly helped. A good confession is sometimes the right beginning, isn't it?"

δ

July 5 [1938]

Dear Dr. Brill,

Thanks for the fine photographs! Very, very good, aren't they! Here is a letter from Carman. Please return it. I think your confessi[o]nal started her right & I hope you'l[l] continue to see her—but the summertime is difficult for it. Please return it. I like her. Maybe I am mistaken.

Have you seen Myron [Brinig]'s Irish Rose?[1] That's what I call it ... Maybe he thought he'd have that kind of suc[c]ess with it, building on the funny combination of the jews [sic] & the irish [sic]. Jeffers still here. Very satisfactory people. Please send a photograph "Greetings to the Taos Theatre"![2]

Your book not come yet.[3] The library will be delighted.

Affectionately,
Mabel

δ

A lost letter from Mabel likely informed Brill of a dramatic incident between Robinson and Una Jeffers that occurred after his recent visit. Brill's comments in his next letter suggest that Mabel attributed the cause of this event to his casual discussions about sex while he was in Taos. On July 16, 1938, a weekly newspaper, *The Horse Fly*, reported that Una was admitted to the hospital for "a gun-shot wound in her left side, self-inflicted while cleaning a pistol last Saturday night" (*Misc. Vol. II*). Apparently motivated by both Mabel's and Brill's liberal attitudes, Robinson had an affair with another guest at Mabel's house, a violinist from New Haven named Hildegarde Donaldson. When Una found out, she attempted suicide, shooting herself with Jeffers's gun in Mabel's bathroom.

In *Una and Robin in Taos*, Mabel furnished lengthy details about Brill's conversations, underscoring how his combined kindness and frankness inspired direct discussions of sexual topics. Una asked him a question:

> "I'd like to know what you think of all this promiscuity in sex that's going on among young people. Why, I've heard they think nothing more of the sexual act itself than we used to think of shaking hands!"
>
> "Nonsense! I do not believe young people are any different now than they ever were. There are no facts to prove it ..."
>
> Una began to raise her voice. "You just ask the boys," she shouted, "I bet they will bear me out!" (pp. 2–3)

After summoning her twin sons, Donnan and Garth, then twenty-two, Una interviewed them in front of Brill, asking, "Isn't it true that girls and boys nowadays think nothing of sex?" While Donnan denied her claim, Garth replied, "It depends" (pp. 3–4). Brill laughed at these conflicting answers.

Another interaction with Brill may also have influenced Robinson's betrayal. With Haig, his white English bulldog, on a chain, Robinson entered the living room where Brill and others were talking. As Mabel described, Haig spied another dog through the screen door:

> Haig bristled and rumbled. His forelegs drove into the rug, his chest swelled. "R-r-r-r-u-m-ph!" he growled and the hair rose on his back.
>
> "Oh!" exclaimed Brill in his loud kind voice, "let him live out his aggression!"
>
> Una looked amazed, and Robin laughed a little one-sided laugh ...
>
> "Come on, Una! Let's let him out!" I cried daringly. (*URT*, p. 12)

Haig was allowed to run after the other dog, "ready to pounce upon him, to devour him in an ecstasy of sudden release" (p. 12). Robinson may have interpreted Brill's comment as license to freely satisfy his own desires.

δ

July 12, 1938

My dear Mabel,

What you write me about the Jeffers is very interesting indeed. That will probably account for the fact that I heard nothing from Una about the pictures[4] that I sent her. But, please do not blame me for this thing. My discussion was based on questions that you people asked, and if Robin acted on it, all power to him! I think Tony sizes him up properly. <u>Ca s'arrangera</u>!

Everything else that you asked for in your letters was attended to—I am sure by this time you have heard from Harry Burton. Bennett Cerf, as I told you, was out of town ...

I have some more pictures of Taos, which I will print and send to you in due time. I also sent a picture to [Dorothy] Brett ...

I still doubt that Carmen [sic] will visit you.

As ever,
[A.A.B.]

δ

Although Brill mentioned contacting Cerf in his effort to get *On Human Relations* published, he could not know that, two days later, on July 13, Alan Collins would break bad news to Mabel, quoting the final decision of an editor at Harcourt, Brace: "Maybe we're just plumb crazy, but it seems to us that she has failed badly." Collins kept trying to interest other publishers, ultimately with no success.

Brill's prediction that Barnes would not go to Taos proved correct. Although she had written to Mabel about her intention to visit—on May 16, 1938, "I am looking forward to Taos," and again on June 28, 1938, "Of course I'm coming!"—she ultimately decided against it, as revealed in a July 20 [1938] letter Mabel received from Myra Kingsley, the astrologer who was to be Barnes's traveling companion. Kingsley explained that although Barnes would not be coming as planned, she herself would arrive in early August. This next letter to Brill is written on the back of Kingsley's letter where Mabel drew two parallel lines next to the first paragraph and noted to Brill: "Right again!!" Mabel also informs him that Thornton Wilder, who lived in New Haven, Connecticut, was visiting her in Taos with his sister, Isabel, also a writer.

δ

c. July 20, 1938

Dear Dr. Brill,

Thornton & Isabel Wilder are now here. Jeffers leave for Carmel Sunday D.V.⁵

Aff.
M.D.L.

δ

Brill's next two letters acknowledge receipt of a number of "communications" from Mabel, including a letter from Hildegarde Donaldson she had likely forwarded in case Una Jeffers presented for treatment. Mabel had written to Una recommending psychoanalysis with Brill after her husband's disastrous affair with Hildegarde. In her continual desire to urge others towards treatment and, some would say, interfere in their lives, Mabel also encouraged Hildegarde to consult with Brill, as she revealed in *Hildegarde: Eight Years After* (c. 1946), a third part of her chronicle of the Jeffers's relationship: "Soon after she [Hildegarde] left Taos I had put her in touch with Dr. Brill" (p. 1).

δ

July 22, 1938

My dear Mabel,

Just a few lines to tell you that I got all your communications, but I have had no chance to sit down and write to you.

I'm not looking forward to having Una come here, but if she should come, I will do all I can for her …

Affectionately,
A. A. Brill

δ

Monday July 25, [19]38 [see Illustration 25]

Dear Mabel,

To repeat I received everything and am returning Hildegard[e]'s letter. I was quite sure that Una will refuse to come here and I am pleased that she made this decision. What would I do with her at this time of the year? I saw the [Robert] Davis photos. I thought they were wonderful. I wrote him thanks etc. Burton has the copy you sent me and told me to let him read it and that he would return it to me … I cannot see why he does not want the whole book. I'm sure he would make a hit with it. If he doesn't want [it] someone will get it. There is nothing new here … Excuse my brevity. I hate to write long hand.

Love,
A. A. Brill

P.S. Saw Carmen [sic] last week & she said
she would not go to you.

δ

Una Jeffers wrote to Mabel on August 3, 1938 explaining her decision not to enter treatment with Brill:

> It was very kind of you to suggest psycho-analysis which would be very interesting any time if one could afford it but I didn't need Dr. Brill to tell me why I was so unhappy & indignant. Robin says if I needed psycho-a-, he needed it worse … [Hildegarde] told him he was being ruined & so on & pressed him to come & stay at her house in New Haven to escape my attentions! Really when I heard from him that he had <u>listened</u> to her I felt so desperate a wound & unhappiness that I could not think (everything for the past 25½ years considered!) that I cared to make one more gesture towards living.

Despite Mabel's urging her towards analysis, Una returned to Carmel with her husband.

Mabel next inquires whether Brill had received a "black and ebony" box from her—later referred to as a "Memento Mori" (Latin for "remember that you have to die") box in a letter to him from January 31, 1939—that is central to a tense scene between Una and Hildegarde in *Una and Robin in Taos*:

> There was a little Italian ebony and silver box … it had a skull and cross-bones and the words "memento [sic] Mori" inlaid in the cover. It was for a token of revenge and dated back to the days when outraged lovers, husbands and wives could appease their anger by killing or castration. An ear or an offending organ would readily fit into it, to be sent in vengeance to anyone deserving punishment. As we started for the dining room Una grabbed it up and shook it in Hildegarde's face.
>
> "Do you see <u>that</u>?" she cried. "I wouldn't <u>hesitate</u> to use it." (p. 36)

Mabel also asks if Brill has received the "big book," most certainly her *Family Affairs*, a 483-page unpublished manuscript.

δ

July 27 [1938]

Dear Dr. Brill,

Glad to know you're somewhere there! I thought you were perhaps in England.

You say you got all my communications but did you get the black & ebony box & the big book? Don't bother to answer if you did ...

A certain peace descended upon us when the Jeffers left! I will never see Una again probably. Tony put his foot down & says we will never have her here again & besides that I am so disappointed to find her out. She gave herself away, & then Robin had his chance to be himself & revealed so much. I cannot any longer take her at her own valuation. Of course my "enemies" here are saying I drove her into a frenzy by "making" Hildegarde flirt with Robin! Then the boys [Donnan and Garth] took to our two pretty little Mexican girls & found them witty, pretty, good dancers, & less clumsy & gauche than the daughters of my friends, so they took them to dances. This enraged my friends! They said I was responsible for it. They said Garth was trying to get "sex experience!" (He has had plenty for several years!) These Mexican girls are well brought up & do not misbehave. Now Brett tells me Una went calling all round town before she left & howled & grumbled about it & said she had not been able to do a thing about it. Apparently blaming me again! Ah me! Well, I'l[l] be blamed till [sic] I die I suppose for everything that ever happens! ...

Harry B[urton] bought only a few pages. I'l[l] tell him to return your mms. I am feeling alright but have to close the Big House. Can't afford to run it.

Love,
Mabel

δ

Burton paid for a portion of *On Human Relations*, as indicated in a letter to Mabel from Edith Haggard dated July 28, 1938: "We are very lucky to have sold that small part for $750." Despite this purchase, her work never appeared in *Cosmopolitan*.

Mabel next reports to Brill on Thornton Wilder's troubled stay in Taos, during which she gave him her "P.A. article," almost certainly *On Human Relations*, to read.

δ

Sunday [after July 27 and before August 2, 1938]

Dear Dr. Brill,

Certainly there is something peculiar about this place. After the Jeffers left a week ago, Thornton Wilder & his sister [Isabel] being here, everything seemed as though we could relax & have a nice time. Thornton had come to work on his play "Merchant of Yonkers" that [Max] Reinhardt[6] is going to produce next month in California.[7] But a peculiar feverishness animated him. I gave him my P.A. article to read. He took it to his room for perusal. He knows all <u>about</u> P.A.[,] knows Freud, went to see him & had several long talks. But he could not rest. Sunday morning he rose & before breakfast walked down the highway & back in the sun without a hat ... The next day he went to a dance in the pueblo without a coat along & caught a chill, he says, from the rain. Then he had a sore throat he would not admit or care for ... I found the P.A. article left by him on my desk ... but he never mentioned it to me. I do not know what he thought of it or what his reactions were. His voice disappeared & from being over conversational & brilliant, he became silent. I insisted on Dr. [Ashley] Pond yesterday who painted it [Wilder's throat] twice but said nothing seemed to be the matter! Still his voice was gone! ... Then his sister came over to breakfast & said he'd been awake all night & had decided he had to go away today ... At 2.30 I took them to the stage & he left in silence smiling wistfully ... They had planned to stay some weeks but now I'm certainly glad they didn't. As he left he murmured: "I am sorry I had to break up like this!" What on earth gets into people here? I am so tierd [sic] of all these performances ... Do you suppose it's <u>my</u> fault?

Love,
M

δ

Extending her self-doubt, Mabel sends the following note to Brill, written on the bottom of Edith Haggard's July 28 letter that expressed relief for selling part of *On Human Relations* but also uncertainty about further sales.

δ

August 2, 1938

Dear Dr. Brill,

I guess my mms affects people badly? Even Mrs. Haggard the agent is cold with it. I guess it hurt Thornton too.

M.D.L.

δ

In Brill's next letter, he scolds Mabel for her readiness to blame herself for Wilder's losing his voice, offering instead his own interpretation of the situation. To support his claim, Brill likely included a copy of his lecture "Art and Neurosis," since a typed carbon, dated March 4, 1938, appears next to this letter in the Luhan archives. Brill had given this talk on radio station WQXR as part of the Works Progress Administration's Federal Theatre Project, providing a definition of a neurotic person as one "whose emotional energy has been dammed up so that it must find an outlet in some roundabout way," and concluding: "Every great artist from ancient times to the present has shown neurotic tendencies" (p. 1).

δ

[c. early August 1938]

My dear Mabel,

Don't you think it is high time to stop feeling guilty and give up your foolish superstitions. I cannot see why you should attribute W's loss of voice to any fault of your own. It is quite possible that he had a cold. He is a pronounced neurotic—people say—so he could have exaggerated his cold to express some complex. Writers are narcistic[8] and the fact that he said nothing about the MSS may mean he didn't read it or he read it and liked it and [i.e., or?] disliked it and forgot about it. That it might have caused his upset is not likely although anything might do it. Who knows what? You are so ready to spank yourself because you have a guilty conscience.

I received the box and find it very interesting and your book in which I read the part referring to the Jeffers ...

Love,
Brill

δ

The book Mabel sent to Brill, *Family Affairs*, had been completed in August 1933 and incorporated the fifty-one pages of *Una and Robin* (January 1933). Here Mabel tried to define the couple's relationship, emphasizing their powerful dynamic in Robinson's own words: "Una <u>likes</u> to make things happen" while "<u>I hate</u> to, but I hate it worse if they don't." She also explained: "At some early moment ... Una took over the responsibility of his earthly life, he gladly giving it into her hands" (pp. 336, 338). (*Una and Robin in Taos*, describing their summer 1938 visit, was not included; Mabel did not finish it until December 1938).

Notes

1. Brinig's novel, *May Flavin*, featured a red-haired Irish woman.
2. The *New Mexico Sentinel* (September 11, 1938) reported on the display at the Taos Theatre of "autographed photographs of famous people," including Brill, Stokowski, and Thornton Wilder (*Misc. Vol. II*).
3. Brill likely was donating one of his own books, perhaps *The Basic Writings of Sigmund Freud*, translated and edited by him and published in 1938, to the unnamed library, possibly the Taos Public Library.
4. Brill is referring to photographs of Robinson and Una Jeffers that he took in Taos. Mabel recalled: "Robin came out, in these pictures, in that familiar pose of his, coached through the years by Una: 'Hold your chin up, Robin!' His shoulders drooped a little ... but he always held his head up" (*URT*, p. 13). Not located.
5. Deo volente, or God willing.
6. Viennese theater director.
7. The play was not performed in California at this time, but instead opened in Boston on December 12, 1938 and then moved to New York, opening on December 28, 1938 and running for only twenty-eight performances.
8. An acceptable spelling for "narcissistic" at this time in psychoanalytic writings.

CHAPTER NINETEEN

Money and a novel

In her next letter to Brill, Mabel encloses payment towards her outstanding balance for treatment with him in New York the previous winter and spring, money presumably earned from the sale of a section of *On Human Relations* to *Cosmopolitan*. She mentions her intention to offer her Big House as an inn to generate revenue, a plan that apparently never came to fruition.[1] Mabel needed money to pay attorneys representing her in a $50,000 slander suit brought by Dr. Charles Kanter in the early summer of 1938 for negative remarks she allegedly made about his medical expertise during a dinner party at her home in Taos. Fortunately, the case was dropped after Kanter claimed that poor health prohibited him from appearing in court, but he was then discovered dancing at an event. *The Horse Fly* (July 23, 1938) announced: "Dancing Doctor's Slander Suit Ends" (*Misc. Vol. II*). Nonetheless, in preparation for the trial, Mabel had accumulated significant legal fees.

δ

Aug[ust] 28 [1938]

Dear Dr. Brill,

It gives me great satisfaction to send you this check out of money I <u>earned</u>! Thanks for your generosity in vastly undercharging me! I think I must still owe you a lot—I don't know how much. Tell me.

I am now trying to plan to open our Big House next season as <u>The Taos Inn</u> if I can find a good woman to run it. I wouldn't want to do that or be there much. I would have it as a quiet summer place for well[-]off people—only letting in our friends & acquaintances. Do you think it a good idea? I must make some money somehow to pay my attorneys & the bank mortgage & my income has dropped to half what it was & [Edward] Greenbaum says I must expect it to decrease steadily with the trustee I have. (I also have paid Eddie G. with my earnings!! So that's fixed to date!)

I have my ole debbil [sic] depression coming down on me again because I am bored & have no humans to exchange libido with here. You know it is an inferior population as a whole & when my visiting friends are gone, at first I am glad to be alone but soon I find it does not agree with me. The Una affair was none too good for me but I weathered it alright. The <u>kind</u> of activity my visitors provided this summer was not congenial! Now I am trying to finish a long psychological novel [i.e., *Water of Life*] I have been working on for 3 years & it is like pulling teeth to fish out an idea! I am up to the last 3 chapters too & can't seem to make it! Last night I dreamed I had stepped over an opening & narrowly escaped falling into it—it was a long wide tin pipe like a vent of some kind. I also constantly dream of going to strangers' houses to stay, & they are not ready for me.

Love,
M

δ

Mabel was admitting to Brill that she was depressed once more in the absence of others to stimulate her energy, and she mentioned two dreams. It is surprising that, in his next letter, he makes no comment about these. As recently as April of that year, Mabel had written in *Psycho-Analysis with Dr. Brill* about his strong interest in dream life, reporting the format of his asking for a dream, her recollection, and then his guiding and inquisitive remarks. The images from her dreams—a narrow escape from falling and the repeated visits to the houses of strangers who are not prepared for her—are evocative perhaps of close calls and unmet longing, but without background and Brill's questions, the dream associations remain unknown. In the following letter, Brill offers Mabel genuine reassurance by placing her distress in context, urging her to shake off her depression and return to writing.

δ

August 31, 1938

My dear Mabel,

… Thanks very much for the check. As I told you before, there was no hurry about your paying me, and I do not know whether you owe me as much as you sent. If you do not, I shall send back the balance.

It is only natural that you should now have a letdown after all the excitement that you had—I mean the excitement of the last 6–8 months. Remember, you have done a lot of things that you never did before. Some of them were undoubtedly beneficial. I am referring to your visit to New York. Some of them were just exciting. Your trial, for instance, was very exciting. Fortunately, it turned out well. Then, the Una affair was certainly very exciting and left a bad impression with you.

Incidentally, I just got a letter from Una, dated August 25th.[2] It is a one page letter in which she thanks me for the pictures of the 4 Jeffers[3] and she adds that it was "fun to hear you talk, you are wise and humorous too—well you should be after all you've heard and seen and pondered! Life is odd and exciting." Then, she tells me about the glorious weather and the sea, and wishes that I could climb the steps to their tower[4] and gaze in every direction … Not a word does she say about the situation, which she undoubtedly knows I know about.

As to your financial condition, of course, I cannot speak about that. You have to be guided by the situation … The only thing is that you have to watch so that you do not get someone who will waste more money for you instead of giving you some income …

If I were you, I would pull myself together and get to work. You take things too seriously. You cannot control the world, but you still would like to. (Omnipotence of thoughts[.])[5]

I am returning your book.[6] I mean the typewritten book.

As ever,
Brill

δ

In Mabel's next letter to Brill, she announces, perhaps as a result of her quickly taking his advice to heart, the completion of her novel, *Water of Life*. She has also finished a chapter entitled "The Money Complex," intended as an addition to *On Human Relations*. Brill replies with enthusiasm for her treatise on money.

δ

Sept[ember] 16 [1938]

Dear Dr. Brill,

The novel is finished & gone to the agent, Curtis Brown. Do you care to read it? I think it is an imposition that you should have to read everything your patients write, I must say! On the other hand you can see in their work[,] more than in any other way, how your efforts have failed or succeeded with them so you should be given a chance if you want to take it. This book is a romantic-psychological one & I suppose it is an attempt to sublimate the Myron [Brinig] fixation. I don't know whether it succeeds or not or whether it has any life in it. I will only know that by its career, I guess. It is full of symbolism & is called "Water of Life" & is laid in an invented environment somewhere in Mittel Europa! There is nothing unconscious in it & perhaps that fact may cause it to be lifeless & to fail. I confess I would like your opinion on it. I could send you a carbon copy. Have ... written another chapter for the "[On] Human Relations" on money, which I will send you to add to your copy.

Love,
Mabel

δ

September 27, 1938

Dear Mabel,

I just read your chapter on the "Money Complex" and I like it very much. I note that I added to it on page 3, at the end of paragraph 2, after the word, "Dreams, fairy-tales and folk-lore."[7] I think it is very well done and in spite of what you think I believe that the whole book is very good. I have added it to my other chapter.

As to your novel, I am very glad that you have finished it. I should be very glad to read it, but unless you can give me plenty of time, I would not ask you to send it to me. Just now I have so many things to do that I cannot pin myself down to anything definite.

I hope that by this time you have shaken off your blockings and are free again ...

Affectionately,
Brill

δ

From her two psychoanalysts, Mabel likely learned about money and its associations. Jelliffe instructed her about the link between body and psyche, as she reported: "Jelliffe had taught me the close connection between excrement and gold in the symbolism of the psyche, and I had observed the relationship between our money-making fixation and the great signs advertising all kinds of laxatives" (*M&S*, p. 516). She was also probably familiar with Brill's writings on this subject, which draw heavily on Freud's ideas that link money and feces, such as in "Character and Anal Erotism" (1908b). Brill (1912) explained (in a chapter whose title, "Anal Eroticism and Character," directly corresponds to Freud's): "The relation between defecation and money though seemingly remote still shows a definite connection. Some of you know that the most obstinate cases of constipation can be cured by psychoanalysis ... We know that misers are called filthy (filthy lucre), and that in mythology, fairy tales, superstitions, and dreams money is intimately connected with feces (goose that laid the golden egg)" (pp. 395–396). Both Jelliffe and Brill certainly believed in money as symbol.

Mabel's six-page essay, "The Money Complex," explored the meanings of money, beginning with: "Money is power ... It bestows a certain sense of security that is often lacking from childhood" (p. 1).

She offered: "Money often becomes the surrogate for the repressed emotions. When people are unable to love freely and to be loved in return, they can find an outlet in the activity of adding gold and silver together and in that way getting a feeling of increased significance" (pp. 1–2). It is impossible here not to wonder about Mabel's own relationship to money: her wealthy family was generous with financial support but stingy with affection and love.

Mabel then discussed the association between miserly attitudes about money and childhood withholding of feces: "He who has an exclusive interest in money is like the child whose early attention is held by the amazing act of defecation. This is not repulsive in the anal eroticism of infancy but in the man it is held to be inferior ... The misers withhold, or are 'close'; they will not let themselves go, they are tight" (p. 3). She also wrote about constipation: "Those who have occasional attacks of it will be found to have them when their money is scarce or difficult to produce. The body portrays the inner life, psychic as well as physical" (p. 3). Mabel was surely convinced that the topic of money was highly evocative and significant.

Mabel's barely disguised autobiographical novel, *Water of Life*, is a story of the relationship between a powerful and unfulfilled woman named Gaza and an artistic, detached homosexual writer named Gendron, inspired by Myron Brinig and, most likely, D. H. Lawrence. In the novel, Gaza, like Mabel, looks outside herself, to nature and eventually to men, for definition and strength. After observing an intimacy between Gendron and a male friend, Gaza is filled with longing and intently pursues Gendron, despite his declaration: "I don't care for women. Nearly all women seem unattractive to me" (p. 171). Reminiscent of Mabel's urgent and destructive appropriation of male artists' energy for herself, as in her relationship with Lawrence, Gaza is determined to bind Gendron to her: "It's no use, Gaza, I know it's no use. I must have peace—and possess my soul. Here I feel you pulling at me all the time! You drag at me." Gaza persists: "There was something in him beyond her knowing and she felt that she must somehow reach it and find out about it and add it to herself" (pp. 195, 197). She then emphasizes the crucial value of connection between people, echoing Mabel's own writing about the Native American life she discovered with Tony: "What we really need are human relationships again! We are all alone and lonely. People never were lonely when they were tribal, clannish, and not individuated!" Gendron insists: "I don't want to be intimate with anybody" (pp. 284, 296). The urgency of Gaza's plea deeply parallels Mabel's lifelong search for people who could satisfy her insatiable needs for reassurance and a sense of her own identity.

Towards the end of the novel, Gendron suddenly acquires insights into the magnitude of experiencing rather than denying his feelings, and he then travels to a dangerous peak in search of Gaza. Drawn to the mountain at the same time, they reunite with intensity and abandon in the scene Mabel referred to in her July 1, 1938 letter to Brill:

> Now Gaza said, "I want your son, Gendron. I think I came for that."
>
> All his secret unused power sprang up in him instantaneously. He took her quickly, possessing her as though she was earth to plow ...
>
> Then the ground heaved mightily under them and a terrific detonation sounded in their ears. The dormant volcano above them blasted out of its crater a stormy shower of hot rocks ...
>
> Gendron had leapt to his feet at the first sundering of the peak. He was standing alone, exposed and sacrificial, when the fragment struck him and he fell like a massacred deer across Gaza's body.
>
> His head was bleeding and it soaked through to her breast. She felt his heart but there was no movement there. (pp. 388–389)

This dramatic ending to Mabel's novel features the kind of destructiveness she herself exhibited with men like Brinig and Lawrence in her efforts to control them and siphon off their life blood to enrich her own. Mabel yearned for intimate bonds with creative men, whose energy and inspiration she craved to feed her own soul. In these efforts, her willfulness often dominated, inevitably damaging her relationships.

Over the next few months, *Water of Life* was rejected by publisher after publisher, and her agents at Curtis Brown were discouraging about its prospects. Haggard had written to Mabel on September 22, 1938: "I'm afraid that there is no chance for the novel in the magazines but, knowing that Harry Burton is interested in everything you do, I am sending a copy to him." This negative response to her writing likely contributed greatly to Mabel's current despair, as revealed in her next letter to Brill.

δ

Sept[ember] 30 [1938]

Dear Dr. Brill,

No. On the contrary, my "blockings" are worse than ever. As I cannot work all the time, (because when I work I work hard & pour out a lot & have to fill up again) I am idle & vacant & hollow as a drum—at the same time throbbing & vibrating with a strong melancholy libido that turns here & there seeking a way out & finds none.

I should think that at 3 months from 60 years of age this physical & psychic tension ... would let up & let [sic] allow me to sit amiably smiling in peace doing <u>nothing</u>. On the contrary if I miss one day of exhausting horseback riding, the next day I am <u>frantic</u>. I have no ideas, nothing but a terrific panicky seeking of the libido who finds no object & no outlet & no interest in life. This is added to, I suppose, by the bi-weekly Theolin[8] (pituitary) injections which whip up energy. I tried to cut them down & relapsed on to [sic] the couch looking vacantly straight ahead.

The Theolin drives me out on the horse, in the car, anywhere. Much of the time I am alone for no one interests me & I am so negative at such periods, I interest no one. I turn to thoughts of Myron believing that if he were here I would be alright yet I know this is only rationalizing & seeking a solution. If I had an <u>idea</u> I would work but nothing turns up in my head! A bad outlook at 60 years I call it.

What say you? I can't go to N.Y. until after Xmas <u>if</u> then.[9] Too poor. I have paid nearly <u>all</u> my dwindled income out lately to lawyers, bank, loan in Santa Fe, taxes, insurance policies. In fact I have managed to reduce living expenses to a minimum. Maybe we spend $350 a month on house & servants & the rest goes to the debts, & by doing so I have also reduced my debts very much but I still owe the bank $5500, Judge [Henry] Kiker $1500, another lawyer $450, & taxes for Nov. & Dec. $400. So you see I am deep in the red & must crawl out somehow for I <u>hate</u> to owe money. If I could work or love or something I could stand it but I can do neither. What would <u>you</u> do?

Love to Rose,
M.

δ

In a passage from *On Human Relations* about the artist, Mabel describes the experience of "blockings": "Unless the life in him moves he is driven wild by its inhibited, damned-up [sic] immobility. The artist must love or sublimate or he will die" (p. 28). For Mabel, obstruction of or lack of access to creative outlets caused her to panic, leaving her depleted and immobilized. She observes about the artist, and likely herself: "If he cannot sing for too long a period he mopes into melancholia, rage, despair. Then he cannot love, or paint, or write, or create in any way" (p. 28). She also explains the artist's tendency to derive identity and purpose through involvement with another, closely paralleling her own urgency towards intimate relationships, as well as her earlier quest for control over men such as Lawrence and her current preoccupation with Brinig: "He often lives concentratedly in the thought of another person. To be with the desired one is heaven, to be separated is misery and annihilation of his sense of being" (p. 27). Mabel was again obsessed with the idea that the presence of a man, currently Brinig, would relieve her depression and liberate her creativity.

Notes

1. There is no mention in Rudnick (1996) of any such use of the house.
2. Not located.
3. Referred to in Brill's July 12, 1938 letter to Mabel.
4. The four-story Hawk Tower on the Jeffers's property in Carmel, adjacent to their home (Tor House), built by Robinson himself with granite rocks, and perched fifty yards above the ocean. He named it Hawk Tower in honor of Una, whom he likened to a falcon (Karman, 1987, pp. 28–29, 90).
5. Brill (1946) describes this term: "Hypnotism is the highest expression of the omnipotence of thought: like a god, you can make everyone do what you want!" (p. 7).
6. Likely *Family Affairs* which Mabel had sent him in July.
7. In the existing typescript, the passage Brill refers to does not include his addition, but reads: "When we assert there is an infantile relationship between gold and excreta how do we determine this? By the tested examination of dreams [here Brill wanted to add 'fairy tales and folklore'] where one is the symbol of the other" (p. 3).

8. Theolin is a drug with the active ingredient Theophylline, used to treat symptoms of asthma, chronic bronchitis, and related obstructive airway diseases. Its adverse reactions include restlessness, hyperactivity, and insomnia.
9. Mabel's next documented trip to New York was not until December 1939.

CHAPTER TWENTY

Dreams, ups and downs

Mabel's next letter to Brill reports a dream with imagery derived from San Geronimo Day, an autumn harvest festival at the Taos pueblo where certain Native Americans, the Koshares, celebrate by climbing a tall pole made from a pine tree peeled of its bark, topped with a sheep and harvest products. As she explained, the Koshares "… give vent to the lawless, undomesticated element in men and in their persons the whole tribe relaxes for a few hours from all rule and all censorship. For these days the Koshari may do as they please, and whatever occurs to them" (*Statue*, p. 152). By participating in observing the Koshares, the members of the tribe are thereby temporarily liberated from social regulations.

δ

Oct[ober] 1 [1938]

Dear Dr. Brill,

One of our dogs named Phillip, attaches himself to one person. At present our cook. If she goes out he suffers so from panic & lonsesomeness [*sic*], tearing around looking for her, that it bores us to death.

Last night I dreamed I was leaving a place but I looked up & saw Phillip had been left at the top of a very high pole with tiny steps up & down it & a small platform at the top. I thought: "Oh dear, I am afraid he won't know how to get down & he may jump over. He is so stupid." Then he turned into John Evans who calmly jumped off the pole into the air & began to fall slowly thro' the large empty space to the ground. My heart stood still as I watched him. I thought it was the end. He fell so slowly—with a vague smile on his face, feet first, that he was able to slowly wave his arms up & down imitating a bird.

I did not see him land because there was a truck standing in the way. My apprehension ceased as well as my interest & I went on.

The dream was drawn from the pole climbing yesterday at the Pueblo for it was San Geronimo Fiesta ... [when the Koshares] are allowed every liberty—can do as they please, no censor, no taboos; all the children are thrilled & fearful when they come around. Well, one of them—the same one, always climbs the tall new pole to get the lamb & presents tied on the top & divides them with the others in the clan. Yesterday he had a harder time than usual. He is getting older. He hates to give up ... He frightened us yesterday—he seemed to falter ... Tony said: "That damn fool! ... Why doesn't that Juanito stop if he can't do it any more? Plenty others in the clan ready to take his place in the pole climbing."

I said: "Perhaps he hates to give up."

Tony said: "Foolish. He wants to be important so everyone will slap his hand when he gets through!" (shake his hand.) [sic]

Now just because I am able to interpret this dream, & because the mechanisms that victimize me are only too familiar & customary, seems no reason for them to fade out. In fact the more I understand them the worse they are!

I do not feel any inclination to go to New York because Myron is away—where I do not know. I wrote him some time ago I might be unable to go this winter. He had previously suggested in a letter I be sure & come & we would have the same nice times as last year. We used to dine out together every other night, (strictly dutch treat!), go to a movie or theatre. Much that I did in the way of contacts etc[.] was motivated by him. If I did not call him for a couple of days he would call me in a fluster, saying he'd thought perhaps I'd gone away. He was looking forward so much to spending the summer here in one of our houses & then I wrote him he couldn't come, on account of John Evans'[s] behavior the night he spent here in May. Jealous of Myron. Myron wrote me how he despised John's incestuous feeling for me.[1] But Myron himself has an incestuous feeling for me. And I for him, of course. So what?

    None of all this takes primary place with me if I can work & sublimate it. The novel is about it. Now I think it's a pretty good novel. However Curtis Brown's agent Mr. Collins writes me he doesn't know if the publishers will like it because, though it is beautifully written, because [sic] it has <u>no plot</u>![2] My god! It has all the plot you can get out of the effect of human relationships on people! That seems to me the only <u>origin</u> of plot!

    I suppose my lack of suc[c]ess in which I feel to be my best work, done this year, is at the root of my failure to move, feel, get ideas & write, at present. Understanding this also has no <u>release</u> in it! I fear I am regressed & am acting pretty inferior. All I really want right now is Myron around & a lot of money to pay my bills! ...

Ever,
M.D.L.

δ

Although Mabel claimed to have interpreted her dream, she did not present any conclusions to Brill, nor did she mention her ambivalent feelings towards her son during his fall. Her initial anxiety about John's jump from the pole and descent through the air ends with her indifference to his landing, an attitude not far removed from her often distant approach towards him.

    Perhaps relevant to Brinig's reference to incest is John Evans's own novel featuring incest, *Shadows Flying* (1936). In a grueling scene, the mother lustfully pursues her son, Runyon, a passage impossible to read without cringing, and without questioning the basis for such lifelong violent emotions in the volatile relationship between Mabel and her son. Runyon has returned home for a visit with his friend Jacob. After they have retired for the night into separate bedrooms, Jacob looks into the hallway and sees Runyon's mother softly knock on her son's closed door: "Her eyes ... glittered intently, full of undisguised passion. From her whole being seemed to emanate an aura of lascivious lechery, a poisonous all-pervading embodiment of all that was wicked and evil" (p. 114). When she tried to touch him, he forcefully pushed her away "with a visible shudder of horror and loathing" and hissed: "You beastly animal! Get into your room and stay there! And if you ever so much as touch me again, so help me God, I'll murder you!" (pp. 115–116). For his novel, Evans certainly had ample material to draw from; the real mother–son relationship was punctuated by passionate attachment, profound mutual jealousies, and discomfort with the intensity of their feelings for each other.

Brill replies to Mabel's last two letters with reassurance of her eventual emergence from her current depression and explains his own theory about mood cycles.

δ

October 3, 1938

Dear Mabel,

The best thing to do when you are in a mood like this is to give into [sic] it and say to yourself that it will pass; the more gracefully you take it, the sooner, and then your libido will come to the surface. Remember, the human organism is no different than any other dynamic structure. Whatever goes up must come down, and it does not stay down either. Otherwise, there would be no progress, no variety, nothing new in life.

You have the capacity to live so fast and do so much while you live that there must come some slump. In addition, you have had quite a lot of emotional tension as a result of your New York visit, the Jeffers, etc. Last, but not least, a big loss financially, which coming as it did, did not contribute to your happiness.

You need no medicines, but of course you always take them, so keep it up.

I am just getting back into the harnes[s], my lectures have begin [i.e., begun][3] and to tell you I am crazy about it would be lying …

As ever,
A.A.B.

δ

In *Basic Principles of Psychoanalysis*, Brill included a section about "Manic-Depressive Psychoses," describing patterns he certainly observed in Mabel:

It is designated by that name because ... it runs in certain phases or cycles. Sometimes the patient is excited, exhilarated, restless, manic, and sometimes he is melancholy, retarded in thought and action; depressed. Suddenly a wave of excitement lasting a few days, weeks, or months ... will come over the patient: the emotions run up and gradually down and remain normal for a period. There then may follow another similar wave. (pp. 221–222)

Brill's faith in the progression of ups and downs that eventually leads to a phase of "normal" moods was a key element in his therapeutic approach to Mabel, often advising her to wait out her emotional fluctutations. Mabel herself, in *On Human Relations*, had written a description of the artist's manic-depressive pattern that seems strikingly autobiographical: "It is the fear that if he is psycho-analyzed to help his depression or to stimulate his creativeness, he may lose the wonderful bursts of exaltation that compensate him for what he goes through. The artist is often a fitful creature with ups and downs. He fits easily into the type called manic-depressive" (p. 27).

* * *

Mabel writes Brill another dream about falling.

δ

Oct[ober] 4 [1938]

Dear Dr. Brill,

Dreamt last night another falling dream. This time very snowy country & hills with very high places & a strange combination of a snowplow, aeroplane & cate[r]pillar tank was crawling up one of these high places, on the edge of a low drop. I was below & in this vehicle our Boston terrier bitch—Betty, was imprisoned. As it climbed higher & she saw me left below she got more & more frantic, then to my horror she found a crack in a window & climbed thro' & hurled herself out & I saw her falling thro' the air from the great height. I saw her strike the snow & looked to see if it had killed her but she was not there in the background. The machine went on & I too left that place. Only sometime after it occurred to me she had penetrated the snow & maybe was suffocating but alive, & that I had not tried to get her out when I was there horrified me. But it was too late. We had come too far to go back. This was very painful to me & full of remorse.

All these dreams are very agonising & seem to be trying to tell me something I should do but I don't know what. I forget what falling means in a dream, specifically. But anyway I feel a little better this morning.

Writing you about it seems to encourage me. I hope it doesn't put too much on you.

Ever,
M.D.L.

δ

Brill identified specific types of dreams and it is quite possible Mabel had read the following passage:

> An unusually interesting typical dream is the *falling dream* ... What the falling dream essentially denotes ... is a repressed pleasure originating from motion, which, as we know, is a fundamental pleasure principle in life. Motion is a passive root of sex, and, as such, has a powerful appeal to young and old alike. Thus from time immemorial ... the way to pacify the child that was unsatisfied with nursing was to rock it. We know that as the child grows older he likes to be taken up by an adult, thrown up in the air, and caught: he experiences a sense of exhilaration and pleasure in the experience. Later on this early emotion repeats itself in dreams, but when that happens we no longer conceive it in terms of pleasure, but, rather, in terms of displeasure. It is now a repressed, a tabooed pleasure. That is why so many men and women have these falling dreams as symbolic of moral falling. (1921, p. 197)

While Mabel claims not to remember the meaning of falling, it is intriguing to ascribe to these dreams Brill's idea of "moral falling," as well as another typical category he described where *"the dreamer identifies himself with some animal"* (1921, pp. 198–199). Both of Mabel's dreams involve dogs falling from a great height, perhaps suggesting, in Brill's view, her moral decline, feared or actual. Each dream also features Mabel's detached interest, as she abandons the site of the fall after only barely investigating the outcome. In the second dream, even after realizing she might have saved the dog herself, she "had come too far to go back" and did not attempt returning. This resignation is somewhat chilling, even though she wrote about feeling pain and remorse in recalling the dream and pondering its significance. It seems worth speculating that Mabel's falling dreams reflect her fractured and difficult relationships with both her son and others. (Brill did not refer to either dream in his next replies to her letters, a puzzling omission.)

Mabel writes to Brill again the next day, inquiring about benzedrine sulfate for her depression, a stimulant that first appeared in clinical literature in 1937 as a treatment for chronic fatigue, depression, and psychoneurosis. Brill responds with both encouragement and caution. Physicians at the time were enthusiastic about its positive effects, citing the highly desirable results of increased energy, optimism, and motivation, but they were also guarded that long-term use might impair circulation.[4]

δ

Oct[ober] 5 [1938]

Dear Dr. Brill,

I have retired to bed with a sore throat & fatigue. Tony was out till [sic] four o'clock on one of his regular sprees … He drinks & gambles & forgets time & place. I never sleep till [sic] he gets home always afraid he'l[l] have a nasty accident after drinking. He comes in slow & dignified as usual, after being out from 9 in the morning till [sic] early the following morning.

The reason of this letter is to ask your opinion on this. Dr. Pond has given me some Benzedrine Sulphate tablets—one before breakfast—to tide me over this depression, ennui, displacement & boredom. One tablet removes <u>all</u> dark thoughts, tension, melancholy & pessimism. They seem to co-ordinate one, and cause a change in the brain mechanism. Dr. Pond does not believe they are habit-forming. But he says I can only find out by experiment & observation if they make me <u>more</u> nervous. They keep some people awake.

I wanted to ask you if you think they are legitimate to use. They give me immense relief from depression in all its symptoms. However should one let <u>nature</u> take its course, & go on & live thro' this familiar rhythm as heretofore in order to reach the customary normality? Does one interfere with the creative mechanisms by not enduring these rest periods?

M.D.L.

δ

Oct[ober] 19, 1938

Dear Mabel,

As to the tablets, I have known about them for at least a few years, and the opinions about their efficacy, etc., are still divided. Some psychiatrists, pretty good ones, have reported good results thru the judicious administration of this drug. Some others have not been enthusiastic about it. They all said that you have to be very careful in its administration, and one of them said that this is a new "drug addiction." Since you wrote to me, I have talked to a man who is a good chemist, and he "pooh-poohed" the idea of its being an addiction drug. That is all I know about it. If it does you some good, I am very pleased, but remember you could have thrown off all those things without it, so do not continue to lean on it ...

I hope that by this time you have cleaned up all the cobwebs and that you are again actively back at work ...

Very cordially yours,
A. A. Brill

δ

Oct[ober] 20 [1938]

Dear Dr. Brill,

... I decided to take your advice & have my depression as "gracefully" as possible. I made up my mind to put myself thro' a course of sprents [i.e., sprints?] while the interesting attitude towards life remains in abeyance. So I pay practically no attention to the vague, unformulated feelings of distaste for life & the attending ennui, & I examined what causes in my environment were legitimately depressing me & I discovered that there has been a slump in Tony's behavior for some time due to drinking that caused him to be very <u>heavy</u> in mind & blood & to lose all his attractiveness & good looks, also to damage his automobile seriously & to lose several of his crops. He has been depressed himself owing to his teeth—having only 3 left on top & his bridge fatally broken. This, he said, made it impossible for him to talk as his words got lost in the empty air of his mouth. It inhibited him very much & he grew more & more inarticulate & silent.[5] I had a serious talk with him & told him I wasn't going to live with a hard drinker & that if he didn't try & succeed in stopping drinking I was going to "take a dose & end it all." He promised to drink no more & has kept to it for nearly a week.

I felt it was not fair to take my customary highballs between 5 & 7 as I always have for so long, & have him looking at me & my friends doing so. So I got all the whiskey out of the house & swore off too. This was quite hard comparitively. [sic] speaking because absolutely the only hour of the day the heaviness, depression, & pessimism lightened for me was between 5 & 7, and no ill affects [i.e., effects?], no disagreements. Whiskey has always agreed with me perfectly. Then while he went to Albuquerque to have his 3 remaining upper teeth out I started five[-]mile walks every morning after breakfast up to the mountains & back with 6 dogs. I must admit this had a certain pleasure in it & the sense of practical action for health's sake. Tony came back last night & had lost 5 lbs[.] already ... This morning he accompanied me on the hike & I guess he will continue. I had a sweet letter from the Hoveys[6] begging us to come & visit & I somehow attributed this to you. We would like to go but we cannot until the work is done here & Tony's teeth (new ones) are in his mouth. Maybe in a month ... Tony says he is going to Mexico with the singing-dancing boys[7] & I may go to Hollywood[8] & visit <u>if I am not too dreary</u> to be a decent guest. You know how I sink down into myself.

I asked Dr. Pond if I was in one of these last summer when instead of depression I had a sourceless dysentary & he said yes. I told him I'd much rather be sick with a physical symptom than healthy & sad & what do you think he said! I thought it so <u>cute</u>. He said: "Well, you go to these psychiatrists & they take all that stuff away from you so you can't get the relief of it!" I asked him if he couldn't please induce a somatic condition for me so I could have that instead of my dark ennui & he said he couldn't ... Everett Marcy is arriving any hour for a few days on his way to N.Y. The show he did the lyrics for ... is soon opening.[9] He has a patron who understands him—Leonard Sillman[10]—who has him stay in his hotel locked up with a stenographer & once in a long while a line comes through & the stenographer puts it down. At the end of months & months he has the lyrics for the show. The night Everett went out with us ... we went to a nightclub called "Tony's"[11] & the woman entertainer sang a song called "Intimate Memories: How I Brought Culture to Buffalo."[12] I had heard it before there & the woman had been introduced to me by Myron & she said: "Do you know Mr. Marcy? He gave me that song." So that was the reason I went back <u>with</u> Everett. I wanted to see how he would act. He paid no attention to it at all. He only turned to me & said in a conversational voice: "I have cried in my sleep for you for years ..."

Ever,
M.D.L.

δ

Apparently, according to Mabel, Marcy's infatuation with her had not waned and still caused him misery, but she seemed unmoved by his feelings, perhaps due to her preoccupation at the time with Brinig.

Mabel next writes to Brill using the term manic depression for the first time in a letter, thus explaining her alternating mood states, and discussing at length her struggle to moderate her "ups and downs." She also refers to Freud's idea of the pleasure principle—a motivating force behind mental life, described by him as the psychic aim of "an avoidance of unpleasure or a production of pleasure" (1920g, p. 7)—and introduces the ideas of the ancient Chinese philosopher Lao Tzu, founder of Taoism.

δ

Oct[ober] 23, 1938

Dear Dr. Brill,

I answered your letter the day before I got it! I am not taking the B.S. [i.e., benzedrine sulphate] tablets—nor the highballs—nothing but a small tablet at night to induce a quick getaway into sleep. Not a sleeping potion—just a starter ...

No, I am doing no head work. I have no ideas, responses, zests or excitements. However I walk two hours every morning and these last afternoons I husk corn for two or three hours sitting with a circle of friends and working like mad. All I do, I do by will and without pleasure. But I do it. I am faintly considering an article in non-technical terms about these ups and downs—entitled "The Golden Mean" from which I will quote from Lao Tzu and also from Freud on the Pleasure Principle. I am groping for an explanation of these recurrent states ... There must be an understanding one could reach somewhat within the terms of Lao Tzu and other philosophers who designate a "middleway" [sic] to go, avoiding extreme states ... [Austen] Riggs,[13] [S.] Weir Mitchell,[14] Bernard Sachs and all the old school psychiatrists were unsuccessful in truly understanding the depressive state, and even today the most modern of them have no better remedy than the others for the duration of the latency of the emotional responses, and they, like the others, recommend a cheerful (if possible) acceptance of the condition and a rest period. The older ones put the sufferer to bed for months! Do you remember the "Rest Cure?"[15] ...

However being a recalcitrant person I cannot rest in resignation without research! I vaguely feel there is a way of life for manic-depressives to discover that could save them from these slumps and I intuitively believe it has something to do with living perpetually in loyalty to a kind of superior standpoint that ignores personal satisfaction—personal pleasure and selfish or self-seeking satisfactions and that—if found—this way of life would afford more than pleasure and could be called, moderately, happiness, balance, serenity ... This is still very vague, and may be forgotten by tomorrow ...

Ever,
M.D.L.

δ

Mabel has just proposed an approach to living guided by downplaying the importance of personal pleasure in an effort to quell potentially destructive urgent feelings, thus arriving at a calm state of being. She continually struggled with ways to balance her emotions, find relief from crippling bouts of depression, and discover new concepts to help her. The idea of the golden mean, a desired midpoint between two extremes (as expressed by various philosophers including Lao Tzu) appealed to Mabel in advocating a life that seeks a middle way. She had also likely learned about the pleasure principle and its regulating force, the reality principle, through Brill's writings: "The child starts its life with what we call the *pleasure principle*; it craves for nothing but pleasure ... Gradually, however, society begins to curb the child; parents cannot give it everything, and it feels, for the first time, the force of repression. The older it grows, the more it has to cope with the *principle of reality*" (1921, p. 136). In *On Human Relations*, Mabel explained in her own words: "For we are all governed by two principles, the pleasure principle and the reality principle. We try to gravitate to pleasure in one way or another and to get away from the hard aspects of reality" (p. 37). She probably took refuge in Brill's assertion that "the manic-depressive patient always recovers under general conditions and never shows any mental scar" (1921, p. 223). This conviction that the patient would return to a state of "normal" is the kind of reassurance Brill offered Mabel in his letters whenever she appealed to him at times of severe distress.

Although Mabel never wrote the article she had mentioned to Brill, she did write extensively about Lao Tzu's ideas in *Notes Upon Awareness*. She recognized in Lao Tzu firsthand knowledge of depression, considering him a kindred spirit—"The multitude have enough and to spare, alone am I as one who has lost something" (p. 142)—and described his approach to managing difficult states of mind: "Lao Tse [another spelling] recommended the practice of non-resistance and the forfeiting of initiative, for doubtless he knew in his own person the fatal results incurred by the untamed ego seeking power for itself and the penalties it must suffer for indulgence in extremes ... He continually advocated moderation and warned against exaggeration" (pp. 142–143). Powerfully drawn to Lao Tzu's teachings of restraint and avoidance of extreme states of being, Mabel concluded her section on him exclaiming: "Who can guess the joy of the golden mean after the frustrations of pleasure and pain?" (p. 158a). In *Notes Upon Awareness*, Mabel dedicated herself to the challenge of finding a middle way, a unity of opposites, when dealing with such contrasting states as pleasure and pain, mania and depression, love and hate.

Notes

1. Lost letter. A 1936 letter from Evans to Mabel, however, reads: "You are mistaken. I <u>do</u> like Myron. What I did not like was the way you were with him."

2. Collins had written to Mabel on September 27, 1938: "It lacks a plot in the accepted sense of the term, and I am afraid that is what most readers want."
3. At this time, Brill taught at a number of New York hospitals, including the New York Psychiatric Institute and Bellevue. He also lectured to detectives at the New York City Police Department and consulted with the Department of Correction in New York (*Psycho-Analysis with Dr. Brill*, p. 8; Brill, 1921, p. viii).
4. Among these early articles is: D. L. Wilbur, A. R. MacLean, & E. V. Allen (1937), "Clinical Observations on the Effect of Benzedrine Sulfate: A Study of Patients with States of Chronic Exhaustion, Depression and Psychoneurosis" (*Journal of the American Medical Association*, 109: 549–554). In a 1946 article, "Benzedrine Sulphate in Clinical Medicine: A Survey of the Literature" (*Postgraduate Medical Journal*, 22: 205–218), W. R. Bett reported on the "often dramatic value in breaking the stranglehold of the depression, restoring 'energy feeling,' and renewing optimism, self-assurance, increased initiative, appetite for work, and zest for living" (p. 208). However, doctors were also guarded, as a 1938 editorial in the *Journal of the American Medical Association* warned that its long-term use was "certainly not without danger, particularly to the circulatory system" (110, p. 901).
5. Tony's usual silences were legendary, as he spoke only broken English and often preferred silence.
6. On October 17, 1938, Carl wrote to Mabel: "This gives us a chance to ask you & Tony if you won't come & stay with us at Beverly Hills ... Don't you think you could feel the urge?" Sonya added: "Do come with Tony!"
7. According to Blue Spruce Standing Deer, Tony's great-grandson, these were men close to Tony—between six and eleven of them, sometimes representing three generations, also referred to in two later letters as simply "the dancing boys"—who provided "reliable" entertainment for Mabel and her guests in Taos. They occasionally traveled by car, in smaller groups of six or so, to dance in other locations, most likely for friends of Mabel's (personal communication, January 27, 2015).
8. Referring to Beverly Hills, where the Hoveys live.
9. Marcy was one of the writers for Sillman's musical comedy, *Calling All Men*, that was intended, after a summer run in Dennis, Massachusetts, to open in New York in November 1938, then again in July 1939, but never appears to have made it to the stage (*The New York Times*, September 30, 1938, p. 24; April 14, 1939, p. 28).
10. Sillman was a producer, director, performer, and writer who collaborated with Marcy on many projects.

11. Tony's speakeasy on West 49th Street (Peretti, 2007, p. 181), owned by Italian immigrant Tony Soma.
12. This song, apparently written by Marcy, is not located.
13. American psychiatrist who founded a pioneering psychiatric hospital in 1907 in Stockbridge, Massachusetts, first called "The Stockbridge Institute for the Psychoneuroses" and then renamed "The Austen Riggs Foundation" in 1919.
14. Philadephia neurologist who treated neurasthenia with the "Weir Mitchell rest cure," as Freud referred to it in 1895 (Oberndorf, 1953, p. 51).
15. A highly regarded treatment for neurasthenia until around 1905: "During the rest cure, which usually lasted six weeks, the patient remained in bed, received no visitors, and was plied with food frequently. It provided a consoling form of treatment for both physician and patient" (Oberndorf, 1953, pp. 50–51).

CHAPTER TWENTY-ONE

Notes Upon Awareness

Mabel next wrote Brill from the Hoveys' home in Beverly Hills, complaining of a depression fueled by the strain of continuing conflict with her son. Out of concern for her friend's emotional state, Sonya had urged Mabel to visit them in California to relieve her immobilizing melancholy.

δ

Dec[ember] 5 [1938] [see Illustration 28]

Dear Dr. Brill,

The old malaise returns. I guess I have to move on soon. Everyone is angelic to me but nothing helps. I am alone too much & there is no one here I <u>like</u> enough to go out after. Being alone turns my thoughts too much to my son who now does not write to me. I suppose this depression will pass like others have but I do not feel very sociable while it is going on. Also [Dorothy] Brett is arriving too this week to stay & I guess I'l[l] get irritable.[1] Tony will let me know his plans soon. He is in San Antonio with the dancing boys.[2] We may meet soon in Taos. I really should stay home when I'm like this. I have been here 3 weeks today & my ticket was for 1 month so it will be next week. I try to exercise & I am working some. I am writing out the Una story though of course I cannot use it. But to get it out of my system!

Love to you both,
Mabel

δ

Despite her despair, Mabel did finish *Una and Robin in Taos*, the second installment in her three-part series about the Jeffers family, while visiting the Hoveys; it is signed and dated "December 1938, Beverly Hills."

In the following letter, Brill acknowledges receipt of her novel, *Water of Life*, and advises Mabel not to dwell on her depressed feelings. He also reports that Hildegarde Donaldson, the apparent catalyst for the Jeffers's violent marital discord during the past summer in Taos, had been to see him—perhaps the same consultation Mabel referred to in *Hildegarde*: "She had one conversation [with Brill] that did not come to anything" (p. 1).

δ

December 7, 1938

Dear Mabel,

I have been so busy that I have not had a chance to answer your former letters, nor have I been able to read the manuscript.

What the average person would just consider a passing mood, your fragment of auto-eroticism strives to get negative gratification by making a "depression" out of it. Do not forget, we all have "ups and downs," and he goes thru life most smoothly who pays no attention to such little bumps. But, I can see that you have had enough of Beverly Hills, which, by the way, is not New York, no matter how much it is cracked up to be. I am assured that your hosts are most delightful people, and I would love to be with them for a month or two, but the background (mean New York background) is not there.

I just read a very good article about you in the Saturday Review of Literature by Miss Sargent [i.e., Elizabeth Shepley Sergeant]. Say, she is an excellent writer. I liked it very much.

Would you believe it—I had a nice visit from Hildegarde. It is too bad that I was not there when she was there. Maybe the

Jeffers affair would not have taken place. I take for granted that Hildegarde gives you all the "dope," so I need not tell you what she told me.

It is interesting to hear that [Dorothy] Brett is going out there ...

Nothing new in the great metropolis. I am uncomfortably busy, but c'est la vie!!

Love,
A.A.B.

δ

Sergeant's article in *The Saturday Review* (November 26, 1938) was a sympathetic portrait of Mabel, provocatively entitled "Sphinx of Taos Desert." The author insists that despite her self-revelation and forthrightness, both in person and in writing, Mabel "is inscrutable and unpredictable" and "... remains an enigma. An enigma, above all, to those who know and like her best" (p. 12). She recalls Mabel's periods of depression, her "quality of adventure," and the "dominating and dramatic aspects of her own temperament" that often resulted in tremendous interpersonal conflict. Sergeant also shows high regard for her subject, describing Mabel as "a sort of forerunner of an American woman" (p. 13) in her independence and insistence upon the value of creative expression. She acknowledges the significant literary impact of her autobiographies, well beyond their nakedly revealing—at times scandalous—admissions. In a concluding passage, Sergeant surmises that Mabel "is best understood by her Indian husband, by her son, ... by her favorite psychoanalyst, Dr. A. A. Brill, of New York, and by a small group of Buffalo friends," as well as fellow artists "who are wise enough to recognize in Mabel Luhan a sort of genius at the mercy herself of the play of negative and positive forces with which all artists have to reckon" (p. 14). Brill would have considered himself accurately portrayed as one among few who had earned entry into Mabel's closest circle.

Myron Brinig sent a note to Mabel on January 10, 1939 about Sergeant's article: "That 'Sphinx' thing has been used so often when people write about you ... You fascinate her, she would like to know what makes you 'tick', but that, I fear is beyond her ... beyond anyone, probably. I know no more about you than I did five years ago; and then you change from time to time." Brinig's letter may have motivated Mabel to attempt a public rejection of being labeled a "sphinx." In an unpublished reply to the editors of *The Saturday Review*, she argued:

> Something persuades me that the time has come when it is right to emerge from a long passivity towards my critics after having left them to fling their arrows at me for years. Wondering myself why this impulse activates me I find it has something to do with the term <u>sphinx</u> which was lately applied to the person who wrote my books and which more than any other epithet seemed ironical to one who has tried very hard to unriddle herself! ...
>
> I had a definite purpose in writing an autobiography in the manner in which I undertook to do it instead of in the accepted way. I wanted to tell about the creature almost any human being has become, stripped of the conscious and unconscious camouflage that is our habit to hide away in. Then in showing what is behind the outer veils and the pretentious attitudes, and by presenting the natural creature as she is, I drew from an analytic reader a comparison with the symbol of the least understood object on our earth—the Sphinx! (*NUA*, p. 272)

Mabel implored her audience to undertake a truthful self-examination, a kind of daily psychoanalytic session: "I challenge my readers to observe themselves objectively and sincerely for one hour a day and to admit what they see and feel. There is no other way to defeat the menace of cruelty and hatred that comes ever nearer to our lives. I beg them to accept the method of self-observation that I have tried to give them and others as it was given to me" (*NUA*, p. 282). In this defense of her candor, she emphasized the common bonds between subject and reader, the similarities revealed beneath the mask.

Brill next writes Mabel about *Una and Robin in Taos*, where she describes dramatic crises in the Jeffers's marriage, including Una's suicide attempt while gripped by extremes of rage and jealousy.

δ

January 14, 1939

My dear Mabel,

I just received your manuscript re: Una, etc.; I shall read it with interest and add it to the material that I have.[3]

It is too bad that Una does not allow you to talk about it publicly, but I can understand her feelings.

It is too bad that you could not stay in Beverley [sic] Hills longer than you did, but I can understand your feelings in the matter. I have about the same sentiments about the movie crowd. They are stimulating perhaps for a little while; one is curious to see what kind of types they represent, but after a while they become monotonous. To be sure, the Hoveys are very interesting, very stimulating to talk to, but they, themselves, seem to be in a whirl of Hollywood society ...

Here, things are the same as ever. I am constantly occupied with one thing or another and am looking forward to the winter's passing ...

Edmund is going to the Sorbonne with the head of his department, Professor [Leigh] Hoadley,[4] who was invited to give a course as an exchange professor from Harvard. He expects to stay there about six months and do the experimental part of the course. Mrs. Brill and I are seriously thinking of going there in May and coming home with him, if it will be possible to cross the ocean by that time.[5]

With greetings to you and Tony, in which Rose joins me, I am,

Affectionately,
A. A. Brill

δ

* * *

Krishnamurti

In January 1939, Mabel sent the spiritual teacher Jiddu Krishnamurti a portion of her manuscript *Notes Upon Awareness: Addressed to Krishnamurti*, with the following note:

> Towards the end of December [1938] at a moment when I was empty and hopeless one of your books was put in my hand, and I read in it what you have to say about awareness. Now I am going to write and tell you some things that led up to that moment of recall.
>
> There have been several people who have appeared at intervals along the way, whose influence served to heighten awareness, awareness of what life had been and what it had become in me. (*NUA*, p. 1)

Krishnamurti proved to be one of those influences for her. While staying with the Hoveys in California and still in the throes of depression, Mabel met a girl at lunch who "came and sat at our table for a few moments and there was something struggling to get through between us" (*NUA*, p. 294). The girl soon gave the Hoveys a book by Krishnamurti to pass on to Mabel, who read his words with fervor. In *Notes Upon Awareness*, she includes the following passage from Krishnamurti's book:

> Now why should you not suffer? When you are happy, when you are joyous, you do not say you must not be happy. You do not run away from joy, you do not seek a refuge from it ... [You] destroy all things which stand in its way, your gods, your moralities, your values, your beliefs, everything, to maintain this ecstasy.
>
> Now why don't you do the same thing when you are suffering? Why don't you destroy all things that interfere with sorrow, the mind's many explanations, escapes, fears and illusions? If you sincerely and deeply put this question to yourself you will see that beliefs, gods, hopes, no longer matter. Then your life has a new and fundamental meaning.
>
> In the flame of love, all fear is consumed. (1938, pp. 18–19; *NUA*, pp. 295–296)

Krishnamurti's words resonated deeply with Mabel's lifelong struggles, inspiring her expansion of *On Human Relations* to incorporate his teachings. At the core of his message is this 1929 statement: "Truth is a pathless land." Krishnamurti (n.d.) believed self-knowledge is not acquired through religion, philosophy, or psychological approaches such as psychoanalysis, but rather through "the mirror of relationship," an individual's observation of his thoughts and feelings in relation to himself, others, and the natural world. This approach would have appealed to Mabel's developing rejection of dogmatic approaches and her embrace of Native American ways.

On the typescript of *Notes Upon Awareness* (erroneously dated April 11, 1938, as internal evidence and correspondence identify the year as 1939), Mabel wrote in her own hand: "Follows here an analysis of psychoanalysis approved by Dr. Brill (Freudian), the first to bring this science to America thirty[-]five or more years ago. His illegible notes on the side are corrections of my language." Another note written in August 1946 further explained: "This book is a consecutive summation of the attempts of one manic-depressive character to discover how to free herself of her disability & vacillation & the various 'methods' she encountered on her way thro' the jungle life!" (p. 1). It is surprising that Mabel asked Brill to read and revise this manuscript, given the predominance of its non-psychoanalytic explorations.

Notes Upon Awareness is a moving chronicle of Mabel's efforts to comprehend her own psychology in her journey through the many approaches she embraced. The manuscript is organized as a long letter to Krishnamurti, with different sections introduced by letters to him—a variation on the epistolary structure of her memoir about D. H. Lawrence, Lorenzo in Taos, addressed to Robinson Jeffers. Mabel details the sources for her developing self-understanding: early consultations with the occultist Mrs. Lotus Dudley; dabbling in Christian Science; immersion in psychoanalysis, with extensive passages about Freud's ideas; and her interest in Lao Tzu's teachings of the golden mean. She expresses to Krishnamurti the pain of recalling her past in her autobiographies and the courage involved in deliberately re-experiencing memories, concluding: "In recollection, then, it seems to us that we live fully at last, as the truth reveals itself to us in the great impact of realization. By means of this <u>abreaction</u> ..., awareness is possible. This awareness of the lost time gradually teaches us present awareness ... I know one can become aware at any moment and in present awareness the whole past can be wiped out of one" (p. 186). Psychoanalysis, with its examination of the past and its impact on the present, had certainly provided Mabel with one method to approach both her memories and her memoirs.

Towards the end, Mabel wonders about the reasons for her constant searchings, asking Krishnamurti:

> The question is, why was I always trying these different methods and these various environments?
>
> This depression and despair always finally drove me to search for an escape from its unendurable misery, so I tried everything that came along, and from all these systems I learned something and the interest in each occupied my wandering unattached attention for a while, and the new activity afforded me an outlet.
>
> But the whole pattern of existence became an alternation between two kinds of escape, one of emotional fixation upon another person, the other of getting out of the agony of this unsuccessful stimulation—which was the only love I knew and was not

> love at all ... Actually the only disinterested love I knew was what I felt for Tony but it was not exciting enough to keep me going. So I sometimes projected myself upon someone else and tried to live more intensely. It always let me down, this vampire means of living! But how long I kept it up! (pp. 286–287)

It was during this state of searching that Mabel had received as a gift the book by Krishnamurti, whose writings helped her reorient herself and live with less fear.

As her next letter to Brill indicates, Mabel had emerged from her depression when she first mailed *Notes Upon Awareness* to Krishnamurti. She also refers to the slander case brought against her by Dorothy Brett the previous summer.

δ

Jan[uary] 31 [1939]

Dear Dr. Brill,

I suppose you will be glad to hear—I am feeling fine again now. Took August, September, October, November, December & a little of January to get over the depression of the summer & all that! Did you ever read the two[-]part piece "Una & Robin"? You <u>had</u> read the 1st part, but not the second. I would like to hear if you felt it was a mellow, mature & balanced account.

You never wrote me if you received that little, sinister, italian [sic] "Memento Mori" black & silver box. I hope it lies on your big table in your office. It should amuse you to see peoples' [sic] eyes fall on it & their <u>unconscious</u> understanding of it which often they are quite unaware of. They just stare at it & know about it. Try this out if you have not. I hope you do not have it in your waiting room. People always crave it for themselves & try to steal it! They just somehow <u>want</u> it; perhaps an unconscious use to put it to at home? It's a very odd bibelot altogether!

You will be interested in the two enclosed letters, which please mail back. You will note that <u>my</u> letter was not what the case was based on. It is not libelous or scandalous. But the case hung on a letter <u>Brett</u> had written. The lawyer for the plaintiff had heard she had always denied hearing me say those things viva voce, in my house to a group, but evedently [sic] she had written a letter to someone saying she _had_ heard me. So she constituted a _witness_ wher[e]by they could prove libel! She would have got 2 years in jail if the case had been tried & as Mr. [Henry] Kiker's witness she had denied hearing me & then the other lawyer had produced her letter!

I _like my_ letter. The jury would have loved it. I shall always be sorry the case was not tried & only dismissed for I am paying the fees just as though it _had_ been tried! ... My income tax return shows over $4000.00 paid to attorneys in 1938! Horrors!

Love to Rose & the children. Are you all well? We are in a blizzard & _like_ it!

Love,
Mabel

P.S. I hope for a month in NY March 15 to April 15 when Tony & boys[6] go to California to dance.

δ

February 6, 1939

Dear Mabel,

I was very pleased to hear from you that you are again yourself, and that you are thinking of coming to New York in March.

I read your "Una and Robin," and I liked it very much indeed, but I regret that I have not been able, as yet, to read "The Water of Life." It is too formidable to tackle with the little time I have at my disposal.

Now, first of all, I wish to say that you know perfectly well that I received the "Memento Mori," because I wrote to you and told you how much I liked it. Secondly, you know that my own desk is always littered with papers and that no one will see it and question it in the condition that it is now. I have already shown it to a number of people, but I had to read for them the inscription [i.e., "Memento Mori"][7] which, of course, will not do if you wish to make any experiment with it. You bet I will not lose it!

Now, as to your complications—between you and me, I also received by the next mail Brett's version of it. You know Brett, so you will understand how excited she feels over it. She swears that as far as she knows she has never written any such letter, and she only hopes that you will not make up your mind that she did until you see the letter, which I certainly believe is a reasonable request. I really feel that Brett is a genuine friend of yours and whatever she did was not done with any intention of hurting, but probably just to disburden herself or something. Be that as it may, I will be interested to hear or see the contents of the letter. Meanwhile, I should like you to be very nice to Brett, because she always speaks very highly of you, and I am sure she did not in any way mean to damage your case. Anyhow, the case is finished and I do not see any reason why Kiker should have revived it in any way except that in a small locality the possibilities for aggressive outlets are very few …

Anyhow, we will talk about it when I see you.

With my best to Tony, I am[,]
As ever,
Brill

P.S. What do you expect to do with "Una & R"? …

δ

Brill quite earnestly urged Mabel not to mistreat Brett, deftly communicating from a position of hearing both sides of the story. Mabel writes Brill next to report on the publishing status of her writing projects, concluding with the final rejections of *On Human Relations*. (In a January 30, 1939 letter to Mabel, Alan Collins regretted that eight publishers had expressed no interest.)

δ

Feb[ruary] 9 [1939]

Dear Dr. Brill,

Don't be silly. Of course I'l[l] treat Brett nicely! At the same time I consider her absolutely half[-]witted & irresponsible. I am waiting to <u>see</u> that letter she wrote.

I hope I will get off in March, the middle. If I am not working I will; I am working pretty evenly now & would not want to interrupt it.

I am not going to do <u>a thing</u> with "Una & Robin." What <u>can</u> I do? I'l[l] leave it in my files & when I die it will be discovered! Then what?⁸ I'm sure I don't know! It is a rare human document, I know that.

About the book "Water of Life"—no one would publish it. They <u>all</u> clamored for another vol[.] of autobiography which I refused—since I consider that completed. I have changed the title to "Eau de Vie" & am going to try for an english [sic] publisher, & try to do it under an assumed name for the fun of seeing what the critics make of it.⁹ All the publishers said it was very well written but not for <u>my</u> "fans"!

The Psycho-analytic mms was also considered good, well written, etc[.] but not easy to <u>sell</u>! So that's that!

Love to you & Rose,
Mabel

P.S. I am 60 yrs this month & <u>still</u> feel quite romantic!

δ

Despite her professed intentions, Mabel apparently did not travel to New York in March 1939, likely due to the sustained period of productive writing she had hoped for. *Notes Upon Awareness* was completed on April 11, 1939. Mabel mailed Jelliffe her "only carbon" copy on April 29, 1939, suggesting in her accompanying letter: "You might like portions to use in yr journal¹⁰—particularly the piece on manic-depression." He replied on May 20, 1939: "I do not find enough that is tangible for the psychiatrist in the Manic Depressive chapter ... I fear, dear Mabel, you are an incorrigible exhibitionist and the value of it undoubtedly must depend on the onlooker. For myself I find it very alluring, at times delightful, again annoying." Mabel answered on May 24, 1939: "I agree with you that Mabel is an exhibitionist if you take her presentations of herself as given in a conscious & more or less scientific spirit." After challenging some of his views on her manuscript, she closed with: "Well—anyway we will see where we come out, you & I, in 10000 years hence—friends I guess anyway." In a somewhat collegial way, Mabel asked both her former psychoanalysts to read what she had written about her growing understanding of her condition and treatment.

Notes

1. Mabel had a strong reason to be irritated with Brett; see Mabel's letter to Brill on January 31, 1939, where she explains that a letter from

Brett about Mabel's allegedly slanderous remarks was introduced as evidence in Dr. Kanter's suit against her.
2. See note for Mabel's October 20, 1938 letter to Brill.
3. Brill already owned the first installment, *Una and Robin* (1933).
4. Professor of zoology at Harvard.
5. Brill's concern likely arises from the current tensions in Europe making future travel potentially dangerous, as the threat to world peace from Nazi Germany under Hitler's leadership was accelerating. Only two months earlier, on the night of November 9, 1938, Jews throughout Germany and Austria had been subjected to violent and murderous attacks during Kristallnacht.
6. See note for Mabel's October 20, 1938 letter to Brill.
7. The words "Memento Mori" were inlaid on the cover of the box.
8. "Una and Robin" was never published.
9. Her novel was not published in England.
10. *Journal of Nervous and Mental Disease*, the journal Jelliffe edited and had owned since 1901.

CHAPTER TWENTY-TWO

Myron

The next communication from Mabel to Brill is either a complete note or part of a lost letter. It contains only the date, location, one word by Mabel, and a clipping from *The New York Times* (May 2, 1939) previewing the publication of Myron Brinig's *Anne Minton's Life*. The book's cover announces: "When Anne Minton steps out on the window-ledge of a Los Angeles hotel and crowds gather below to watch the spectacle of her distraction, her own life rolls backward in the novelist's mind and the lives of others are quickly affected in the present."

δ

May 5 [1939]

Taos,

Horrors! [with a vertical line in Mabel's hand indicating the following passage]

BOOK NOTES
    A new novel by Myron Brinig, author of "May Flavin," is being brought out by Farrar & Rinehart on June 5 under the title "Anne

Minton's Life."[1] It is the story of one fevered day in the life of a tragic exhibitionist.

δ

In Brill's next letter to Mabel, he forcefully defends not having time to read all the material she sends him, since she had by now mailed him over 600 pages of manuscripts, including *Una and Robin, Una and Robin in Taos, Water of Life, On Human Relations*, and "The Money Complex." He then reveals his intrigue about the true identity of Brinig's new heroine, implying Mabel may be the inspiration.

δ

May 8, 1939

Dear Mabel,

Your long silence was appalling, and when you finally broke the silence by telling Mrs. Brill[2] that I never read anything that you sent me, I can understand why you were mad at me. The fact of the matter is that when you get an attack of logaria [i.e., logorrhea],[3] and keep on turning out manuscripts of enormous dimensions you cannot expect a man who has to earn his livelihood to drive away all his patients and read the manuscripts. Besides, I have so much confidence in you that I know, Brill or no Brill, you will do what you like anyhow. Moreover, when the winter starts, I am in a whirl of all kinds of situations and I become, as it were, preconscious and just drift along. When I heard from you last, you were displeased about your visit to the Hoveys. I could understand you perfectly, although we both agree that the Hoveys are darn nice people.

I take for granted that now you are, as they say in the army, "as you were," and again working with the fantasies of certain innane [sic] young people like the author of May Flavin. I, too, am now interested to find out who Anne Minton is. The only clue that I have is that the heroine's name begins with "M," which sounds somewhat familiar, and that it is the story of a tragic exhibitionist, which is not so familiar. You evidently have had very few communications from Myron;[4] otherwise, you would have known something about it, and you may be all wrong, but when I saw this, I recall that he did something similar in the past. He wrote a novel in which he brought in a couple rather unfavorably, whose hospitality he was supposed to have enjoyed for some time.[5]

I received a sort of a gossipy letter from Carl, in which he tells me of Brett's leaving, and about Sonya [Levien]'s nephew[6] having had such a wonderful time with you and Tony.

Vacation is coming. We wanted to go to Europe, but in view of the uncertainties, we decided not to go ...[7]

Here, there is nothing new. I am working on a number of manuscripts ...

Hoping that every [sic] is as beautiful in Taos as ever, I am, with kindest wishes to you and Tony,

Affectionately yours,
A. A. Brill

δ

Brill's insinuation that Mabel is not a "tragic exhibitionist" is somewhat puzzling; many would certainly label her as such. In fact, as just quoted, Mabel admitted as much to Jelliffe. Brinig, however, wrote Mabel on May 10, 1939, insisting his book was not based on her: "No, it is not about you."

Mabel next describes to Brill in painstaking detail her physical and emotional distress. Drawing from Brill's earlier advice, and from the language of psychoanalysis, she expresses her understanding of the importance of waiting for this phase to pass—the same counsel, in fact, that he offers in his immediate reply to her.

δ

Sunday [June] 11th [1939]

Dear Dr. Brill,

Would have answered you sooner only I have been laid up for a week. I suddenly realized I couldn't go on coping with the place, such a lot to do in the spring & all boring—all the animals eating each other, dogs killing turkeys, snakes getting chicks, hawks getting pigeons, horses kicking the gander & killing it—it all seemed too much. So I lay down & sent for Dr. Pond & he found I had high blood pressure & told me to lie down & rest for a week. So I did ... Then he took a blood count & urinalysis because I have been suffering from a draining sinus for 2 months ... Dr. Pond found the urinalysis ok but the blood count proved anemia. Having tried drops of ephedrin[e] & suctioning into the sinus cavity, & hot rags with argyrol [sic][8] packing & getting only temporary amelioration, he has decided on another "program." Tomorrow he is going to give me a shock of insulin[9] in the afternoon with a box of candy beside me! Now all I tell you is what he tells me & none of it may be true—he may be telling me false diagnosis since you & I have convinced him I am impressionable, suggestible & hysterical, I think! But anyway I have lost about 4 lbs[.] in a week. That I can diagnose for myself with my scales. And I feel rotten. Weak, depressed, incapacitated, and simply reeking with that Tedium Vitae as of old. Nothing seems worthwhile for though I feel I have overcome the crude egotism that always ruled me, still the movement of life passes me by & does not use me for more generous purposes than are found in the exercise of the Pleasure Principle! So I feel I have no ego & no superego either. No wishes, no libido, no nothing. And this is very sad.

Meantime in the middle of this Myron rented one of our houses & is in it with a maid, & keeping house & seemingly very happy & content to be here. His book which he brought me, is about a girl that jumped from a ledge. He took that young man that did it[10] & transposed it into a girl in Los Angeles & the story is about the effect of the sight of her on people watching from the street, & how the spectacle of the sharp choice between life & death shocks them into a feeling of the value of life, & in spite of the traps & tangles of life how it is preferable to its loss. The book is quite good in fact & full of humanity. The girl is defective, has a persecution mania, & is useful only in her leap to death by which she brings these other desperate people back to the reality of adjusting themselves to life's imperfections. She makes them feel they are relatively well[-]off since they are still alive while she is dead.

I don't know whether this chronic sinus low[-]grade infection that flares up at times since a long time, is the cause of my occasional weakness & depression or whether it is vice versa. I only know I have no feeling of interest in life now that my ego is subdued! An illusion or two such as most other people enjoy being activated by would be enlivening. But here I am sixty & sensible &

unable to kid myself any more [sic] at all. The only thing to do is to know it, I guess, & be aware of what reality there is in it & wait to see what next. If I had more energy I could still accomplish things but it seems to have leaked away.

We have had a lot of flu & streptococcus infections here ... But I hadn't it—I just lost my pep by accident or by too much awareness![11]

Ever,
M.D.L.

δ

June 14, 1939

Dear Mabel,

Well, there is nothing new. You are a little depressed as you have been over and over again before. It means that you are trying to bring to the surface a stratum of libido which does not wish to come up, and after you form a precipitate,[12] it will come up. I do not believe that all the physical conditions you mention are responsible for it, but you are always fussing around with them. I would be very careful in taking insulin. I do not see why you should take anything ... I do not think the sinus has anything to do with the condition.

It is also funny that you should worry about losing four pounds. What harm would that do you? Suppose you lose forty? You will get it back again. Stop pitying yourself and say to yourself: "The cycle is moving and I happen to be at the present time turned away from the sunshine, but it is turning rapidly and will get there soon." Besides, Myron is there, and that ought to help. I read a review of his book[13] and I felt quite relieved when I saw that he did not refer to you.[14]

In brief, the best thing is to do nothing about the sinuses except sunshine, and if your nose bothers you, do what my secretary does—she always puts a 10% solution of argyrole [sic] into her nose and it is invariably effective, so get yourself a small bottle of about two or three drams of 10% argyrole [sic] with a nose dropper, and put it in one side and let it run out the other side. Have a lot of kleenex [sic] around so as not to stain your things. As I recommended this to my secretary, I can tell you it is alright.

Everything here is about the same.

> With my cordial greetings and best wishes,
> I am[,]
> Affectionately,
> Brill

δ

In a further response to her letters about her depression and physical complaints, Brill again reassures Mabel of the inevitability of a return to herself. In her reply, she mentions the famous actress Lillian Gish, star of the movies *The Birth of a Nation* (1915) and *The White Sister* (1923), who was coming to Taos to work with Brinig and the American writer Frank Waters on a film script.

δ

June 23, 1939

Dear Mabel,

Just a few lines in response to your last two letters. I do not know what to say about your taking insulin. He [Pond] gives you so few unites [sic] that there is nothing to worry about, but you may recall that you felt very enthusiastic about benzadrine [sic]. I know all about insulin. I introduced the man who was the first one to use it to the psychiatrists.[15] In psychiatry it is gradually being given up. They are just beginning to find out that whereas in shocking doses it produces temporary changes, it does not fundamentally do anything ... Whenever a new drug comes out, we are all willing to use it.

As far as you are concerned, I can see that you are going thru the usual thing, and I have no doubt at all that you will soon be yourself. You are the type of person who forces out so much libido at a certain period that there is bound to follow a sort of dormant period. That is the penalty of being <u>extraordinaire</u>!

What you tell me about Myron is very interesting[.] I have not read his book, but I have read a number of reviews.[16] For all I know I may not read it, but the reviewers for the most part speak well of it ...

Please always convey our love to Tony.

> As ever,
> [A.A.B.]

δ

June 29 [1939]

Dear Dr. Brill,

Thanks for your nice letter. I don't know just what system Dr. Pond is using on me but whatever it is it works. With 10 units every other day the Insulin [sic] stimulates & co-ordinates the nerves & I seem to have a little more energy every day & to be less shaky & week [sic] & unsociable ... One's "Verdamndest"[17] attitude is increased & one feels more serene & philosophical. I cannot say I have any ideas for work yet & I just rest & eat & putter around the house & garden & embroider & have one or two people to dinner every night & find life quite pleasant that way. In fact I feel as if, if this state lasted, it would not be at all a miserable old age after a pretty intense life. When one is sixty to be able to relax & enjoy small matters is not so bad.

... Lillian Gish has not arrived yet so Myron is on tenterhooks. He is still lacking in irresistibility!

Love,
Mabel

P.S. Tell Rose I <u>just</u> found her little thimble in my workbox & am sending it on ...

δ

Mabel next reports to Brill on Gish's tireless activity in Taos after arriving to work on her script. The fourteen-page preliminary draft in the Luhan archives, finished in Taos on July 24, 1939, indicates that "The Birth of the Films" was written by Gish, Brinig, and Waters, with its foreword explaining the writers' intentions to tell the "true story of the birth of motion pictures and the great influence of the silent film" (p. 1). The script was never made into a movie.

δ

July 21 [1939]

Dear Dr. Brill,

Just a bulletin: Am still rather submerged but trying to cope. Lillian Gish is here ... working with Myron & another friend I roped in on it, on a movie that will be a history of the silent pictures with Lillian Gish as the central figure. She gently ousted

Myron from his house & moved in, dog & all, & no one knows how long it will last. They are working hard—she is like flexible steel & never tires but the young men get tierd [sic] of 12-to-12 hours & they are chafing. I get her from 4.30 to 6.30 in the P.M. & take her driving—sometimes have to have her for dinner. In a favorable light she looks 20 & must be near 50. All last eve I noticed Tony staring at her silently & asked him afterwards what he had been thinking & he said: "No life left in that face. Too many people been lookin' at it."

A very cunning letter from Edmund [Brill] sending two friends to me from Wood's Hole—[William and Lyle] Boyds.[18] He said: "They have that partly unconscious, partly conscious <u>drive</u> to comprehend things transcendent which characterises those few who are actively working toward an expansion of consciousness." See how seductive? Of course he knew that <u>should</u> make me ask them to lunch. Not to disappoint him I invited them for today tho' I feel my own "<u>drive</u>" is sadly latent!

I sent Rose her thimble? [sic] Did she get it? I have only had 1 dose of Insulin [sic] in 3 weeks ... It begins to occur to me that my enfeebled state is merely being 60 years old!

Love,
Mabel

δ

Mabel's comment about her age sparks a response from Brill, expressing his belief in the return of her irrepressible energy and his faith in the stimulating recharge that usually results from her having guests.

δ

August 16, 1939

My dear Mabel:

My secretary[19] is bzck [sic] from her vacation, so now I can dictate a few lines to you in answer to your two letters. To be sure, they do not require much answering. They were your characteristic, chatty, newsy missives. I can see that you are emerging from your emotional lethargy, and I am sure that by this time you are your old self.

In a way, you are right when you say that it is probably due to the fact that you are sixty. I say "in a way" because I do not think that age will ever very much influence your activities. The best thing is not to think of getting older. It does not mean a darn thing anyhow. Just follow along on your laid-out trails and do what you please.

It is hot as hell here, but I am spending most of my time in the city. I do some writing and read, and the splendid isolation to which I am occasionally subjected is not bad.

By this time you must have a house full of interesting people, to whom you are giving all kinds of generous entertainments, and thus attaining gratification yourself.

Affectionately,
[A.A.B.]

δ

In her next letter, Mabel elaborately describes to Brill a large gathering in Taos of family and friends, many of whom he knows. She also proclaims the severity of her son's "mother complex," a diagnosis she had made as early as c. 1921 in a letter to Leo Stein about the complexes of her Taos guests:

> Andrew Dasburg staid [sic] ... for four months but his mother complex grew worse & worse ... Bobby [Jones] has a family complex & 2 mother complexes ... John Evans also has a mother complex which makes him very jealous of all my friends except Tony (strange to say)—& really when all these mother complexes sat down with me at my table this summer I couldn't eat a thing—it was so tense!

Mabel clearly believes her son is unhappily married to his second wife Claire, particularly after moving his family to Bagaduce Farm in West Brooksville, Maine around 1935. (In a letter to his mother from that time, he had written: "Well, perhaps I will make a better farmer than either a banker or an 'author.'")

δ

Aug[ust] 30 [1939]

Dear Dr. Brill,

To keep you au courant with family affairs:

John Evans has been ill all summer he writes me. The first letter I had in 6 weeks. He is rotting away in his mother complex that is transferred onto Claire.

Then 2 days ago the Evans girls (his)[20] & Alice & Edgar Rossin[21] & Joan Lewisohn[22] arrived for a couple of days ... They baffled me. They were in gayest spirits the first day then the next day all seemed sunk into lethargy & moodiness. I don't understand girls—never having been one myself—or perhaps more strictly speaking, never having been anything else. I liked Joan & would have liked some chance to talk quietly with her but there were too many people in every room! We met on the common ground of our amazed appreciation of Rilke's Elegies[23]—the most developed [sic] poetry ever written, I guess.

The second day of this gathering Sara Brisbane McCrary[24] ... drove up from Albuquerque ... on her way back from Reno where she has been getting a divorce from Tex.[25] Do you remember them? She asked, wistfully I thought, after you.

She told me an added bit of the terrific Brisbane Saga. Her brother Seward[26]—about 23 or 24 I believe, back from abroad began to develop a neurosis—vague fears, etc. Their old family doctor, Dr. [Leopold] Stieglitz,[27] sent him to a Dr. Schreiber[28] to be analysed (twice a week at $30.00 an hour). Sara thought Seward might be haunted by a vague rumor around New York that Arthur Brisbane had married his own daughter (Phoebe[29] the daughter of his long-time, lifetime mistress Emily Cary!) Sara thought Seward might unconsciously be fearing he was the incestuous offspring & that if Dr. Schreiber brought it up in him he might go right off the handle for his mother is an extreme manic-dep. & has to be kept in hot water[30] at times—very violent ... Sara talked about this danger to Dr. Stieglitz but he pooh-poohed it. "Your father was an intelligent man," he said. Sara, in despair, tried to get an appointment to talk to Dr. Schreiber but could not for a week ahead. So she had to telephone him & discuss such a matter quasi-publicly & warn him to spare Seward the shock. He said: "If such a thing is true we know how to handle these matters, you know." But Sara had no confidence in him. She says she is sorry you couldn't have had Seward to handle …

You may see her one day, I think. I am so sorry for her & for them all. What a man Arthur was & how he marked all who were near him.

The Evans girls got time to confide to me that John is going to seed & to pieces on that lonely farm, completely under Claire's thumb & that they are holding all that together by will alone.

Love to Rose,
Mabel

P.S. Oh yes, I forgot to tell you. Myron is buying my small house in Placita[s],[31] a mile from here. He simply forced me to sell it & at a good price too …

δ

Before Brinig bought her house in Placitas, Mabel had hosted another writer, Frank Waters, in her characteristic spirit of offering rooms at her properties to artists and writers. Waters, a native of Colorado, had first visited Taos in the summer of 1937 when he rented Spud Johnson's house. After meeting Tony Luhan at an Indian dance, he was then introduced to Mabel, reluctantly so, as he had heard much negative advance press about her. But Waters was surprised: "She was friendly and warm and it destroyed my bad impressions of her immediately. I liked her very much" (Rudnick, 1996, p. 178). At Tony's and Mabel's invitation, he lived in their house in Placitas during that winter and a year later returned to stay in Tony's house, devoting himself to writing. Both Tony and Mabel were important figures for Waters; he described Tony as an "older brother" and credited Mabel with first exposing him to Eastern philosophy, initially through reading her copy of the *I Ching*, the sacred Taoist text (Rudnick, 1996, pp. 178–179).

Waters wrote *Pike's Peak: A Family Saga*, also called the Colorado mining trilogy, which includes: *The Wild Earth's Nobility* (1935), *Below Grass Roots* (1937), and *The Dust Within the Rock* (1940). The story is based on the life of Waters's grandfather, Joseph Rogier, who had arrived in Colorado in 1872, quickly become wealthy through his contracting business, but had then lost his fortune in mining. Waters explained the theme of his trilogy, focusing on the meaning of Pike's Peak: "Such high mountains are regarded throughout the world as repositories of psychic energy, places of access to higher consciousness. And it's this psychical aspect with which this novel is concerned," including Rogier's "projection of his own unconscious self upon the physical Peak" (Adams, 1985, p. 22). A high mountain as a prominent character in a story would certainly have appealed to Mabel, whose own novel, *Water of Life*, ended with a sexual encounter on a peak whose dormant volcano suddenly erupted and killed the male character, as discussed earlier.

In the following letter to Brill, Mabel asks for assistance in distributing copies of the first two books of Waters's trilogy to Theodore Dreiser and Sam Lewisohn. Apparently, she also included a September 5, 1939 letter from Waters to Brill, as it appears next to hers in the Luhan archives: "Mrs. Luhan in her consistent effort to help me has written the enclosed notes regarding a Guggenheim Fellowship I am applying for."

δ

Sept[ember] 5 [1939]

Dear Dr. Brill,

Please do me a favor, will you? I am sending you the 2 books of a trilogy written by a friend here who wants to get the Guggenheim Fellowship[32]—& I want Dreiser & Sam Lewisohn to sponsor him. I wouldn't ask them if I didn't believe in him. Dreiser should appreciate him on account of his solid realistic fiction, Sam on account of his story of gold mining & Cripple Creek, the engineering & the artistry of telling about it.

What I am asking <u>you</u> is to send the two volumes to each of these, Dreiser & Sam Lewisohn, because I don't know their present addresses, & <u>include my notes</u> please in the packages. I am sure I am right in trying to further the work of Frank Waters.

All goes well here.

Ever,
Mabel L.

The 2 copies of each of the two volumes will come to your office soon from the publisher.

δ

September 6, 1939

Dear Mabel,

First of all, I was very interested in your pen dream,[33] which shows very nice symbolism. Secondly, I am glad to hear that you sold the small house to your friend. It means that he will be a steady visitor in your immediate environment, which, to say the least, will add some zest to speculation.

As far as John Evans is concerned, I am not at all surprised. I thought of that when I read his last book on the incest problem [i.e., *Shadows Flying*]. I am sure, however, that John will know how to solve his problems.

What you tell me about Sara Brisbane is also interesting. Both you and I expected that the thing would not go on—and here it is! The man to whom her brother goes[34] has never had any experience or training in this line of work. As a matter of fact, he was educated to be a pathologist or a surgeon, but found it convenient and profitable to assume a different imagery. Dr. Steiglitz [sic] is an old family physician; I believe he is about 80 or more, and undoubtedly means well.[35]

Here, everything is about the same. The summer is over, the air is crisper, and the joie de travaille [sic] may be asserting itself. So far, I would still prefer to do something else!

As ever,
[A.A.B.]

δ

Sept[ember] 11, 1939

Dear Mabel,

Just a line to let you know that I have done exactly what you asked me to do for Mr. Waters.[36] I received the four books from Liveright and two were sent to Dreiser, and the other two I expect to deliver myself this evening when I am going to call on Sam. The letters have already been sent.

Cordially,
[A.A.B.]

δ

This collaboration to promote writers was an interesting extension of the relationship between Mabel and Brill. He seemed to trust her recommendations and was willing to reach out to his friends to support her.

Notes

1. Anne Minton and her sister Marion are staying at a Beverly Hills hotel. Anne ventures outside onto the window ledge. When Marion finds here there, "either about to jump or at least with the thought in her mind," she pleads: "'Anne, what are you doing out there?' ... 'Come in. Come in, dear.'" Anne replied, "'Don't bother me. I want to think ... It's wonderful out here. But I want to be left alone'" (pp. 18–20).
2. How Mabel communicated this to Rose Brill is unknown. No letter to her exists and it seems highly unlikely Mabel had been in New York.
3. Excessive wordiness.
4. Not true, as there are four letters from Brinig to Mabel from January to July 1939 in the Luhan archives. They are, however, soon to become estranged.
5. Likely referring to Mabel and Tony, who hosted Brinig in one of their guesthouses during the summer of 1933 (www.glbtq.com/literature/brinig_m.html, retrieved January 21, 2014). This Brinig novel could be *The Sun Sets in the* West (1935) or *The Sisters* (1937).
6. Unidentified.
7. In March 1939 the Nazis had invaded and occupied Czechoslovakia as part of their plan to expand the German Reich, and, at this point, Germany and Austria were united as Axis powers. Brill did not tell Mabel that, in addition to visiting Edmund in Paris, he had hoped to see Freud, on what would have been their last visit before Freud's death in September 1939. He had written to Freud on January 15, 1939: "I shall surely visit you in the Spring ... I expect to come with Mrs. B. about the middle of May and pay a short visit to that part of Europe still accessible to us. I shall surely take advantage of your invitation and visit you" (SFA).
8. The brand name of a liquid silver-protein compound that can be used on the mucous membranes as an antiseptic.
9. Insulin shock therapy was first introduced to the United States in the mid-1930s by Manfred Sakel, an Austrian psychiatrist who had discovered often marked improvement in the mental functioning of psychotic patients after insulin-induced convulsions or comas. Sakel emigrated to the United States in 1936 and was hailed for his novel treatment for schizophrenics. Eventually, however, doctors found that gains were only short-term (Sabbatini, n.d.).

10. On July 26, 1938, John William Warde leaped to his death from the 17th floor of the Hotel Gotham in New York. Like the heroine in Brinig's novel, Warde remained on the window ledge for hours, from 11:40 am to 10:38 pm when he jumped. "The Man on the Ledge" from *The New Yorker* (April 16, 1949, p. 34) tells the story of Warde's suicide and the efforts his sister and others made to coax him back inside.
11. Most likely a reference to *Notes Upon Awareness*.
12. In chemistry, an insoluble solid that is separated from a liquid solution.
13. Brill likely read the review of *Anne Minton's Life* in *The New York Times* (June 11, 1939).
14. Brill will not be relieved in two years if he reads Brinig's 1941 novel *All of Their Lives*, in which the heroine is based on Mabel and killed by lightning while she gallops on her horse in New Mexico.
15. Most likely Manfred Sakel, the pioneer of insulin shock therapy, as discussed in note 9.
16. Another review had been published in *The New York Times* on June 19, 1939.
17. A word apparently made up by Mabel combining the German "verdammt" (meaning damned) and the English "damnedest."
18. William Boyd was a professor of immunochemistry at Boston University's School of Medicine. Edmund Brill worked at the Marine Biological Laboratory in Woods Hole, Massachusetts.
19. Laura Buck Herb.
20. Evans had three daughters with his first wife Alice Henderson—Natalie, Nancy, and Letitia—and another, Bonnie, with his second wife Claire Spencer.
21. Alice Henderson became Alice Rossin when she married Edgar Rossin after she and Evans divorced in 1932.
22. One of the four daughters of Sam and Margaret Lewisohn.
23. The Bohemian-Austrian poet Rainer Maria Rilke's *Duino Elegies*, a cycle of ten elegies published in 1923. The poems address the human condition, existential suffering, and themes of life and death.
24. Arthur Brisbane's oldest daughter.
25. Her husband J. H. R. McCrary.
26. Seward Brisbane, a real estate executive in New York.
27. Leopold Stieglitz, brother of Alfred Stieglitz, was a New York physician who treated many prominent families. In Brisbane's obituary, Stieglitz was named as his doctor (*The New York Times*, December 26, 1936, p. 1).
28. Unidentified New York psychiatrist.
29. Brisbane had married Phoebe Cary in July 1912, who was distantly related to him through blood. They had six children together, four daughters (Sara, Emily, Alice, and Elinor) and two sons (Seward and one who had died).

30. Hydrotherapy was a popular treatment in psychiatric hospitals beginning in the 1910s. Either immersion in a bath of hot or cold water or tightly wrapping a patient in water-soaked sheets was found by some doctors to help decrease symptoms of violence and agitation (Adler, 1917, pp. 66–70).
31. Mabel owned a house in Placitas, a community north of Taos.
32. Waters was not awarded the fellowship.
33. In a lost letter.
34. Dr. Schreiber, the unidentified psychoanalyst mentioned in Mabel's August 30, 1939 letter.
35. In fact, Stieglitz was only seventy-two at this time.
36. Brill also wrote to Waters the same day: "My dear Mr. Waters, Following Mabel Luhan's instructions, I have sent two of your books to Theodore Dreiser, and two to Mr. Lewisohn. They have also by this time received the letters which Mabel wrote to them."

CHAPTER TWENTY-THREE

A salon revived

Mabel returned to New York at the end of December 1939 and stayed until April 1940. On January 1, 1940, she moved into One Fifth Avenue, noted by *Time* as "that swank Greenwich Village tower" (January 22, 1940, p. 80), where she planned to host salons in the spirit of her earlier New York gatherings at 23 Fifth Avenue from 1913 to 1917. An article in *The New York World-Telegram* (January 5, 1940)[1] proclaimed (with an incorrect date): "1918 Salon Revived by Mabel Dodge: Author Hopes Her New At-Homes Will Have the Same Kind of Crowd." Mabel reminisced about the attendees of her previous salon, including Hutchins Hapgood, John Reed, Carl Van Vechten, Walter Lippmann, and Bobby Jones: "They were a wonderful group, young and enthusiastic, and full of ideas. Some are not young any more and some are dead. Many became famous." Mabel remembered the fervor that flourished at her gatherings: "All who came believed in something. They were magnetic. They had radiance. It was a time of transition, changing patterns. We all felt that something was going to happen." In 1940 Mabel hoped to attract a new crowd to her revived salon: "There must be youngish people who crave for something more satisfying than café society ... We all know there's a kind of disintegration going on. I'd like to give them something to think about ... I'd like these evenings to bring results." Twenty-seven years later, Mabel was still devoted to providing a stimulating atmosphere where people, young and old, could have meaningful conversations and energizing interactions.

"Mabel's Comeback," an article in the January 22, 1940 issue of *Time*, described her as "a spry, 60-year-old, brown-eyed grandmother from Taos, N.M., with long greying bangs, horn-rimmed glasses, a thirst for new experiences" who "was convinced by her son, Novelist John Evans, that a salon is needed. Mabel hopes to get a crowd like the old one" (p. 80). It is interesting that Evans reportedly suggested the revival of her old salon, particularly given their recent tensions.

In the *World-Telegram*, Mabel announced the schedule for her upcoming evenings, which she planned to host until the spring: on January 12, Thornton Wilder was to discuss James Joyce's new novel, *Finnegans Wake* (1939); on January 19, Brill would speak about psychoanalysis: "'I am having Dr. Brill,' Mabel Dodge explained, 'because it was in my home that he first talked about psychoanalysis to a lay group. Some left in great disgust. Those were days when new subjects were thrilling to some and horrifying to others. Birth control and psychoanalysis were sensational.[']" In a January 28, 1940 letter to Stein and Toklas, Wilder described the salon topics: "The first Friday night it was on Civil Liberties; the second: T.W. will elucidate eight pages of Finnegans Wake; the third Psychoanalysis and Medicine" (Burns & Dydo, 1996, p. 254).

The *World-Telegram* report inspired the journalist Margaret Hoover to contact Mabel for an invitation to the Brill evening. In a letter dated January 10, 1940, Hoover mentioned this article and reminded Mabel "[W]e did meet several years ago when you were staying at Dr. Brill's house" when she was assigned to interview Mabel for the Scripps Howard newspapers: "You welcome young people to your Friday evening salons. I am young—25, to be exact—and acutely interested in the subjects you are discussing, especially psychoanalysis. Would you be so kind as to invite me to the salon over which Dr. Brill will preside?"

From California, Sonya Levien was caught up in the excitement over the revival of Mabel's salon, and wrote on January 27, 1940: "We are all green with envy—that New York should have you instead of ourselves. Also, what you are doing sounds so exciting—amusing, stimulating,—and we can't be with you! ... And now I hear that Brill is going to talk!" Mabel's resurrected salon certainly generated heightened expectations of reviving its original dynamic energy. It is a testament to the power of

Mabel's enduring influence that her return to New York to restart her salon was the subject of such interest and debate.

In Brill's next letter to Mabel, he testily explains his preferences before he agrees to speak at her salon.

δ

January 16, 1940

Dear Mabel,

... Now, don't forget—I do not want to come there and argue with a lot of nuts. I have enough of that! Let me remind you that if you will have a big crowd there, I will not talk, and if I talk, there will be no arguments about treatments and different schools, and all that. If you want different schools, have them appear in a row. I have had enough of that, so please remember, and don't get angry if I change my mind about talking.

I think you made a mistake in asking me to talk, and I believe you can still change it. You did not announce me,[2] and so you can ask some other people to start talking and I will be very pleased to listen.

As ever,
Brill

δ

Brill did appear as the designated speaker at Mabel's salon on Friday evening, January 19, 1940. The following day, Wilder wrote to Mabel:

Dr. Brill—while inspiring every confidence as a menschenkenner—gave us that extended parallel between an amoeba and a man and I was horrified—it did not rise above the level of midnight beer-discussions when we were sophomores at college ...

I divined last night that the discussion would get nowhere if it remained in generalities and my apparently dull question to Dr. Hornay [i.e., German psychoanalyst Karen Horney] was an effort to bring her back to a discussion of the Aggression Instinct and its various expressions, but I did it badly and it misfired.

It is fascinating to picture Brill and Horney in the same room, perhaps debating points of difference. Unfortunately, the details of this evening were never recorded, so it is left to our imagination to recreate the atmosphere.

Although she burst upon the New York scene energetically hoping to invigorate and inspire, it was not long before Mabel experienced fatigue and half-hearted feelings about her renewed salon, as she revealed in a letter, c. late January 1940, to Spud Johnson:

> I have been trying to revive the old at[-]Home evenings once a week, at the same time still struggling with that liver & gall bladder which makes me so sluggish & down ...
>
> You can't imagine how eager people are for something in a home—a house—and apartment. They are dead tierd [sic] of night clubs & don't like "halls." So when I have these Fridays I have to protect myself or we'd get pushed out the windows by crowds! The night Thornton "elucidated eight pages of Finnegan's [sic] Wake," I discovered a large party going on in the hall outside—people who couldn't get in ... It is no fun except afterwards & I don't know why I do it except I was sort of begged into it.

The revived salon apparently did not last as long as Mabel had initially planned; references to it soon fade away in letters and contemporary periodicals. In his January 28, 1940 letter to Stein and Toklas, Wilder acknowledged its demise: "I had much hope that it would be a Something, but it wasn't. It takes a will of iron, and Mabel hasn't that, so it's petering out" (Burns & Dydo, 1996, p. 254).

On February 3, 1940, *The New Yorker*'s "Talk of the Town" featured a piece on "Mabel's Tony":

> We dropped in on Mabel Dodge Luhan, who, as you've undoubtedly heard, is back in town reviving her salons of yesteryear, largely to ask about her celebrated, and fourth, husband, Tony, a Pueblo Indian who is due to come to New York from their home in Taos, New Mexico sometime in February. Mrs. Luhan ... told us that Tony, who, like herself, is over sixty, will probably not have too good a time here; he's visited the city before and, as a confirmed outdoors man, objects to having everything go on under roofs ... He dislikes oysters, and Mrs. Luhan doubts that he'll react much more favorably toward her salons, if he attends any. "He would probably get little pleasure out of such topics as civil liberties and

'Finnegans Wake' and psychiatry," she said, referring to recent discussions *chez* Luhan ...

Tony's full name is Antonio Lujan ... The discrepancy in spelling between his surname and his wife's is attributable to her resentment of her Eastern friends' mispronunciation of Lujan, which is pronounced "Luhan." Tony has an Indian name, too, but has never told his wife what it is, being reserved about Indian affairs practically to the point of complete silence. "In the beginning I used to ask him about things like that," Mrs. Luhan told us, "but he never answered." She doesn't mind this a bit; Tony lives his life, she lives hers (and writes about it), and everything is amicable. (pp. 14–15)

This piece on Mabel and Tony reveals how fascinating their relationship was to readers of *The New Yorker* and beyond. Mabel had crossed a line few had even approached, dramatically marrying outside her race and culture. The negotiation of their differences was a hot topic among many.

Mabel left New York in April 1940, joining Tony on his trip to Mexico as a delegate to the First Inter-American Conference on Indian Life, organized by their friend John Collier who was still Commissioner of Indian Affairs. They then returned to Taos.

* * *

Brill next writes to Mabel in quick response to a lost letter of hers that must have recounted the troubling recent visit to Taos of her son, John Evans, and his family. Brill addresses directly the fulfillment of Mabel's childhood urge to punish her temperamental father by reaching across racial lines to join her life with Tony's. (In fact, Mabel confessed: "I often wished one of those old men in the Pueblo had been my father instead of the frustrated, tortured man I had known and turned away from in my childhood!" [*Statue*, p. 45].) This letter contains the first mention of Freud's death, a loss that deeply affected Brill. Freud had died on September 23, 1939, and Brill wrote a number of tributes to him, including one where he admitted that "the news of his death is a severe shock," and accurately predicted: "I have no doubt that in the course of time some of Freud's views will be modified. New ideas will come to replace them. I am convinced nevertheless that the luster of the man and the glory of his great achievements will remain undimmed no matter what may take place in the future" (1939a, p. 409). May Romm, a colleague, recounted of Brill at this time: "Many of his friends (myself included) noticed a definite change in him after Freud died. A good deal of his buoyancy, his enthusiasm, and his lust for life seemed to have evaporated. There was a sadness in him that he could not conceal. He told me that, when he was informed of Freud's death, some part of him also died" (1966, p. 222).

δ

Thursday the 25th [c. July 25, 1940]

Dear Mabel,

  Just read your second letter and my secretary being away I am writing longhand as I did not wish to let you wait. Mabel you are so suggestible and hence easily discouraged or the reverse. In this case I can see your side perfectly. John, poor fellow![,] has no insight into real life else he would not have imposed on you such a burden. As I recall the plan he was to visit you with his family—the two little ones. There was never any question of anyone else. But being infantile when it concerns you he saw no reason why he should not take others especially as it fitted into the scheme of his & Claire's situation. And you, as I said, in your enthusiasm had no objection. But au fond you spoiled it <u>uncons'ly</u> because you were so intent on doing everything possible for John—feeling of guilt: need for punishment. But there is a limit to self-inflicted punishment, there is, there must come a reaction and that resulted from John's inordinate craving for more and more. Asking for another week when he should have known that you all were surfeited. As a matter of fact you were all unconsciously aware of everything but continued it in order to bring about this denouement. At all events, it ended better than it might have. It was good that you discussed it and I give you credit for it.

  Your arguments with John about the future state of society are symbolic of your whole life, your own resistance to your mother etc. The blind force of "Hitler" appeals to you as a personification of your own blind rage since early childhood. You wished to destroy everything and avenge your father—that is why an extra-tribal attachment—you & Tony worked well while the sexual element participated and continues to do so without it. But in accepting Tony's conservatism—religion—ceremonials—etc. you are only harking back to your own background from which you ran away. If you only tell yourself the facts—if you can—you'll not become disturbed and think it is all wrong and it may as well disappear. Nothing disappears, as nothing is ever destroyed, fluctuations between love and hatred do occur and will continue ad infinitum …

Well I am here. I go to the family for the week end[3] [sic] and am working the rest of the week not with patients but writing. Now that Freud is dead I have to finish up many things which I am doing, and have accomplished much already. Rose is not so well.[4] I do not know what it is, it is not her heart condition but she refuses to be examined …

… Now don't invite me to come to Taos. I know that I'd be welcome but I do not think I can go so far away from home. Nothing however would please me better.

Also about two weeks ago I received a letter from the caster of my head which stated that [Nison] Tregor[5] owed $111. on it etc. I sent the check and it was brought to me last Friday.

Gioia adopted a little girl of 6 months about 10 wks ago. She could not become pregnant despite the fact that the medicos found no reason for it and she did not care to wait longer and continue Tommy as an only child. She will be glad to have one or two more should they come. A lovely little girl named Lynn.

Well stop brooding over some of your putative transgressions. You have no real cause to complain. You have done much more than the average mortal and can do a lot more. Why worry about people who do not understand you who are unable to see things unless dissected for them. We who look at things more or less under the guise of eternity should know better.

At any rate I love you just as much as ever.

Affectionately,
A. A. Brill

P.S. Mention me to Tony. I do not think that there is something wrong with his thyroid[6] but that's entre nous.

δ

This long and very personal letter ended with Brill's observation that he and Mabel had similar perspectives on life: "We who look at things." This parallel comparison must have been particularly reassuring to

Mabel, as was the comforting: "At any rate I love you just as much as ever."

Brill answers another lost letter from Mabel in which she apparently reported on some kind of accident.

δ

December 30, 1940

My dear Mabel,

... I am very sorry to hear of your accident and I am inclined to feel that although the accident was genuine, the continuance of the disease is, as you say, unconsciously desirable. But, now that you know it all, why don't you get well? You had a good rest, and there is no use of making an invalid out of yourself.

I also read the letter which you wrote to Lorber[7] in which you state that you and Tony might come to this city.[8] I think it would do you both good to have a change.

What you say about John and Claire is not so good. It means that John's behavior is very abnormal and I hope that he will soon realize it and try to change it. He is evidently satisfied to play the mother role. However, there are so many things between heaven and earth that one could discuss for a long time that I had better stop.

With my best wishes to you and Tony for this coming New Year, I am[,]

As ever,
Brill

δ

Notes

1. In Hutchins Hapgood Collection, Beinecke Rare Book and Manuscript Library.
2. In fact, she had, in the *World-Telegram* article.
3. To Allenhurst, New Jersey.
4. It is unknown what then ailed Rose.
5. A clipping from the *American Journal of Psychiatry* (1948, *104*) reports that at the dedication ceremonies of the Brill Library at the New York

Psychoanalytic Institute: "[A] bronze bust of Brill was unveiled. The sculptor was Olem Nemon, the same who executed the statue of Freud which is also in the Institute" (p. 667). A notation by Edmund Brill on this clipping indicates: "This bust was later replaced by a better one done in 1940 by Nison Tregor" (SFA). A recent search at the Brill Library, however, only located the Olem (or often referred to as Oscar) Nemon bust. The present location of Tregor's bust is unknown.

6. It turns out Brill was likely wrong about Tony's thyroid. As Mabel recounted in *Doctors*, Tony's right thyroid had shown signs of swelling and Dr. Lovelace had recommended "x-ray treatments" for six weeks, then surgery. It is unclear from Mabel's account whether Tony had cancer, but the result of this surgery was Tony's "throat was shrunken on one side, gradually his hair fell out, and not long after he became impotent. But the major effect of this operation was that he lost his singing voice and that was a real tragedy for him" (p. 47).
7. Perhaps Herman Lorber, a doctor on Park Avenue in New York.
8. It is unknown if they made a 1941 trip to New York.

CHAPTER TWENTY-FOUR

Surgery in New York

Nearly two years pass before another existing letter exchange between Mabel and Brill. During this time she remained in Taos with Tony, continuing to entertain friends at the Big House, and Brill was immersed in his diverse life of teaching, writing, practicing psychoanalysis, and family.

In 1942, Mabel consulted with several doctors in New Mexico about urinary pain, yielding no diagnosis; one doctor in Santa Fe eventually recommended: "Mabel, I think you'd better go to New York and find the best urologist you can and get this situation cleared up" (*Doctors*, p. 49).

In lost letters, Mabel had evidently written to Brill at least twice about her painful urinary symptoms. When he next replies, he cannot help but wonder, with his characteristic psychoanalytic slant, whether her symptoms have a psychological component, and he suggests she might try to cure herself through insight or come to New York for better treatment. Brill also mentions he is preparing to deliver the Salmon Lectures at the New York Academy of Medicine, an annual series begun in 1931 as a memorial to Thomas William Salmon, a psychiatrist who died in 1927.

δ

Wed[nesday] September 12, 1942

Dear Mabel,

I was very pleased to hear from you and I wish to apologize for not having answered one of your letters. I am very pleased that you have been thoroughly examined and found negative. The fact is that your first letter worried me and probably accounts for my not answering it. I should think that by this time you'd know that it is best to go to some modern clinic for a check up [sic] instead of fussing around with a quondam physician in a small community. However I am very glad that you are now well. There may well be something psychic about anything that concerns you but I feel that with your insight you should be able to work it out and perhaps see it. I often think that your "repetition compulsion" makes you blind and you just repeat the pattern.

Rose is getting quite well. Her B.P. came down and if she would only stop fussing with every little thing and take it easy she would get along well but you know her she cannot change herself now. So she occasionally has some pain and sometimes even tells me about it ... I am busy with all sorts of outside matters but mainly with patients and writing. I am to deliver the so-called Salmon Lectures at the N.Y. Academy of Medicine which I am formulating in my mind.

Why don't you come <u>East</u>.

[A.A.B.]

δ

In a letter to his son, Edmund, from the summer of 1942, Brill had admitted: "To be elected for these lectures is supposed to be a great honor, but somehow I am not very thrilled by it. However I shall give them" (SFA). The culmination of each series was a published collection of the papers; Brill's *Freud's Contribution to Psychiatry* was the resulting volume. He considered this book his "psychiatric autobiography ... a résumé of my own experiences in relation to what I consider the greatest epoch of psychopathology" (p. 9). His lectures covered such topics as "The Sexual Etiology of the Neuroses," "Paranoia and Its Relation to Homosexuality," and "Psychoanalysis, Art, and Religion." He dedicated the book "To Dr. Rose Owen Brill, my wife, who unwittingly inspired my quest for Freud's psychoanalysis, and whose patience and encouragement sustained me in the struggle to establish it in this country" (p. 5). Delivered three years after Freud's death, these lectures served as a tribute to the lasting impact of his teachings.

* * *

Writing to the actress Fania Marinoff, Carl Van Vechten's wife, from the Gladstone Hotel in New York on December 13, 1942, Mabel announced that she had traveled east "on a moment's notice to Dr. Brill for a couple of weeks & would love to see you" (CVVC). However, Mabel was not to remain at the hotel for long, as she reported:

> I went to New York alone and I asked my old adviser, Dr. Brill, whom he thought I should go to. He said immediately, "Dr. Ruben [i.e., the gynecologist Isidor Rubin] is the best man here, although he's growing a little old. I will telephone him and you go up and see him this afternoon."
>
> I went to his house up on Park Avenue where he had his office and he put me on a table and invaded me with his forefinger and explained, "Why, dear, you have a tumor on the bladder as big as an orange. I'm going to put you to bed in Mt. Sinai Hospital." ... He operated on me the next day, and I had a very peculiar time. He removed the tumor all right but he perforated the intestine and the abdomen and produced a fistula which took me six months to clean up. (*Doctors*, pp. 49–50)

On December 16, Mabel wrote again to Marinoff, this time from the hospital, reporting, "The doctors shot me in here yesterday for an operation tomorrow!" On December 19, Mabel appealed to her: "Come & see me some day now am just better but still weak" (CVVC).

Brill and Rose both visited Mabel when she was recovering at Mt. Sinai. She developed disturbing hallucinations after a procedure to drain her infection, and asked her doctor to summon Brill:

> I began to have delusions ... I found myself trying to cross the field between the desert and the Tony House to find something I had lost. But worst of all was the knowledge that it was nonsense to have blacked out the windows in the usual wartime precautions for I knew I was in the hands of the Germans. The whole hospital was

manned by German spies, nurses and doctors, and even patients. I could not speak of this to any of them, not even to Dr. Ruben [sic] when he came in the morning. It was a fixed conviction. All I asked him was to please telephone Dr. Brill to come and see me.

    Dr. Brill and his sweet wife, Rose, came up and he seemed overcome and unable to deal with anyone as crazy as I was. He looked at me, walked up and down the room and then went to the door and stood looking up and down the hall hoping somebody would come and cope with me. Rose, on the contrary, sat down and said, "What's the matter, Mabel?" But as a nurse was on the other side of the bed—one of those German spies—I could only say, "Can't I see you alone?"

    She said, "Certainly." And to the nurse she said, "Leave her with me one moment." The nurse went out and Rose closed the door.

    "Rose," I whispered, "nobody knows but we are in the hands of the Germans. Everybody in this hospital is a German. They are all waiting for the attack. Soon we are going to be bombed."

    Rose replied, "Never mind, dear. We will get you out of here before that occurs." And so she quieted me. (*Doctors*, pp. 50–51)

It is fascinating that Brill himself, in Mabel's recalled memory, was apparently overwhelmed by her condition and unable to offer comfort, whereas Rose knew how to ease her confusion. Mabel remained in the hospital for a couple of weeks and then returned to Taos to complete her recovery.

    In his next communication with Mabel, Brill acknowledges that she had written him a number of now lost letters about healing from her surgery. He then touches upon a sensitive and highly charged subject: her mothering skills. John Evans had been hired by the Department of the Interior and wrote to Mabel on March 14, 1943 that he would be leaving for Alaska soon and needed to find a place for Claire and his children to live while he was away. He did not ask if she would be willing to host them, and it is quite possible Mabel wrote to Brill feeling slighted and hurt. He discourages her from even considering such a request, boldly questioning her maternal aptitude: "Did you ever have it?" Brill knew well Mabel's feelings of inadequacy about being a mother to her own son. In *European Experiences*, she recalled the aftermath of John's birth: "No milk came for the baby and they had to put it on a bottle" (p. 52). She admitted: "My maternal sense, blotted out in the struggle between

Parmenter [her gynecologist and lover] and myself, which took all my energy, left nothing for John of tenderness or attention. As my mother before me, I left my child to nurses" (*FA*, p. 7). In this letter, Brill again suggests that Mabel use her recent hospital stay as a subject for her writing. She may have taken his advice with *Doctors: Fifty Years of Experience*, completed in 1954.

δ

May 24, 1943

Dear Mabel,

I waited purposely before answering your letters, because I wanted to be sure that the fistula is closed forever. I know it is, and I am very glad that you have nothing to complain about, at the present time, except the ordinary disturbances of life.

What you write me about Claire and the children does not in any way surprise me. I think it's much better that they should not be with you. Children of that age are always troublesome, at best, and it requires a youthful, simple mind—a loving mother—to stand for all these vagaries. You have been away from it for too long to take it up again. Did you ever have it?

In your place, I would begin to think of some literary production. You will recall that I asked you to write about your hospital experience, including your delirium. It would be interesting, and you could get a kick out of it ...

I am carrying on, as usual, and reading your description of the bucolic munificences, I felt it would be nice if I could live that way. However, I would probably get tired of it very soon ...

As ever,
A. A. Brill

δ

Brill's next letter to Mabel, yet again in response to a lost one from her, reports on a patient of his whose mother-in-law, Elizabeth Sage Hare, is a friend of Mabel's. Hare was a painter and a wealthy patron of the arts. Her son, David Hare, was an artist who had married Susy, the daughter of Labor Secretary Frances Perkins. Susy had recently been hospitalized at the Pennsylvania Hospital for the Insane, where John Appel was the treating psychiatrist. Elizabeth Hare had written to Mabel at this time, appealing for her help in contacting Brill: "Dr. Appel there thinks when she was well enough she should have analysis and thinks it should be Brill, it is important it should be the best, Dr. Appel thought there was only a slight chance of Brill taking on anyone new and David was writing you to help him there."

δ

September 14, 1943

Dear Mabel,

I should have answered your letters before, but the fact of the matter is, that my secretary,[1] whom you knew, left me some time ago, and thereafter I didn't have anyone.

Now, first I am glad that you are doing well and keeping so busy.[2] I always enjoy your communications, and the last one telling me about [John] Collier's marriage,[3] was particularly interesting. It seems that the older man gets, the more he is attracted to the younger generations. I am wondering however, whether this venture will last long.

Concerning the Hares. As you are so interested in Mrs. H[are]. I saw the young people and found them both very mixed up. Susey [sic] has left the sanitarium about a month or so ago. I just received a letter from David, and they expect to be in New York on the 20th of this month. I will take her for treatment. The family situation is not only confused, but also burdensome—constitutionally speaking. But, as you are a friend of the mother, and I was also very much urged by Drs. [Earl] Bond[4] and [John] Appel to take an interest in this patient; I decided to see what I can do ...

Cordially yours,
Brill

δ

In two more letters to Mabel, Brill comments on many details contained in lost communications from her. He is pleased to hear about Mabel's new house, likely the River House in Embudo, 2000 feet below Taos, where she and Tony spent weekends for a break from the high altitude in Taos. Brill then reports on his contact with their varied mutual relations, in and out of therapy, and continues to urge her to write about her hospital experiences, particularly her delusions, even going so far as to suggest a title.

δ

October 13, 1943

Dear Mabel,

It is always nice to hear from you, particularly when you don't complain of illness. I am very pleased to know that you are well and I have no doubt at all that you will continue to be so. As to falling in love, why don't you do so? It becomes increasingly difficult, I find, to fall in love nowadays.

I have not yet received the book,[5] but I am sure that I will read it with interest ... I am very interested in the house that you bought. From your description it must be wonderful, and I am sure it will do you a lot of good. At any rate, it is a new interest, and as it also fits in with your physical condition, I think it is a fine thing.

The new organization bids fair to give you something to do in the nature of gratification ...

You did not for a moment imagine that John would go out of your life altogether. A son always wants more and more milk from his mother, and so I am not a bit surprised at the wire that he sent you.[6]

Occasionally, I see one of the Evans girls, I think it is Nancy, but I have not seen her this fall as yet. She seems to be doing very well ... As to Susy [Hare], we just decided that she should come to me for treatment ... I have already seen and will see again the older Mrs. [Elizabeth] Hare, and Miss [Frances] Perkins is coming to see me next Saturday. I understand she hasn't got much love for you, and that being the case, she is probably not in sympathy with the whole thing. The case is rather uncertain as far as prognosis is concerned, but given a clear field, I have been able to do much with such cases.

In closing, I wish to say that your best bet is to sublimate, so sit down and write the book that I asked you to write, the title of which should be something like "The Sojourn in a Hotel Dieu."[7] I am sure if you are not running away from the disagreeable situation and will try to recall the peculiar views that obtruded themselves on your mind while you were there, you could produce something worthwhile reading.

Rose joins me in sending our best to you ...

Affectionately,
Brill

δ

January 3, 1944

Dear Mabel,

Thank you very much for [Arthur] Koestler's new book[8] about which I heard a great many nice things. I shall read it, I am sure, with much enjoyment.

We have gone through the holidays in the usual manner. I did not do much celebrating. Somehow the holidays hold no allure for me. I did not even go to Sam and Margaret [Lewisohn]'s cocktail party. I felt that I could dispense with all the nice ladies and gentlemen who were there. Instead I worked some and enjoyed my grandchildren.[9] By the way, do you hear anything from John [Evans] and his family? ...

Thank you again for sending me this book, and wishing you and Tony a very Happy and Healthy New Year, I am,

Affectionately,
A. A. Brill

δ

Notes

1. Laura Buck Herb.
2. Likely a reference to her current chairmanship of a community project to benefit the Taos public schools.
3. Collier married his second wife, Laura Thomson, in 1943. He would marry again in 1957.
4. The superintendent at the Pennsylvania Hospital for the Insane.
5. Most likely Arthur Koestler's new book, *Arrival and Departure* (1943), referred to in Brill's next letter.
6. Lost telegram.
7. No manuscript by this name exists in the Luhan archives.

8. *Arrival and Departure* is a novel about the moral conflict in the main character, in treatment with a Freudian psychoanalyst who helps him discover an important childhood event through his unconscious, thereby allegedly freeing him to make a decision.
9. Brill's grandchildren, Tommy and Lynn, are 7½ and 5.

CHAPTER TWENTY-FIVE

Mabel's birthday

Mabel turned sixty-five on February 26, 1944 and hosted a birthday party in Santa Fe, hoping A. A. and Rose Brill would join her there at La Fonda Hotel for the celebration. In a lost communication, she had written to him about her current physical complaint of urinary frequency, likely the symptom he minimizes in his next letter as due merely to psychological causes. Although Brill sends a telegram announcing that he and Rose cannot come, he promises another trip, which never happened.

δ

February 23, 1944

Dear Mabel,

In the first place, I wish to congratulate you on your birthday and wish you many returns of this day.

I am very glad that you are in the La Fonda and that you are busy as I see with Brett's exhibit.[1]

I am returning John's letter and I think your behavior about it is proper.[2] As to your other difficulties, I shall write you a letter in a few days about it. I do not believe it is anything at all except your marked ambition, if you will remember what I told you before.[3]

With my cordial greetings to you and Tony, I am,

> Affectionately,
> Brill

δ

February 25, 1944

TO: MRS. TONY LUHAN
    FONDA HOTEL
    SANTA FE NMEX

SORRY WE CANNOT MAKE TRAIN CONNECTIONS HOPE YOU WILL UNDERSTAND WE WILL TRY LATER LOVE TO BOTH

> ROSE AND A[.] A.

δ

Even though Brill did not make it to Mabel's party, he was certainly thinking of her at this time, as is strikingly revealed in a letter to Mabel from Elizabeth Hare on March 2, 1944:

> I heard through Dr. Brill that you were having a birthday party on your 65th birthday ... Brill was very funny, we were talking of very serious things when he suddenly said "do you know it is Mabel's 65th birthday on Friday." It shows ... the M.D.'s work by suggestions or associations and it reminded me of your kindness in communicating with Brill in [sic] Susy's behalf. He is doing an A.1. job with her.

Hare's report of Brill's inserting the fact of Mabel's birthday into an analytic session is fascinating evidence of the close overlap between the personal and professional in his work with patients.

In Mabel's next letter to Brill, she inquires whether he has a copy of her novel, *Water of Life*, since Viking Press is considering it for publication.

δ

March 3 [1944]

Dear Dr. Brill,

Well, that Birthday Party was quite a thing. It roused up the town. What was amusing was that my neuritis or whatever it is in or near bladder & the accompanying frequency ceased an hour before the party & did not return all afternoon, evening, & night. In fact I did not have to get up once all night. Since then it has returned but with less pain ...

What I am writing about is that there is a New York publisher who has an agent here, & they want to read my novel "Water of Life" & I can't remember what I did with the original copy! I only have a carbon copy ... If I don't find out who I gave the first copy to I'l[l] have to have it all re-typed! Gosh! Maybe I gave it to you or Frank Waters ... Could you wire me collect here if <u>you</u> have it or if you know what I did with it? ...

The only one I didn't hear from on the big birthday was John [Evans]! Ho! Hum!

Love to you both,
Mabel

δ

March 6, 1944

Dear Mabel,

Now that your birthday party is over and you are of age, I think your other symptoms should disappear. As you can see, when you were emotionally occupied, the symptom did not bother you.

A symptom of this kind is a sign of an inordinate ambition, and I am sure that is a representation of how you still feel about life. That is why I am pleased that you are thinking of publishing a new novel. But I can only tell you that you never gave me the novel and I never heard of it before. You must have given it to somebody else, you say Frank Waters. Probably you did. At all events I am wiring you that I haven't got it.

Affectionately,
AAB

δ

Brill's recollection that he is unfamiliar with her novel is completely incorrect: he had acknowledged receiving "the manuscript" on December 7, 1938 and reported to her on February 6, 1939 that he had not yet read it. There are no indications in either of their letters that he returned the manuscript to Mabel, and yet it is not among his papers at the Library of Congress. Despite all her efforts, including this recent one, *Water of Life* was never published.

In Mabel's last existing letter to Brill, she presents herself in good spirits, with confidence and an energetic, self-reflective voice. She reports on her recent activities, including her successful efforts in joining with her friend John Dempsey, the current governor of New Mexico, to secure a pardon for a Taos man. She also issues another invitation for the Brills to meet Tony and her in Santa Fe at La Fonda.

δ

Tuesday [after March 3, 1944]

Dear Dr. Brill,

Well, here we are at home after a great roistering time in Santa Fe—I had a fine time & lots of fun & everybody loved me & gave me parties, & Tony & I had to go to Albuquerque for the weekend to rest & have low altitude & get ready to come up here & cope again. I got yr telegram[4] ringing on the 'phone the minute I stepped into the door yesterday. Thanks. I have given someone that novel & I can't remember who. Three publishers refused it 3 years ago. They said it was "well-written of course" but they were scared of it. Homosexual, lesbian, decadence, et al. Now a young exploiter wants to try & sell it to <u>his</u> publishers (Viking Press) ...

While in Santa Fe I worked like I like to & can, got a pardon for a nice Taos Mexican man in the Penn. [i.e., penitentiary] in Santa Fe who made a mistake & killed his son[-]in[-]law last June, & he is coming out in a few days after serving 6 months for manslaughter—the shortest term anyone ever served here, I guess. Governor [John] Dempsey, my pal, & others got him out for us ...[5]

Then Collier is in a jam & his light o'love Dr. Sophie Aberle[6] & her husband William Brophy[7] are on their way <u>out</u>. She was made superintendant [sic] of the 22 pueblos & mismanaged everything & her husband was indian [sic] lawyer & supposed to protect the indians [sic] & he only protected the indian [sic] employees (including

Sophie) & there was pending a congressional investigation of all that & Collier, always one jump ahead, got them 3 month jobs outside the Interior Dept[.] to investigate <u>malaria</u> & that is only the first step in there [sic] departure from the Indian Service. So I have started activities to have Judge [Henry] Kiker made the indian [sic] lawyer ... So tho' I am not boasting to you I am telling you I did not <u>only</u> go to parties & stay up all night every night! ...

Now really sometime you & Rose must come out to Santa Fe & stay in that nice hotel in lovely rooms & good food with us next door to you & we'l[l] have a lot of fun.

Tony just came in & I told him I'm lonesome! I guess I like people & wangling things!

Love to you both,
Mabel

δ

March 14, 1944

Dear Mabel,

Spring is in the air and I take it that it is in the air in Taos. I am sure that you will be very busy and that you will forget all about your morbid anatomy.

But what you say about Santa Fe appeals very much to Rose and me. You know I have been there and I liked the restaurant very much. It was there that I met Margaret Sanger with her husband[8] and took a picture of her[9] while I was on my way to you. You probably forgot it. I wouldn't like to go there in the winter time. I was there in the summer time and it was lovely. I liked the whole layout and the food was good. I hope it still is.

But if you will listen to my advice, I would write something on your last operation. You know, what I suggested. But like everybody else, you probably hate to think of it. I was very interested in what you said about the Indian affairs and I just read this morning that there is going to be an investigation of the whole department.[10] When I heard that Collier married, I sent him a letter of congratulations. Never heard anything from him.

I am glad that you did more in Santa Fe than just amuse yourself, but I question whether it was worthwhile taking out a man from prison after six months when he committed murder. He might kill somebody else there.

We still have no cook and Rose delights in cooking. I can't say that I always had the same feeling about it. But she seems to be getting along very nicely. With my very best to Tony, I am,

As ever,
A. A. Brill

δ

Brill's final existing letter to Mabel is in response to two lost ones from her. In his usual manner, he responds quite specifically to the content of her letters, so it is possible to imagine what she had written. She must have communicated about her current writing projects. The Rydal Press had plans for a new edition of *Winter in Taos* in the fall of 1944, announcing in its flyer the addition of an afterword of twenty-five pages. The flyer states this new issue will be limited to the number of advance orders received, on account of "shortage of paper, and other restrictions ... It is doubtful that this well[-]known work will be reprinted again before the end of the war" (Luhan, *Winter in Taos: Reviews*). Given the absence of any reviews in 1944, as well as no indication of the book's reissue in any library records, it seems this project was abandoned, likely a casualty of the war and its effect on the publishing industry. Almost certainly, Mabel also updated Brill on writing about her recent hospital experience, a project he persistently encouraged. He might have been dismayed that it appeared only as part of Chapter IV in *Doctors*, and not as a book, as he had hoped.

δ

May 2, 1944

Dear Mabel,

This is in answer to your two letters on the introduction[11] to "Winter in Taos" and to thank you for the very beautiful book on the War Ceremonials of the Navaho.[12]

The most important reaction is that you are active which pleases me very much. Keep on writing and I am sure you will soon have a very interesting book ... I haven't read any of the works, that is, your introduction nor have I had a chance to look at the book of drawings, except very superficially. I am sure it will be of great interest. In fact, it looks fascinating.

At all events I am glad that both of you are back and at work ...

Rose read your letters and was very pleased to know that you are both back and busy. Will write to you again soon.

As ever,
Brill

P.S. I like your afterthought to Winter in Taos. B.

δ

Based on his last comment, it seems Mabel had sent Brill a copy of her afterword. In these pages, as excerpted in the Rydal flyer, Mabel described the war's effect on her sensibilities and priorities since first writing her memoir of life in Taos:

> Now it seems as though those years were passed in the calm that precedes a storm. The peace that filled this valley and other hills and dales and towns was the peace that kills, a peace carrying hidden in its heart its own destruction.
>
> Suddenly the rulers of the world were impelled to defend the way of life we all knew, and to attack the forces that were inimical to it ...
>
> Let it all break down and be destroyed. Let the old lovely antique furniture crack up and disappear, let the plumes and long velvets and damasks decay and be thrown to the flames. (*Winter in Taos: Reviews*)

Mabel then proclaimed: "If we lose what we called civilization, and also culture, ... we gain now something else. What shall we call it? ... I suppose it is the return to earth, the mother whom we had almost forgotten and from whom alone we get our life—though for so long we had looked skyward to an invisible heaven for our *raison d'etre*" (*Winter in Taos: Reviews*). Here Mabel fully embraced Native American culture with its emphasis on drawing meaning and solace from the rhythms of nature. The poignancy of her claim that "the mother" is the sole source of vitality is aching in its painful contrast with her own barren childhood.

Although this is the end of all existing correspondence between Mabel and Brill, a later letter from Brill's son indicates they saw each other at least once more in New York before Brill's death.

Notes

1. Mabel's positive review of Brett's show of paintings at the Museum of New Mexico was entitled "Mabel Dodge Luhan Stresses War Impact in Brett Show" (*Santa Fe New Mexican*, February 19, 1944).
2. Lost letter and unknown behavior.
3. Although it is unknown which specific remark Brill is referring to, he writes Mabel two weeks later, on March 6, 1944, stating his opinion that her urinary frequency is due to "an inordinate ambition."
4. Lost.
5. The specific details of this event are unknown, despite a search of the Governor Dempsey Collection in the New Mexico State Archives.
6. Physician and anthropologist. In 1935, Aberle had been appointed by the Bureau of Indian Affairs as superintendent of the United Pueblo Agency. As early as 1936, Mabel had accused Aberle of poor management of the Indian tribes she was charged to oversee (Rudnick, 1984, p. 264).
7. An attorney.
8. The birth control advocate and her second husband, James Noah Henry Slee, a businessman. Sanger had attended at least one of Mabel's New York salons and was likely planning a visit to Mabel in Taos at the time Brill had met her, as the *Albuquerque Journal* (July 14, 1937) reported on "Mrs. Sanger in Taos": "Margaret Sanger, internationally known leader of birth control movements, was scheduled to arrive here to be the guest of Mabel Dodge Luhan" (in Luhan scrapbook, *Taos II*).
9. Not located.
10. Brill may have read the article in *The New York Times* from that same day, "House Votes Inquiry into Indian Affairs" that reported: "America's oldest minority, the American Indian, received some attention today in the House of Representatives, where a resolution authorizing an investigation into his current situation was passed" (p. 13).
11. Although Mabel may have also intended a foreword to this new issue, none was publicized or appears in her archives. It is also quite possible that Brill may have mistaken her afterword for an introduction.
12. Most likely *Where the Two Came to Their Father, a Navaho War Ceremonial* (1943) by Jeff King (New York: Pantheon).

CHAPTER TWENTY-SIX

Final years

Almost a year later, in March 1945, Mabel and Tony went to New York for a meeting with the publishers Smith and Durrell, who were considering, but ultimately declined, her novel, *Let's Get Away Together* (Rudnick, 1984, p. 313). Completed in 1945, the book remains an unpublished 454-page typescript, dedicated to "The servicemen honorably discharged from the United States Army." The setting of the novel is Taos, which Mabel envisioned as a sanctuary for those people disillusioned by war and modern life. The main character is Johnny Carruthers, who joins the army and after the war marries the sister of a soldier friend. They move to Taos where they learn life skills from both a Native American and a Mexican, eventually establishing a cooperative business.

On May 5, 1945, *The New Yorker*'s "Talk of the Town" featured a piece on her new novel:

> When we were informed the other day that Mabel Dodge Luhan was back in town, we polished up a couple of durable aphorisms and hopped over to her apartment, at the Gladstone, for the ritual visit. We found her in good health and spirits, a state of mind

which she ascribed to the fact that she had recently finished writing a novel ... It gave her practically no trouble at all; it wrote itself.

"I really had nothing much to do with it," she said ... "It just flowed from my pencil. Dr. Brill, the psychiatrist, had told me that soldiers who are discharged from the Army want to get away to a place in the country. That's exactly the way Johnny, my favorite character, felt." (p. 17)

Even though Mabel mentions Brill, there is no record of their meeting during this trip.

A year later, after the atomic bomb ended the war with Japan, Mabel again offered "the undomesticated magical state of New Mexico" (p. 221) as an escape from the emotional and physical ravages of World War II, in a 1946 *Southwest Review* article, "Holiday from Science?" She described Native Americans as exceptional in their ability to live respectfully in the world without destroying the land and others. When a group of Taos Indian soldiers returned from the war, one of them observed: "We saw everything all smashed by the white man's ideas. So we decided our way is the best in the whole world for us" (p. 222). Mabel was concerned about where humankind might be headed after unleashing nuclear power. Living in Taos, there was no way not to be keenly struck by the contrast between the peaceful, communal life in the Taos pueblo and the stark reality of the Los Alamos nuclear research facility, only seventy miles away.

* * *

In August 1946, Mabel entered another period of depression and sought help from her Taos physician, Ashley Pond. She had consulted with him before about her despairing moods, but usually in conjunction with writing to Brill. This time, however, no letters to Brill exist; one can only wonder whether she wrote any and, if not, why not. Finding no relief from Pond, Mabel then reached out to Dr. Eric Hausner in Santa Fe, who instructed her to discipline herself to write one, and only one, paragraph each day: "He said it was important; but I could not do even so little for a while" (*Diaries*, p. 1). Eventually, on August 18, 1946, she was able to produce the following:

> The Magic has gone out of Taos for me. Now I have said it.
> There is no more magnetism in the place that I used to believe, with Lawrence, was one of the great magnetic centres of the world.

Is it perhaps, though, that there is no magnetism in me at present? In a depressive condition, one feels deprived of the vital spark that enables one to see and feel an outer world that is imbued with wonder and mysterious force and beauty. (p. 2)

Hausner's prescription of writing is strikingly similar to Brill's insistence upon the power of work—writing in particular—as therapeutic. And Mabel's observation about the limiting lens of depression recalls her insights in earlier letters to Brill.

On August 25, 1946, in response to receiving no acknowledgment from Dr. Pond of a letter she had written to him, and judging Dr. Hausner as being "short and curt with me," Mabel wrote in her diaries: "Why am I so touchy? Is it a sense of guilt that makes me ready to imagine people are turned against me suddenly? ... What a sore and inflamed ego this must be that is always finding an ache from someone's touch. Why should it be so sore?" Mabel remained achingly aware of her inner torments, her sensitivities, and her intense need to be liked by others, as she admitted: "I think I am always afraid of adverse opinions of myself" (p. 5). With this vulnerability, she lived her life susceptible to emotional and physical collapse whenever she lacked enough affirmative feedback. Brill had always played an important role for her: a trusted, reassuring presence who rarely ignored her pain.

In true Mabel fashion, she later emerged from this period of depression triumphant and again self-assured. In the last entry of her diaries, dated August 31, 1946, she announced her return to engagement with life: "The doctor's remedy: one paragraph a day, not read over, not shown to anyone, hidden away. Well, it worked, after I got it started! The ideas and the dreams began to well up and melt away the hard block of ice in me, the lovely, exciting nervous energy poured along the trails, and one! two! three!—I was off!" (p. 7). She then reflected on her relationship to Taos and Tony:

> Sometimes I have felt this place and this life would kill <u>me</u> if I did not <u>get away</u> from it. Sometimes I feel I am starving to death here. And I have no real roots like Tony has, so I am very disconnected. <u>My</u> only root is in him and in my relationship with him, a relationship that has by now transcended the elementary sex life, the outlets of talk or activities in common that we had in the first years together. Now we are one in some deep sense below the surface life. (p. 10)

And she claimed her status as a woman breaking new ground in the world at this time:

> I <u>am</u> a pioneer. I have already done things successfully that everyone said were impossible and impracticable [sic]. Didn't <u>everyone</u> say I couldn't marry an Indian and "put it across"? (Across what? The color line? The culture line? No! Guess what, you who read this!)
>
> I married Tony and even made Indians fashionable, at least to know and admire and dream about, if not yet to legally espouse! Unless I <u>die of it</u>, I suppose anyone would say I made a success of miscegenation; and I do not intend to die. (p. 11)

Defying many odds, Mabel had established herself as a trailblazer in cross-cultural relations with her unapologetic insistence on the merits of her own choices.

After surfacing from this latest depression, Mabel continued to write. In 1947, she published her last book, *Taos and Its Artists*, a tribute to the artists who thrived on her beloved New Mexican landscape, including Dorothy Brett, Andrew Dasburg, and Marsden Hartley. Closer to her heart, however, was the memoir she finished this same year, *The Statue of Liberty*. As she announced to Edmund Brill in 1949 (mistakenly dating the book 1948): "Last year I wrote my best book—(at least I think so.) But as it was all about the Indians & myself, I could not show it to anyone not even a publisher. I put in it all I know of the Indian life & culture, secret things I had picked up." The manuscript, dated October 26, 1947, is dedicated to Dr. Hausner, "who persuaded me to write it." Mabel had remained silent for years about the details of her relationship with Tony, ever since 1918 when she wrote about their first night together in her tepee on the last page of *Edge of Taos Desert*. As she explained in the foreword to *The Statue of Liberty*: "I have never felt like writing <u>our</u> book, of all that came after we took that step of union at last, unbreakable as we had both foreseen it would be. But I did not know why I had never been able to tell it" (p. 1).

Encouraged by Dr. Hausner, who seems to have replaced Brill as her muse, Mabel struggled towards an understanding of what prevented her from writing: "I cannot find us where I thought we had been" (p. 4). Although she believed she would describe "the radiant days and nights we had lived out together all these years" (p. 3), she remained stuck and then realized she was looking for happiness and harmony to write about, whereas in fact: "I could not write of happiness. There had not been much happiness in our painful existence. It had been 'more wrestling than dancing!' It had been stormy and full of conflicts, not only with the world but with each other" (p. 4). Thus liberated by her admission—"I vaguely understood: 'Work and go free. Nothing but work can help if one is made as I am. Work to know, work to tell what you know. Work to find the truth'"—Mabel wrote an achingly honest version of her relationship with Tony:

> We have injured each other—torn each other apart, inhibited each other and removed, one from the other, the legitimate satisfactions of our so different mores ...
>
> (Yesterday I told Tony our lives are so divided from one another by different interests and activities that we do not pass an hour or the day or night together ...
>
> He linked together the fingers of both his hands and trying to tear them apart again he groaned, "I can never get away from you. Every minute no matter where I am, my heart is with you."
>
> And I said, "I know it ... I guess we are together no matter what we do"). (p. 6)

One of the most sensitive parts of this memoir is Mabel's account of getting syphilis from Tony before their marriage in 1923. To speak of something so private now helped her feel less ashamed. She admitted:

> In volume four of "INTIMATE MEMORIES" I avoided referring to the terrible secret that underlay our marriage but I have come to realize that nothing can be truly understood about people and the cause of their behavior unless the inescapable facts of their flesh and blood are known ... All my years I have been victimized by the mysterious fatalities of the flesh ... I have been made helpless and shamed. (p. 8)

Despite the horrors of their ordeals with syphilis and the end of being lovers after such assaults on their bodies ("that was gone for good"), Tony and Mabel were meaningfully connected for the rest of their lives: "But we were never separate or cold or lost to each other again. We have truly always loved one another and nothing can come between us—not even death. I am sure" (p. 183). Mabel, in fact, remained married to Tony until her death.

* * *

Brill's remaining years

From 1944 until his death in 1948, Brill continued his teaching, private practice, and writing. During this time, he published articles, book reviews, translations, obituaries, chapters, and introductions to books, always broadening his already significant contributions to psychoanalytic literature. When Columbia University School of Medicine (as it was called then) opened its Psychoanalytic and Psychosomatic Clinic in 1944, the first of its kind in the United States, Brill was quoted in *Newsweek* (October 2, 1944) as saying: "Psychoanalysis is another branch of psychiatry and has always been. I am pleased that it is finally openly acknowledged. By recognizing it, it can be taken away from the quacks" (p. 84). On December 16, 1947, only months before his death, the New York Psychoanalytic Society and Institute dedicated its library to him: the Abraham A. Brill Library. In his address for the ceremony, the psychoanalyst C. P. Oberndorf praised Brill's immense influence:

> Indignation at psychoanalysis, levelled [sic] principally at Freud's sexual theories and interpretation of dreams, found immediate expression in medical circles in America. Brill bore the brunt of much of the attack and so skil[l]fully and courageously that now, after forty years, psychoanalysis has become accepted and respected in American medical circles …
>
> Perhaps no one has done quite so much to spread and preserve the work of psychoanalysis in English as A. A. Brill. ("Notes," 1948a, p. 139)

Brill replied: "My friends, in dedicating to me this imposing and well[-]equipped psychoanalytic library, you have amply recompensed me for the little I have done to advance Freud's views here" ("Notes," 1948a, p. 141).

A. A. Brill died on March 2, 1948, almost four years after his last existing written communication to Mabel Luhan. She and Tony had visited him at some point before he died, as indicated in a letter from Edmund

Brill on August 19, 1949: "We were delighted to see you and Tony in N.Y. even though it was such a flying visit last time. Sorry though that AAB at that time already felt that he was not well even though the doctors said all was perfect. He had always believed that one knows, consciously or unconsciously, when anything is wrong."

Brill's choice of topic in his presentation to the Vidonian Club on December 7, 1946, sixteen months before his own death, seems eerily prophetic and perhaps informed by his unconscious: "Thoughts on Life and Death." He addressed his talk to the New York psychiatrists who comprised this elite social and professional club, and published it in the *Psychiatric Quarterly* in April 1947. In addition to events that may have focused him on end-of-life issues (the recent horrors of the Holocaust, the carnage of World War II, as well as the death of close colleagues like Smith Ely Jelliffe in 1945), it is worth wondering whether Brill's sense of something medically amiss inside him drew him more strongly to contemplating death. On the other hand, his awareness may have been more conscious, as Romm wrote that when talking with Brill during his last years, "[H]e repeatedly referred to his acceptance of the idea that life was running out for him" (1966, p. 222).

In "Thoughts on Life and Death," Brill assembled evocative quotations about death and wrote compellingly about modern man's fear of it and the consequences of such an approach to life. He included the following passage from William Cullen Bryant's poem "Thanatopsis," a work Brill considered "... the most beautiful and most consoling description of the end-in-view. What could be nicer than 'to be a brother to the insensible rock'?":

> Earth that nourished thee, shall claim
> Thy growth, to be resolved to earth again
> And, lost each human trace, surrendering up
> Thine individual being, shalt thou go
> To mix forever with the elements
> To be a brother to the insensible rock.
> (p. 204)

Brill described his perspective on fear of death: "It would be better to accept reality—live well and die contentedly" (p. 207). He continued:

> It is the fear and the struggle at the entrance that makes death so terrible. For study actually shows that long before the individual

> really dies he merges into a dreamy state which is full of tendencious [*sic*] wishes. That may be the reason for the fact that dead people often show smiles on their faces. I have gathered considerable material which I must publish before I "pass over," showing that when death is actually near as in a sudden accident, the individual either goes through a sort of "blackout" or if it happens to be prolonged he is deceived into a feeling of pleasure rather than pain. (p. 207)

Brill did not have the chance to publish his research about the moments before death, but one can hope that he remembered his own words and found their truth before he died. The final quotation in his article is again from "Thanatopsis": "Approach thy grave,/Like one who wraps the drapery of his couch/About him, and lies down to pleasant dreams" (p. 211).

CHAPTER TWENTY-SEVEN

After Brill's death

When Brill died, he left behind his wife, Rose, his son, Edmund Brill, his daughter, Gioia Bernheim, and two grandchildren. His obituary in *The New York Times* (March 3, 1948) identified the cause of death as "a heart ailment" and described him as "an outstanding teacher and practitioner of psychoanalysis" who was "the first to introduce the writings and teachings of Prof. Sigmund Freud to the English-speaking world" through his translations. In fact, the article reported: "Many new phrases, now become household words, such as 'libido' and 'Oedipus complex,' were first introduced into the American language by Dr. Brill" (p. 23).

The New York Psychoanalytic Society organized a meeting to commemorate Brill on March 30, 1948. A number of prominent psychoanalysts paid tribute to him, recalling his crucial role in introducing psychoanalysis to the United States while defending its theories and practice throughout his career. (Given Brill's professed objection in "Thoughts on Life and Death" to obituaries that feature only the departed's virtuous qualities—quoting as he did the proverb "'*De mortuis nil nisi bonum*' [about the dead say nothing but good]" [p. 208]—he might have taken issue with some of the extravagant memorial speeches.)

Lorand acknowledged Brill had been "a fatherly friend to me" (1948, p. 2) and admired these qualities in him:

> He was always cheerful, witty and above all friendly. He fought courageously for everything he believed to be right. A benevolent physician, he was glad to be of service and never refused to see anyone who called on him. Saturdays he kept open for free consultations, a practice which he referred to jovially as his 'free clinic'.
>
> His energy was limitless. He continued with his practice, teaching and lecturing until the day he was hospitalized … The warmth of his personality, his simple method of communication, the characteristic twinkle in his eye, his enthusiasm, made his presence always enjoyable. He was a philosopher, keen and eager to understand the riddles of human problems. (1948, p. 3)

Lorand reported on Brill's decision against writing a memoir:

> Just a few weeks before his death, he mentioned having been approached to write his autobiography. He said he would like to write it but thought it a complicated project, especially since it involved so many prominent contemporary figures of the literary and artistic world. He felt that it might become somewhat of an exposé. In connection with the idea of writing his autobiography he became very thoughtful and said, 'My heart is as old as my body and I have much to do yet'.
>
> He was preoccupied with thoughts of death. (1948, p. 3)

If Brill had somehow found a way to navigate the perils of producing an autobiography, he would have fashioned a valuable account of an influential life well lived and immeasurably enriched by the artists and writers he had known intimately. Mabel would certainly have figured prominently in his memoirs since she had introduced him to many of the movers and shakers of the period.

At this same meeting, the psychiatrist Adolph Stern, president of the Institute, echoed Lorand's description of Brill as energetic, courageous, outgoing, and tenacious: "Brill, by nature, was not inclined to be neutral. He was for or against as a rule, and as a rule unequivocally so" ("Notes," 1948b, p. 299). After learning of Brill's death, Ernest Jones wrote to the psychoanalyst Philip Lehrman: "He was a man of unimpeachable integrity ... I always admired his unyielding spirit and constancy. His generosity and readiness to help wherever he could were unfailing" ("Notes," 1948b, p. 300). It is all of these qualities in Brill—his attunement, tenacity, energy, and passion for life—that kept Mabel so strongly connected with him until the end. Although they could disagree when he was sternly against something she was doing, they nonetheless had remained in responsive communication with each other for almost thirty years.

In his memorial address, Oberndorf described Brill more frankly, with a directness that would likely have pleased him:

> In debate Brill found no difficulty in maintaining his position. He would not be dissuaded, discouraged, terrified or intimidated, for the faith of his convictions was solid. He yielded ground to no one and pugnaciously returned to resume the contest. When aroused, Brill spoke with provocative candor and flashes of temper, but his anger and resentments did not linger.
>
> Notwithstanding his unconventional bluntness, Brill made few permanent enemies. Perhaps it was his integrity, his sincerity, his honesty and forthrightness which eventually reconciled bitter, elder opponents to respect and even admire the outspoken younger man whose ideas had nettled them. Indeed Brill had an unusual number of friends who could depend upon his aid and loyalty, and who will ever miss his geniality, hospitality, enthusiasm and warmth. I am privileged to have been one among them ...
>
> In conversation and with his friends Brill was witty, quick at repartee, entertaining and gay, often enlivening his remarks with a well-told anecdote or joke—sometimes having an earthy flavor. Often when stirred, he became fervid, impetuous and impulsive, and thoughts seemed to explode from his mind. (1948, p. 153)

Oberndorf's description matches Mabel's portrayals of Brill during his two visits to Taos in 1937 and 1938, when he told jokes at a party and engaged in spirited debate with Una Jeffers. All these tributes captured the vital presence of a man who would be greatly missed.

After her husband's death, Rose wrote to Mabel (c. April-June 1948), puzzled that she had received no condolences from her: "I have waited until my spirits rose a little to tell you of our surprise of no communication from you relative to Abe's death March 2d. We can imagine no reason for anger on your part, and we've been so sorrowed and stricken." Rose also acknowledged Mabel had been in recent contact—apparently a lost letter sent after a visit to New York, months before Brill died: "It was nice of you to send the message after your sudden departure"—but closed her letter "Fondly, but sadly." Mabel's response to learning of Brill's death is unknown, but she did send a telegram to Rose sometime after receiving this letter. Although Mabel's message is lost, Rose's next letter to her, from December 1948, revealed its content:

> I do want you to know how deeply I appreciate your kind [tele]'gram while I have been living thru' many dark hours in the depth of my sorrow. There is nothing quite so wonderful as expressions of sympathy, and yours meant a great deal to us ... As inconsequential as I feel I shall always be happy to know you wish to continue a friendship, the depth of which you really don't know, acquired thru's [sic] A's frequent expressions of his esteem and your worthiness as friend and writer over so many years.

Mabel remained in touch with both Rose and Edmund Brill for several years after Brill's death, with five existing letters from Rose to Mabel, three from Edmund to Mabel, four from Mabel to Edmund, but none from Mabel to Rose. Mabel wrote to Edmund on August 23, 1949, "I still miss AAB in my mind" and closed her letter with: "Write again & give my love to Rose. We never forget you all." In December of 1949 or 1950, Rose wrote to Mabel: "We have been hungering to hear from you! Have you thrown us over? I have needed such understanding friends as you." On July 1, 1950, Mabel inquired of Edmund: "How is Rose? How is everything?" On August 19, 1951, Mabel wrote again to him: "Wherever are you & where is your mother? I haven't heard from either of you for ages." In this letter she announced: "I have donated all of my correspondence (letters from your father among them)[,] mms's, scrapbooks, all kinds of literary papers, to the Yale University Library for the benefit of future scholars & student research." Edmund's reply on August 23, 1951 contained an untruth, either a misunderstanding or an outright lie, as mentioned earlier: "Mother says all of Dad's personal letters from you were destroyed when his professional and more personal files were thoroughly burned upon his death. Nothing significant would remain of these." Edmund Brill, in fact, did include Mabel's extant letters to A. A. Brill as part of his own gift to the Luhan archives at the Beinecke Rare Book and Manuscript Library, sometime between 1966 and 1977. The last existing letter is from Rose to Mabel, c. February 1952, in which Rose acknowledged Mabel's health problems, closing with: "I always had much love and admiration for you, and have many tho'ts of you, and hope you are benefitting by your treatments. Love to Tony, too."

* * *

After Brill's death, Mabel relied even more on her Santa Fe doctor, Eric Hausner, for emotional sustenance. When she wrote *Doctors* in 1954, she honored him in the final chapter, "Valedictory," emphasizing his "peculiar healing power that is difficult to analyze" (p. 71). Mabel explained that he (like Brill) "has rarely given me medicine, but always advice" (p. 68) and, echoing her relationship with Brill, told Hausner in a December 7, 1955 letter: "I feel you know already anything I myself fight to express." She had triumphed in finding another trusted confidant.

Mabel spent the last decade of her life in Taos, slowed by physical ailments—high blood pressure, a number of strokes, and cataracts that greatly impaired her vision—but her spirit never dimmed. (After a cataract operation in San Francisco, she punched a nurse in the face when told not to move, thereby tearing the stitches and requiring another surgery [*Doctors*, pp. 66–67].) After these strokes, John Evans and his wife Claire moved to Taos to be closer to her. Tragically, Mabel also suffered from dementia, often leaving her unsettled and confused, preventing her at times from even recognizing her husband. She and Tony, however, had become increasingly dependent on each other in their final years, and he remained at her side until her death. Tony's great-grandson, Blue Spruce Standing Deer, recalled that being in the presence of Mabel and Tony was always to witness their "powerful love for each other" and "a certain look that belonged to them only" (personal communication, January 27, 2015). Mabel died on August 18, 1962 from a heart attack, Tony the following year, in 1963, honoring his earlier promise, as stated by Mabel, "that if anything happened to take me away from the earth he would follow me" (*NUA*, p. 178a). She was buried near her Taos home—ironically in the cemetery named for Kit Carson, the legendary frontiersman who killed Indians in New Mexico while a soldier in the Civil War—and Tony was buried away from her, in a graveyard at the Taos pueblo.

APPENDIX

Psycho-Analysis with Dr. Brill

by Mabel Dodge Luhan
1938 (unpublished manuscript)

I was sitting in front of Dr. Brill and there was a great wide mahogany table between us. It was a fortress, a rampart, making everything very impersonal. The room was large and long and high and it was built to be a drawing room—now with Dr. Brill in it, it alternated between serving as a withdrawing room and a vomitorium with less accented moments of mere association and recall.

"I want to work on a problem of work," I said. "I don't want to do autobiography any more. I am through with the purpose I carried out in those four volumes that took ten years to write, and re-write so I could publish them. I made a certain picture of what life I had seen, as I saw it at certain periods—and I think I showed something important; by showing the earlier, more obscure difficult years and working up to the last volume in 1916 and their conditions, I believe I showed that it is possible to overcome their conditioning if one is lucky—finally—in love. Don't you think one can transcend almost everything, Brill? The bad heredities, the repressions, and the ignorances of environment—and even the stars themselves?"

"Certainly," he answered. "One can overcome anything so long as one wishes to and provided one finds out how. How do you know you want to stop writing autobiography?"

"Oh, I don't know. I'd like to write a novel or something quite different from what I have already done."

"All novels are autobiographical in one way or another," he answered.

"Wish fulfillments, exhibitions of self—... In fact people are always writing about themselves except when they are reporting upon pure science."

"Well, I know; as a matter of fact I don't see how one can know anything except what happens to oneself—"

"And not always know they know it, or that they are telling it even while they don't know it," he observed.

He looked very owlish as he spoke. This man is a bird, I remembered. He has features like a bird, and his eyes are hooded sometimes like a bird's, and he loves birds very much.

"Well, anyway I want to do another kind of work now, but every time I tried to work last summer nothing came out of me but more direct autobiography! Always autobiography! What a word! Why do we have to have those latin [sic] or greek [sic] words in our language? Why can't doctors speak English, and why can't lawyers talk like real people?"

"Wait a minute, wait a minute! You are too impressionable. You are mad because of something—what is it? Not the language—surely. That is merely a cover[-]up. Well what do you <u>think</u> you want to write?"

"<u>I</u> don't know. I have no idea. I want to <u>write</u>. I want that free flowing semi-unconscious euphoria that one experiences when one thinks one is writing and really something else is doing it, and the phrases appear on the page, and one re-lives again more intensely than ever before the hours, colors, tastes, all the emotions of life, though one may be sitting in a cold room with a bad light."

"Ah! Then you still do want to write what <u>you</u> feel, do you? Or do you want to feel again?"

"<u>No</u>. How stupid. I just want to write. When I write I am alive—when I don't I am nothing. I don't like anybody, I am bored, I am dead. I only rouse myself to be even half-nice for one person. You know who. Here I am back in New York with you and I don't know what to do with myself most of the time. I feel bored, frightened. I don't like to cross the streets—I have no self-confidence—it is more than that—I have no <u>self</u>—"

"Well that is enough for now." He fingered through a small book and then said:

"Come tomorrow at eleven and we will see ..."

In the hours between I thought of how much I would tell him the next day. Sitting in front of that table with the large bland window behind him while one's eyes rested upon the far away, kind, and impersonal sky, cloudy and unrevealing one saw into the past more easily, more immediately, than when looking at the burning blue of the southwestern heavens.

But I had forgotten this man's clear and cold technique. It was not to be a long delightful recitative that I would indulge in.

"Well," he said when I seated myself and prepared to tell him my nicely prepared recollections, "give me a dream." "Oh! I don't believe I dreamed last night. Yes I did, too!" I added as one came floating back. "I dreamed …"

"You remember that one is all the actors in one's dream—the different aspects of the person. Well, what does this dream suggest to you?"

"My goodness! Really! I don't think I feel like that. Maybe I do, though," I added swallowing hard.

How describe the peculiar and infinitely variable course of a psychoanalytic ordeal? For ordeal it is and must be since all change is painful, and all organic growth means change; change of boundaries, measurements, attitudes, stubborn resistances, efforts to stay put.

Does anyone suppose there is no pain involved when a tree drives its roots deeper, and expands its girth? Well, a psychoanalytic experience is as mysterious, as solemn, as organic as such a growth. And then, added to the blind imperious drive of nature consider the scientific, conscious, rational, directive force of a human being who is wise enough to let nature take its course, while at the same time he steers the course upward. He must stimulate growth, he must prune away dead matter, and while he stimulates he must also insist upon order and pattern, so the inconvenience of mere lavish sprawling fruitfulness does not make havoc among the neighboring plants. What a good gard[e]ner the psycho-analyst has to be if he would bring to life the arrested growth, if he would start the natural momentum that has been blocked, and keep it in its own place. Something like Moses to city earth Brill has been to city people who were, like the trees in Central Park, planted and just left to do all the rest themselves.

A man like Brill never concerns himself with what solution the patient will find. He does not care what the patient's answer to life is so long as he does answer, that he lives again, that he grows in grace, and that therefore life goes on. He has an infinite faith in life, in its richness, its variety, its ingenuity. He has sat for many years before many people with the big table separating them, and he has often seen the amazing miracle take place before him, often, the miracle of a person's discovery that all the answers are within himself, unsuspected for long yet forever ready. He has felt, I am sure, what some of us who are not scientists would call a mystical sense of the wonder of life. Certainly he could say if he would: "Here before my eyes the god rises and reveals himself."

And what is the process that induces this acceleration and birth?

And why is there still so much misunderstanding about this process that is bringing new life to people, and creative functioning where before there was misconception about the nature of man and ignorance of his own power?

Can it be that people want to remain blocked and stagnant, and that as one man said to me only lately: "I like my inhibitions?" [sic]

Did the trees in New York look as though they liked their neglect? There is still so much fear—fear of freedom, fear of life, fear of, perhaps, the responsibility of being alive. Because some gigantic shock struck a little child in its tenderest hours, must a man go crippled all his days for ever afterwards and like it? Because one grows so accustomed to the stammering of adolescence and so firmly fixed in a broken speech must he rationalize his defect and call it good? Why? Perhaps it is because there must be acceptance of a bitter truth, an admission that the years were wasted and uneven, never whole, never full—that life has gone by in broken inharmonious rhythms, that it has gone by and cannot be brought back: that one can only go on from now. Perhaps to one who would be forced to admit a whole life's failure to live, it is easier to say one will go on so to the end rather than plunge into the dark waters of such a reality even if the last third portion of the whole could be full of light and ease. Perhaps. But it is hard to realize one has been stunted— and that now all one can do is to make the best of the remains. And what this science called "Psychoanalysis" consists of—this method of knowing oneself, this curious dream system—and its attendant associative process, how is it possible to tell, except by going through it? Can a tree tell of its growth, can a man describe in mere intellectual phrases what life is?

Psycho-analysis is so evidently a life process, a mode of becoming, that all the books written about it have never yet been able to describe what it is. To no man calling himself a psycho-analyst can the books of Dr. Freud mean very much beyond an interesting intellectual discovery unless that analyst has himself submitted to analysis in the hands of a good technician. After he has done so he will never be dogmatic, he will not try to lead his patient in any arbitrary way, or determine what the result shall be. He will sit before his patient and with a certain humility and respect he will watch for the god to rise and lead the man.

*　*　*

So Brill sat there behind his big table—patient—generally patient—and as the obstacles rose up to the surface and the arguments bubbled forth he gave occasional instruction. Oh certainly. There are well[-]known patterns, no one escapes them very far. Too far escaping leads to Bellevue. There are well[-]grounded phases from infancy to maturity, in the individual as in the race. On these he can give instruction. Most people in our civilized era do not proceed on an even tenor from childhood to old age, gently emerging from one chapter to the next.

What Edward Carpenter[1] called "the soul's slow disentanglement" is usually a matter of dealing with oneself in a fumbling way and with the obstacles that block the sweet slow progress, or of leaving it to life and having life crack down and dislodge the stone before the door of the tomb. But the new science of psychology hastens and softens life's more tragic manner of setting the man free. One can learn, then, of the phases of youth, that are good and natural in infancy and in youth, that become grotesque and offensive and ugly if prolonged. Narcisesism [sic] for instance is not so unlovely in a boy who sees himself in the still lake—but in the older man it is sad—not to say horrible.

There are several such phases but it is not for me to tell of them here for I have neither the science nor the surety to write about what I have learned. I have heard Dr. Brill lecture to the graduate detectives of the Police College and tell them in very simple terms the interpretations the new psychology places upon what are called sexual crimes, in an effort to make these men more tolerant and more understanding towards the unfortunate creatures whose compulsions have driven them to extreme imprudence. After listening to his course I do not believe these men can ever again rush their captives into police stations without listening to the faltering excuses, nor knock them out, or curse at their vile and indecent behavior. I have heard him talk before the psychiatric groups, and I have read many of his papers. In these ways I have learned a great deal but not enough yet to write about the subject with any authority.

I can tell, though, that in this instance of my own effort to readjust myself that slowly the inhibited feeling for life began to rise again. That again there seemed to me to be wonderful people in the world and amazing things to tell about them; that color came back into life as the life in me moved once more. The man behind the table must have known what he was doing, and what he refrained from saying, but he only seemed to watch and to repeat over and over: "What did you dream?" and "What does that suggest to you?" Does it seem very simple? Perhaps it is. Perhaps after all <u>life</u> is very simple.

After such an hour as is sometimes very hard to face through Dr. Brill would get up and say:

"Well—let's go home and have some lunch," and we would go around the corner to the house, and in the dining room there would be a good meal ready and friends smiling, and the birds there in their cages against the wall. And generally Dr. Brill would stop beside one and wave a finger at a finch he likes and say:

"Come on, Hansi! Sing! Come on, now," and soon the finch would pipe up and trill his little song, and Dr. Brill would laugh and say: "<u>Again</u>. Come on now, Hansi! <u>Sing</u>," and the bird would repeat the tune. I suppose it was not very different from what goes on all day in the office, though the good man never waves his finger there, nor is he insistent in any audible way. But yes, perhaps he is saying inaudibly, compellingly all the time: "Come on, now, <u>Sing</u>! Come on," and then finally he sees the god rise.

Note

1. An English socialist poet and philosopher.

REFERENCES

Adams, C. L. (Ed.) (1985). *Frank Waters: A Retrospective Anthology*. Athens, OH: Swallow Press.

Adler, H. M. (1917). Indications for wet packs in psychiatric cases; An analysis of 1,000 packs given at the Psychopathic Hospital, Boston, Mass. In: W. E. Fernald, G. M. Kline, & E. E. Southard (Eds.), *Bulletin of the Massachusetts Commission on Mental Diseases (Vol. 1)* (pp. 66–70). Boston: Wright & Potter.

Brett, D. (1933). *Lawrence and Brett: A Friendship*. Philadelphia, PA: J. B. Lippincott Company.

Brill, A. A. (1908). Psychological factors in dementia praecox, an analysis. *Journal of Abnormal Psychology*, 3: 219–239.

Brill, A. A. (1912). *Psychoanalysis: Its Theories and Practical Application*. Philadelphia: W. B. Saunders [reprinted Philadelphia: W. B. Saunders, 1922, 3rd edn].

Brill, A. A. (1921). *Basic Principles of Psychoanalysis*. Garden City, NY: Doubleday [reprinted Garden City, NY: Doubleday, 1949].

Brill, A. A. (1931a). Professor Freud and psychiatry. *Psychoanalytic Review*, 18: 241–246.

Brill, A. A. (1931b, October 17). What's wrong with cities? *The Saturday Evening Post*: 20–21, 44, 48, 50.

Brill, A. A. (1938, March 4). Art and neurosis. Typed carbon, MDLC.

Brill, A. A. (1939a). Sigmund Freud—1856–1939. *Psychoanalytic Quarterly,* 8: 409.

Brill, A. A. (1939b). The concept of psychic suicide. *International Journal of Psychoanalysis,* 20: 246–251.

Brill, A. A. (1940). Reminiscences of Freud. *Psychoanalytic Quarterly,* 9: 177–183.

Brill, A. A. (1942). A psychoanalyst scans his past. *Journal of Nervous and Mental Disease,* 95: 537–549.

Brill, A. A. (1944). *Freud's Contribution to Psychiatry.* New York: W. W. Norton.

Brill, A. A. (1946). *Lectures on Psychoanalytic Psychiatry.* New York: Alfred A. Knopf.

Brill, A. A. (1947a). Psychotherapies I encountered. *Psychiatric Quarterly,* 21: 575–591.

Brill, A. A. (1947b). Thoughts on life and death. *Psychiatric Quarterly,* 21: 199–211.

Brill, A. A. (n.d.). *Ned: Our Starling; Re: Cryptamnesia* [sic]. Unpublished manuscript, SFA.

Brinig, M. (1939). *Anne Minton's Life.* New York: Farrar & Rinehart.

Burnham, J. (1991). The new psychology. In: A. Heller & L. Rudnick (Eds.), *1915, The Cultural Moment: The New Politics, the New Woman, the New Psychology, the New Art, and the New Theatre in America* (pp. 117–127). New Brunswick, NJ: Rutgers University.

Burns, E. (Ed.) (1986). *The Letters of Gertrude Stein and Carl Van Vechten, 1913–1946.* New York: Columbia University.

Burns, E., & Dydo, U. (Eds.) (1996). *The Letters of Gertrude Stein and Thornton Wilder.* New Haven, CT: Yale University.

Byrne, J. (1995). *A Genius for Living: The Life of Frieda Lawrence.* New York: Harper Collins.

Coke, V. D. (1979). *Andrew Dasburg.* Albuquerque, NM: University of New Mexico.

Collier, J. (1963). *From Every Zenith: A Memoir; and Some Essays on Life and Thought.* Denver, CO: Sage.

Dreiser, T. (1924). The mercy of God. *The American Mercury,* 2: 457–464.

Eastman, M. (1927). *Venture.* New York: Albert & Charles Boni.

Edelstein, L. (1943). *The Hippocratic Oath: Text, Translation and Interpretation.* Baltimore, MD: Johns Hopkins University Press.

Evans, J. (1936). *Shadows Flying.* New York: Alfred A. Knopf.

Fadiman, C. (1937, September 18). "The Making of a Squaw." *The New Yorker*: 96–97.

Fass, P. (1969). *A. A. Brill—Pioneer and Prophet.* Unpublished master's thesis, Columbia University, New York.

Fortune, C. (1993). The case of "RN": Sandor Ferenczi's radical experiment in psychoanalysis. In: L. Aron & A. Harris (Eds.), *The Legacy of Sandor Ferenczi* (pp. 101–120). Hillsdale, NJ: Analytic Press.

Freud, S. (1908b). Character and anal erotism. *S. E., 9*: 167–176. London: Hogarth.
Freud, S. (1912e). Recommendations to physicians practising psychoanalysis. *S. E., 12*: 111–120. London: Hogarth.
Freud, S. (1920g). *Beyond the Pleasure Principle. S. E., 18*: 1–64. London: Hogarth.
Freud, S. (1939a). *Moses and Monotheism. S. E., 23*: 3–137. London: Hogarth.
Friedman, S. S. (Ed.) (2002). *Analyzing Freud: Letters of H.D., Bryher and Their Circle*. New York: New Directions.
Gabbard, G. O. (1995). The early history of boundary violations in psychoanalysis. *Journal of the American Psychoanalytic Association, 43*: 1115–1136.
Hale, N. (1971). *Freud and the Americans: The Beginnings of Psychoanalysis in the United States, 1876–1917*. New York: Oxford University Press [reprinted New York: Oxford University Press, 1995].
Hale, N. (1995). *The Rise and Crisis of Psychoanalysis in the United States: Freud and the Americans, 1917–1985*. New York: Oxford University Press.
Hapgood, H. (1939). *A Victorian in the Modern World*. New York: Harcourt, Brace & World.
Hugo, V. (1862). *Les Misérables*. Paris: J. Hetzel [reprinted New York: Modern Library, C. E. Wilbour (Trans.), 1931].
Jeffers, R. (1938). *The Selected Poetry of Robinson Jeffers*. New York: Random House.
Jelliffe, S. E. (1933). Glimpses of a Freudian odyssey. *Psychoanalytic Quarterly, 2*: 318–329.
Jones, E. (1948). Notes. *Psychoanalytic Quarterly, 17*: 300.
Karman, J. (1987). *Robinson Jeffers: Poet of California*. San Francisco: Chronicle.
Kellner, B. (Ed.) (2003). *The Splendid Drunken Twenties: Selections from the Daybooks, 1922–1930, Carl Van Vechten*. Urbana, IL: University of Illinois Press.
Krishnamurti, J. (1938). *Revised Report of Fourteen Talks Given by Krishnamurti*. Hollywood, CA: Star Publishing.
Krishnamurti, J. (n.d.). The core of the teachings. Retrieved June 7, 2011, from http://www.jkrishnamurti.org.
Lawrence, D. H. (1928). *The Woman Who Rode Away and Other Stories*. New York: Alfred A. Knopf.
Lorand, S. (1948). A. A. Brill: 1874–1948. *International Journal of Psychoanalysis, 29*: 2–3.

Luhan, M. D., Published Works
Luhan, M. D. (1924). Change. *Palms, 2*: 136–138.
Luhan, M. D. (1924). The ballad of a bad girl. *Laughing Horse*; [reprinted Taos, NM: Willard Johnson, 1927].
Luhan, M. D. (1932). *Lorenzo in Taos*. New York: Alfred A. Knopf.

Luhan, M. D. (1933). *Intimate Memories: Background.* New York: Harcourt, Brace.

Luhan, M. D. (1935). *European Experiences: Volume Two of Intimate Memories.* New York: Harcourt, Brace.

Luhan, M. D. (1935). *Winter in Taos.* New York: Harcourt, Brace.

Luhan, M. D. (1936). *Movers and Shakers: Volume Three of Intimate Memories.* New York: Harcourt, Brace.

Luhan, M. D. (1937). *Edge of Taos Desert: An Escape to Reality: Volume Four of Intimate Memories.* New York: Harcourt, Brace.

Luhan, M. D. (1946). Holiday from science? *Southwest Review, 31*: 221–224.

Luhan, M. D. (1947). *Taos and Its Artists.* New York: Duell, Sloan & Pierce.

Luhan, M. D., Unpublished Manuscripts, MDLC

Luhan, M. D. (c. 1923). *Inevitable.*
Luhan, M. D. (1929). *An Intimation.*
Luhan, M. D. (1933). *Family Affairs.*
Luhan, M. D. (1933). *My Attitude in the Writing of Autobiography.*
Luhan, M. D. (1933). *Una and Robin.*
Luhan, M. D. (1938). *Change of Life.*
Luhan, M. D. (1938). *On Human Relations: A Personal Interpretation.*
Luhan, M. D. (1938). *Psycho-Analysis with Dr. Brill.*
Luhan, M. D. (1938). *The Money Complex.*
Luhan, M. D. (1938). *Una and Robin in Taos.*
Luhan, M. D. (c. 1938). *Water of Life.*
Luhan, M. D. (1939). *Notes Upon Awareness: Addressed to Krishnamurti.*
Luhan, M. D. (1945). *Let's Get Away Together.*
Luhan, M. D. (1946). *Diaries.*
Luhan, M. D. (c. 1946). *Hildegarde: Eight Years After.*
Luhan, M. D. (1947). *The Statue of Liberty: An Old Fashioned Story of Taboos.*
Luhan, M. D. (1954). *Doctors: Fifty Years of Experience.*

Luhan, M. D., Reviews of Memoirs, MDLC

Luhan, M. D. (1932–1939, n.d.). *Lorenzo in Taos: Reviews.*
Luhan, M. D. (1933). *Background: Reviews.*
Luhan, M. D. (1935). *European Experiences: Reviews.*
Luhan, M. D. (1935–1948). *Winter in Taos: Reviews.*
Luhan, M. D. (1936, n.d.). *Movers and Shakers: Reviews.*

Luhan, M. D., Scrapbooks, MDLC

Luhan, M. D. (1911–1928, n.d.). *Intimate Memories, Vol. 7.*
Luhan, M. D. (1912–1927, n.d.). *Intimate Memories, Vol. 6.*
Luhan, M. D. (1913–1937, n.d.). *Misc. Vol. I.*
Luhan, M. D. (1913–1937, n.d.). *Taos.*
Luhan, M. D. (1914–1928, n.d.). *Untitled.*
Luhan, M. D. (1930–1933, n.d.). *Lawrence.*

Luhan, M. D. (1932–1935, n.d.). *Intimate Memories and Letters.*
Luhan, M. D. (1933–1936, n.d.). *Lawrence, Vol. II.*
Luhan, M. D. (1934–1937, n.d.). *Movers and Shakers.*
Luhan, M. D. (1935–1938, n.d.). *Winter in Taos.*
Luhan, M. D. (1936–1939, n.d.). *Misc. Vol. II.*
Luhan, M. D. (1938–1939, n.d.). *Taos Vol. II.*
Lynn, D. J., & Valliant, G. E. (1998). Anonymity, neutrality, and confidentiality in the actual methods of Sigmund Freud: A review of 43 cases, 1907–1939. *American Journal of Psychiatry, 155*: 163–171.
Mukerji, D. G. (1923). *Caste and Outcast.* New York: E. P. Dutton [reprinted Stanford, CA: Stanford University Press, 2002].
Notes (1948a). *Psychoanalytic Quarterly, 17*: 138–141.
Notes (1948b). *Psychoanalytic Quarterly, 17*: 299–300.
Oberndorf, C. P. (1948). A. A. Brill. *Psychoanalytic Quarterly, 17*: 149–154.
Oberndorf, C. P. (1953). *A History of Psychoanalysis in America.* New York: Grune & Stratton.
Peretti, B. W. (2007). *Nightclub City: Politics and Amusement in Manhattan.* Philadelphia, PA: University of Pennsylvania Press.
Romm, M. E. (1966). Abraham Arden Brill: First American translator of Freud. In: F. Alexander, S. Eisenstein, & M. Grotjahn (Eds.), *Psychoanalytic Pioneers* (pp. 210–223). New York: Basic Books.
Rudnick, L. P. (1984). *Mabel Dodge Luhan: New Woman, New Worlds.* Albuquerque, NM: University of New Mexico Press.
Rudnick, L. P. (1996). *Utopian Vistas: The Mabel Dodge Luhan House and the American Counterculture.* Albuquerque, NM: University of New Mexico Press.
Sabbatini, R. M. E. (n.d.). The history of shock therapy in psychiatry. Retrieved March 8, 2012, from http://www.cerebromente.org.br/n04/historia/shock_i.htm.
Sergeant, E. S. (1938, November 26). Sphinx of Taos desert. *The Saturday Review*: 12–14.
Steffens, L. (1931). *The Autobiography of Lincoln Steffens (Vol. 2).* New York: Harcourt, Brace.
Stein, L. (1950). *Journey into the Self: Being the Letters, Papers, and Journals of Leo Stein.* E. Fuller (Ed.). New York: Crown.
Sterne, M. (1952). *Shadow and Light: The Life, Friends and Opinions of Maurice Sterne.* C. L. Mayerson (Ed.). New York: Harcourt, Brace & World.
Van Vechten, C. (1922). *Peter Whiffle: His Life and Works.* New York: Alfred A. Knopf.
Webb, J. (1980). *The Harmonious Circle: The Lives and Work of G. I. Gurdjieff, P. D. Ouspensky, and Their Followers.* New York: Putnam.
Woods, K. (1937, September 19). "Mabel Dodge Luhan's 'Escape to Reality' in Taos." *The New York Times Book Review*: 3.

INDEX

Photographs are denoted by *italic*. Principal treatment of a subject is entered in **bold**. The contents of notes are indexed with an "n" after the page number.

Mabel Dodge Luhan's writings are indexed under Luhan, Mabel Dodge: writings. She is referred to as "Mabel" in sundry subheadings through the index.

Epithets in parentheses after an entry, e.g. (son) or (husband), refer to relationships with Mabel.

Full details of Brill's letters to Mabel appear under Brill, A. A: letters to Mabel. Full details of Mabel's letters to Brill appear under Luhan, Mabel Dodge: letters to Brill.

Brill's writings are also gathered together under Brill, Dr. A. A.: writings.

23 Fifth Avenue, xxiv, 43–**46**, 153
291 gallery, 44

Aberle, Dr. Sophie, 288, 292 n6
Abraham A. Brill Library, 272–273 n5, 298
abreaction, 109–110, 243
Academy of Medicine, New York, 187
Adams, Ansel, 1
Addison's disease, 159–160, 165
Adler, Alfred, 199
Adrian, *16*
All of Their Lives (Myron Brinig), 263 n14
American Journal of Psychiatry, 272 n5
analyst/patient relationship, xxiv–xv
Anne Minton's Life (Myron Brinig), 249–251, 262 n1–263 n13
Appel, Dr. John, 280–281
Armstrong, Hamilton Fish, 177 n17
Armstrong, Helen Byrne, 174, 177 n17

Arrival and Departure (Arthur Koestler), 282–283 ns5, 8
Austen Riggs Foundation, 236 n13
Austin, Mary, 67, 74

"Bad Girl in the Pansy Bed" (D. H. Lawrence), 106
Bagaduce Farm, 257
Barnes, Carman
    Brill treats, 190–191, 203
    clay bust unveiled, 188
    introduced to Mabel, 184
    mentioned, 183
    unrealized plan to visit Mabel in Taos, 205
Beinecke Rare Book and Manuscript Library, Yale University, xxiii, xxv, 6, 304–305
Bendix, Vincent, 182, 188, 191
benzedrine sulphate, 229–230, 232, 235 n4, 254

319

320   INDEX

Berlin Psychoanalytic Institute, 137, 140
Bernheim, Gioia
  birth of son, 149
  getting married, 119–120, 126
  in analysis, 82
  mentioned in father's letter, 141
  on Mabel's paintings, 6
  origin of name, 36
  recalls Mabel and Tony Luhan visiting, 179–180
Bernheim, Philip, 119, 147 n9
Bett, W. R., 235 n4
Big House, Taos *see also* Los Gallos; Taos
  Brill at, 193
  entertaining at, 189, 275
  photograph of, *10*
  plans to create an inn, 213–214
Bleuler, Eugen, 33, 53
Blue Spruce Standing Deer, 235 n7, 305
Bonaparte, Marie, 57
Boyd, William, 256, 263 n18
Brentano bookstore, 72
Brett, Dorothy
  Brill mentions, 237, 239
  Brill seeks to vindicate, 246
  brings slander case against Mabel, 244, 247–248
  exhibition of paintings by, 285, 292 n1
  reports on Mabel's driving, 111 n4
  with Mabel and Frieda Lawrence, 26
Breuer, Josef, 110
Brill, Dr. A. A., **32–37, 51–57, 298–305**
  23 Fifth Avenue evening, 45, 266
  advice from Freud, 89
  approach adopted with Mabel, xxv, 227
  approach as perceived by Mabel, 185–186
  approach to confidentiality, 82, 104, 191
  "Art and Neurosis" (lecture), 210
  "Ballad of a Bad Girl," 85–86
  bronze bust of, 273 n5
  Caste and Outcast, reading of, 91
  chapter devoted to in *Movers and Shakers*, 180, 183–185
  death of, 298–300
  described by Spud Johnson, 195
  dreams identified by, 228 *see also* dreams
  enthusiasm for Freud, 31
  Freud's death, 269–271
  grandchildren of, 283 n9
  hospitals employed by, 82 n2, 147 n6, 235 n3
  interest in sex, 23, 204
  Jelliffe and, 37–38
  letters from Mabel, *see* Luhan, Mabel Dodge: letters to Brill
  letters to Mabel
    c. fall 1916, 55
    c. fall 1916, 56–57
    August 27, 1917, 60–61
    March 18, 1919, 64–65
    August 11, 1922, 68–69
    September 4, 1922, 69
    March 15, 1923, 75–76
    May 1, 1923, 78–79
    September 26, 1923, 81–82
    February 26, 1924, 85
    c. spring 1924, 86–87
    October 6, 1924, 91
    May 7, 1925, 98–99
    July 27, 1925, 99
    August 11, 1925, 100
    January 8, 1926, 101–102
    March 16, 1927, 103–104

INDEX   321

April 9, 1928, 105–106
May 3, 1928, 107–108
August 29, 1928, 109
November 9, 1929, 116
January 20, 1930, 117
May 25, 1930, 119–120
September 19, 1930, 121
February 27, 1932, 122–123
April 12, 1932, *14*, 124
March 29, 1933, 129
October 26, 1935, 140–141
December 5, 1935, 143–144
December 13, 1935, 146
June 30, 1936, 149–150
September 15, 1936, 151–152
November 17, 1936, 154
December 21, 1936, 155
August 11, 1937, 166
September 2, 1937, 168–169
September 15, 1937, 170
October 11, 1937, *19*, 171–172
November 13, 1937, 173–175
December 10, 1937, 175–176
March 26, 1938, 182
April 8, 1938, 183–184
April 11, 1938, 184
April 14, 1938, *21*, 187
May 11, 1938, 190–191
June 28, 1938, 198–199
July 12, 1938, 205
July 22, 1938, 206
July 25, 1938, *25*, 206–207
c. August 1938, 210–211
August 31, 1938, 215–216
September 27, 1938, 217
October 3, 1938, 226
October 19, 1938, 230
December 7, 1938, 238–239
January 14, 1939, 240–241
February 6, 1939, 245–246
May 8, 1939, 250–251
June 14, 1939, 253–254
June 23, 1939, 254
August 16, 1939, 256–257
September 6, 1939, 261
September 11, 1939, 261
January 16, 1940, 267
July 25, 1940, 270–271
December 30, 1940, 272
September 12, 1942, 276
May 24, 1943, 279
September 14, 1943, 280
October 13, 1943, 281–282
January 3, 1944, 282
February 23, 1944, 285–286
February 25, 1944, 286
March 6, 1944, 287
March 14, 1944, 289–290
May 2, 1944, 290–291
lifelong correspondence with Freud, 36
love of birds, 102, 312
Mabel, D. H. Lawrence and, 89–90
Mabel, expresses love for, 172
Mabel, Maurice Sterne and, 59–62
Mabel leaves Taos to see, 88
Mabel psychoanalyzed by *see* Luhan, Mabel Dodge: psychoanalyzed by Brill
Mabel wants autographed photograph of, 201–203
Mabel writes about Myron Brinig to, 17, 216, 220
Mabel's affection for, 158–159
meets Robinson and Una Jeffers, 16
mockingbird request by, 101–102
New York Psychoanalytic Society, 5
Oberndorf and Lorand describe, 302–303
obituary of, 301
on fulfillment, 193–194
on hypnotism, 221 n5

on *Lady Chatterley's Lover*, 109–110
on Los Gallos logo, 11
on outlets, 117–118 n3
on qualities required of an analyst, xxvi
on Robinson and Una Jeffers, 198
on the value of work, 54, 89
on two of Mabel's husbands, 86–87
passion for photography, 23
photographs by, 23–24
photographs of, 5, 18
Police College lectures, 311
requests Mabel to express her feelings for him, 107
Sons and Lovers manuscript, 98
speaks at Mabel's revived New York salon in 1940, 266–267
Time magazine article critical of, 18
Tony Luhan as antidote to, 73
translator of Freud, 23
visits Freud, 68
visits Taos, 163, 193–196
writings by
   Basic Principles of Psychoanalysis, 89, 226
   Basic Writings of Sigmund Freud, The, 211 n3
   "Character and Anal Erotism," 217
   "Concept of Psychic Suicide," 167
   Freud's Contribution to Psychiatry, 276–277
   Ned: Our Starling, 102
   Psychoanalytic Psychiatry, 118 n3
   "Psychotherapies I Encountered," 32
   "What's Wrong with Cities?," 54, 89
Brill, Edmund
   claims Mabel's letters to Brill were destroyed, xxiii–xiv, 304–305
   employment of, 263 n18
   Harvard, 141, 149, 161 n2
   maintains contact with Mabel, 304
   Sorbonne trip, 241
Brill, Gioia *see* Bernheim, Gioia
Brill, Rose
   fondness for Mabel, 108, 170
   Freud sends postcard, 68
   health of, 276
   Mabel in hospital, 277–278
   maintains contact with Mabel, 304
   tries to tone down husband, 194
   upset that Mabel doesn't acknowledge Brill's death, 303–304
Brill, Thomas Owen, 161 n1
Brill Library, 272–273 n5, 298
Brinig, Myron
   Anne Minton's Life, 249–251
   character inspired by, 218
   contacts Mabel regarding article about her, 239
   film script by, 255
   John Evans jealous of, 225, 234 n1
   Mabel claims he lacks superego, 164
   Mabel's fixation on, 17, 216, 219, 221, 224, 232
   May Flavin, 201–203, 211 n1
   mentioned, 183–184
   notes on, 262, ns4, 5
   novel adapted for cinema, 176 n8
   photograph on horseback of, 17
   rents and buys from Mabel, 252, 259
   works with Lillian Gish, 254–255
Brisbane, Arthur, 258, 263 n29
Brooks, Mabel, 182–183
Brophy, William, 288

Bryant, William Cullen, 299
Buck, Laura, 164, 202, 263 n19, 282 n1
Buffalo, New York, xxiv, 3, 39, 115, 239
Buffalo Courier Express, 181
Bull, Nina, 144–145
Bureau of Indian Affairs, 168, 292 n5
Burghölzi clinic, Zurich, 33–34
Burnham, John, xxiv
Bursum Bill, 74
Burton, Harry
  Brill warns Mabel, 198
  Cosmopolitan, 188, 192–193
  interest in Mabel's work, 219
  mentioned in letters, 197, 199, 201, 203, 207–208
Byrne, Janet, 98

Calling All Men (Leonard Sillman), 235 n9
Candelario, John, 29
Carpenter, Edward, 311–312 n1
Carson, Kit, 305
Cary, Emily, 258
Cary, Phoebe, 258, 263 n29
Caste and Outcast (Dhan Gopal Mukerji), 90–91
Cathartic Method, 110
Cerf, Bennett
  Brill as contact for, 196–198
  letter to Mabel, 22
  mentioned, 205
  Random House, 192
  wants *quid pro quo* from Brill, 199–200 n3
Charcot, Jean-Martin, 33
Chicago Herald Examiner, 134
Christian Science, 243
Clark University, Massachusetts, 36, 46
Cleveland Plain Dealer, 181
Collier, John
  affection expressed for Mabel and Tony Luhan, 177 n12
  Bureau of Indian Affairs, 168
  Bursum Bill campaign, 74
  love affair of, 288–289
  Mabel's deteriorating relationship with, 168
  marriage of, 280, 282 n3, 289
  syphilis investigation and, 114
  visits Taos, 67
Collins, Alan, 192, 205, 225, 235 n2, 246
Colorado Springs Fine Arts Center, 165
Columbia University, 32, 298
Concha, Eliseo, 196–199
Coriat, Isidor, 149–151
Cosmopolitan, 188, 191–193, 209, 213
Croton-on-Hudson, 49, 53, 156
Curtis Brown Ltd, 188, 192, 202, 216, 219

Dasburg, Alfred, 173–174, 177 n16
Dasburg, Andrew
  consults Brill, 47, 51, 56
  diagnosed with Addison's disease, 159–160, 165
  Mabel meets, 44
  Mabel's marriage to Tony Luhan and, 77
  marries and divorces, 111 n3, n6
  mentioned in letters, 79–80, 106–107, 109, 166
  one-man show of paintings by, 110 n1
  Taos and, 29, 67
Dasburg, Marina, 174, 190–191
Davis, Robert Hobart, 197, 202, 206
Dell, Floyd, 47, 153
Dempsey, John, 288, 292 n5
Dodge, Edwin (second husband), 43–44, 50–51, 55, 144

Dodge, Mabel *see* Luhan, Mabel Dodge
Donaldson, Hildegarde, 204, 206–208, 238–239
Draper, Muriel, 101, 133, 143–145, 151
Draper, Paul, 104 n5
dreams
  Brill's devotion to, 52–53, 214–215
  Mabel's after seeing Frances Wickes, 113
  Mabel's falling dreams, 214–215, 227–229
  Mabel's syphilis dream, 78
  San Geronimo Day and, 223–224
Dreiser, Theodore, 89, 183–184, 188 n2, 197, 260
Dudley, Lotus, 66–67, 243
Duino Elegies (Rainer Maria Rilke), 263 n23
Duse, Eleanor, 43

Eastman, Max, 54, 57 n1, 108, 111 n7
Embudo, 280
Evans, Alice (first daughter-in-law), 115, 120, 134, 146 n1, 263 ns20, 21
Evans, Claire (second daughter-in-law), 257–258, 270, 272
Evans, John (son), **41–43**
  abnormal behavior of, 272
  aftermath of birth of, 278–279
  allowance cut off, 146 n1
  Brill on, 120, 270, 272, 281, 285, 287
  daughters of, 263 n20
  Department of the Interior job, 278
  difficulties with mother, 115, 134–135
  divorces first wife, 120
  effect on of mother's marriage to Tony Luhan, 80
  Eliseo Concha and, 196
  incestuous feelings and interest in, 224–225, 261
  jealousy of Myron Brinig, 225, 234 n1
  Mabel buys property for, 98
  Mabel dreams of, 224–225
  Mabel's concerns over his mother complex, 257–259, 261, 281
  moves closer to Mabel, 305
  novel by, 225–226
  photograph of, with Mabel, 3
  photograph of, with Tony Luhan, 9
  remarries, 134
Evans, Karl (first husband), 40, 115
Evans, Mabel Ganson *see* Luhan, Mabel Dodge
Evans, Nancy, 115

Fadiman, Clifton, 153, 171
falling dreams, 214–215, 227–229 *see also* dreams
Fechin, Alexandra, 165–168
Fechin, Nicolai, 165
Federal Theatre Project, 210
Ferenczi, Sándor
  International Psychoanalytic Association and, 36
  interprets Brill's dreams, 53
  letters from Freud, 57
  Sándor Rádo and, 137
  takes patient on holiday, 80
Finnegans Wake (James Joyce), 266, 268
Finney Farm
  Brill finally approves of, 54
  Mabel leases, 49, 90
  Mabel returns to from Taos, 88
  Orage's weekend groups at, 101
Fraser, Jimmy, 8
Freud, Sigmund, 34–38, **45–47**

advice to Brill, 89
American avant-garde embrace, 56
analyzing Brill's dreams, 53
approach to confidentiality, 82
Brill follows, 45
Brill introduces to English speaking world, 301
Brill to translate, 199 n3
Brill visits, 68
Brill writes to about Jelliffe, 52
Cathartic Method and, 110
champions unconscious, 31
death of, 262 n7, 269–271
friendship with patients, 57, 80
Rádo's changing opinion of, 147 n7
statue of, 273 n5

Ganson, Mabel *see* Luhan, Mabel Dodge
Gilpin, Laura, 1, *10*, *29*
Gish, Lillian, 254–255
"Glimpses of a Freudian Odyssey" (Smith Ely Jelliffe), 37
Greenbaum, Edward, 164, 177 n9, 214
Greenwich Village, New York, 31, 47
Guggenheim Fellowships, 260
Gurdjieff, G. I., 101–103, 114, 164

Haggard, Edith
  Mabel's agent, 188, 210
  On Human Relations, 192–193, 208
  on *Water of Life*, 219
Haig (dog), 204
Hapgood, Hutchins, 44, 47, 60
Harcourt, Alfred, 127, 130, 143
Harcourt, Brace publishers, 127, 135, 171, 205
Hare, Elizabeth Sage, 279, 286
Hare family, 279–281
Hartley, Marsden, 29, 44

Hausner, Dr. Eric, 294–296, 305
Hawk Tower, 221 n4
Hearst, Randolph, 31
Henderson, Alice, 80, 99
Hitler, Adolf, 248 n5, 270
Hoadley, Professor Leigh, 241
Hoboken, New Jersey, xxiii
Hoover, Margaret, 266
Horney, Karen, 267
Horse Fly, The, 203, 213
Hospice de Bicêtre, Paris, 33
Hovey, Carl, 166–167, 169–170, 174, 189, 193
Howard, Roy, 182
Hugo, Victor, 129, 146 n2
Huxley, Aldous, 125
hydrotherapy, 264 n30
hypnotism, 221 n5

India, 91
Institute for the Harmonious Development of Man, 101
insulin, 252–256, 262 n9
Inter-American Conference on Indian Life, 269
International Psychiatric Association, 36
International Psycho-Analytical Congress, 1936, 176
Interpretation of Dreams, The (Sigmund Freud), 31, 53

Jeffers, Robinson
  described by Spud Johnson, 194
  has affair, 203–204
  Lorenzo in Taos and, 120, 122
  Mabel in New York, 189
  Mabel writes to, 123
  on Brill, 196
  on his wife, 199 n2
  photograph of, with Mabel, *16*

visits Taos, 23, 189, 193–194, 196, 203–205, 208
Jeffers, Una
attempts suicide, 203–204, 214
Brill and, 196, 198, 303
frequent guest at Taos, 16, 23
husband describes, 199 n2
photographed by Brill, 211 n4
praises *Lorenzo in Taos*, 125
psychoanalysis recommended for, 206–207
twin sons of, 204, 208
women and satisfaction, 194
Jelliffe, Smith Ely, **37–38, 49–53**
"Ballad of a Bad Girl," 86, 106
Brill and, a comparison, 158
chapter devoted to in *Movers and Shakers*, 156–157
death of, 299
follows Freud, 31
journal owned and edited by, 248 n10
Mabel enters psychoanalysis with, 46, 49–53
Mabel learns from, 217
Mabel refers to in correspondence, 47
Mabel's correspondence with, 49, 51–52, 67–68, 72, 85–86, 105–106, 150, 156, 179, 247
Sterne's antagonism for, 55
theories on disease, 160
Time magazine photograph of, 18
Jews, 248 n5
Johnson, Grace Mott, 56, 109, 111 n6, 173–174
Johnson, Walter, Willard "Spud"
Alexandra Fechin and, 165–166
article about Mabel, 189, 194–195
"Ballad of a Bad Girl" published, 106

Laughing Horse magazine, 13, 86
Mabel writes to, 104, 268
Jones, Ernest, 35, 302
Jones, Katherine, 200 n3
Jones, Robert Edmond, 101
Journal of Nervous and Mental Disease (ed. Smith Ely Jelliffe), 248 n10
Journal of the American Medical Association, 235 n4
Journey into the Self (Leo Stein), 47–48
Joyce, James, 266
Julia, 9
Jung, Carl
Brill in Zurich with, 33
Brill on Jelliffe and, 52
Frances Wickes as Jungian, 113
interprets Brill's dreams, 53
Mabel's knowledge of, 131
Mabel's psychoanalytic evenings and, 45

Kańczuga, 32
Kanter, Dr. Charles, 213, 248 n1
Kiker, Judge Henry, 220, 245, 289
King, Jeff, 292 n12
Kingsley, Myra, 205
Klein, Melanie, 80
Knopf, Alfred, 13, 108, 110 n2, 122, 200 n3
Koestler, Arthur, 282
Koshares tribe, 223–224
Krishnamurti, Jiddu, 198, **241–244**
Kristallnacht, 248 n5

La Fonda Hotel, 285–286, 288
La Posta, 116–117 n1, 152
Lady Chatterley's Lover (D. H. Lawrence), 105, 109–110, 110 n2
Lane, Nancy, 111 n3
Lao Tzu, 232–234, 243

Laughing Horse magazine, 13, 85–86
Lawrence, D. H., **71–74, 88–90**
　advice to Mabel, 111 n4, 127
　"Ballad of a Bad Girl," 13, 84–85
　death of, 26, 95, 121
　"disloyalty and treachery of," 93
　fictional character based on, 218
　Lorenzo in Taos (Mabel Dodge Luhan) *see* Luhan, Mabel, writings by
　Mabel and Tony Luhan and, 83
　Mabel appraises, 123–124
　Mabel credits for her writing, 131
　Mabel disappointed by, 16
　Mabel, Gurdjieff and, 103
　Mabel renews contact with, 83
　Mabel's correspondence with, 71–72, 83–85, 90, 92–93, 95, 103, 120–123, 127
　Mabel's lack of modesty, 10
　on *Background*, 95
　on Brill, 123
　phoenix image, 176 n1
　photograph of, 12
　portrait of, by Robert Hobart Davis, 197
　sadism of, 95
　serious threat to Mabel, 88
　Sons and Lovers manuscript, 97–98; value of, 98
　Taos, xxiv, 12, 67, 71–74, 83–84, 88, 90, 95, 177 n10
　various works of, read by Mabel, 71
Lawrence, Frieda
　jealousy of, 74
　nickname, 72
　objects and then consents to publication of *Lorenzo in Taos*, 121–122
　photographs of, *12, 26*

　Sons and Lovers manuscript and, 98
　visits Taos, 71, 122, 177 n10
Lawrence and Brett: A Friendship (Dorothy Brett), 26
Lehrman, Philip, 302
Lescaze, William, 182
Levien, Sonya
　concern for Mabel, 237
　encourages Mabel to see Brill, 169–170
　in Taos with Mabel, 166–167
　letters to Mabel, 166–167, 190, 266
　Mabel and Brill and, 181
　on revival of Mabel's salon, 266
　on *Winter in Taos*, 177 n11
　wants Brill to treat her son, 190
Lewisohn, Joan, 258
Lewisohn, Sam, 152, 161 n3, 174, 260
Library of Congress, 35, 288
Lippmann, Faye, 173, 177 n15
Lippmann, Walter, 123, 172–174, 177 ns15, 17
Lorand, Sandor, 302
Lorber, Herman, 273 n7
Lorenzo in Taos (Mabel Dodge Luhan) *see* Luhan, Mabel, writings by
Los Gallos, Taos, *10–11*, 24, 116, 118 n2, 203 *see also* Taos
Lovelace, Dr. Richard, 159–160, 273 n6
Lower East Side, New York, 32
Luhan, Mabel Dodge
　23 Fifth Avenue, 44–46
　65th birthday party, 285–287
　article about in *Saturday Review*, 239
　birth of, 39
　birth of son, 41–42, 278–279
　Brill, her fondness for, 134 *see also* Brill, A. A.

Cerf, Bennett, letter from, 22,
    199–200 n3
childhood of, 39–40
D. H. Lawrence and *see*
    Lawrence, D. H.
death of, 30, 305
driving, 107, 111 n4
ego, on the, 164
empathy with others, xxvi
enthusiasm for Freud, 31
exhibitionism of, 247, 251
fictional portrayals of, 95, 107–
    108, 263 n14
first orgasm, 40–41
Frances Wickes and, 113–115
golden mean, 233–234
Gurdjieff and, 101–103
health problems of, 251–253,
    277–278, 305
hysterectomy, 115
Indian affairs and the Bursum
    Bill, 74–75
Jelliffe, Smith Ely, correspondence
    with *see* Jelliffe, Smith Ely:
    Mabel's correspondence
    with
Krishnamurti and, 241–244
Lao Tzu, 232–234
letters from Brill *see* Brill, A. A.:
    letters to Mabel
letters to Brill
  April 24, 1925, 97
  September 14, 1930, 121
  October 22, 1935, 137–138
  November 4, 1935, 142
  November 30, 1935, 143
  August 3, 1936, 150–151
  September 24, 1936, 152–153
  November 21, 1936, 154
  March 4, 1937, 159–160
  July 3, 1937, 164–165
  August 8, 1937, 165–166

  August 28, 1937, 167
  September 17, 1937, 171
  November 7, 1937, 172–173
  December 10, 1937 (before), 175
  March 23, 1938, 182
  April 8, 1938 (before), *20*, 183
  May 8, 1938, 190
  June 24, 1938, 196–197
  June 24, 1938 (after), 197–198
  July 1, 1938, 219
  July 5, 1938 (before), 202
  July 5, 1938, 203
  c. July 20, 1938, 206
  July 27, 1938, 208
  July 27, 1938 (after), 209
  August 2, 1938, 210
  August 28, 1938, 214
  September 16, 1938, 216
  September 30, 1938, 220
  October 1, 1938, 223–225
  October 4, 1938, 227–228
  October 5, 1938, 229–230
  October 20, 1938, 230–232
  October 23, 1938, 232–233
  December 5, 1938, *28*, 237–238
  January 31, 1939, 244–245
  February 9, 1939, 246–247
  May 5, 1939, 249–250
  June 11, 1939, 251–253
  June 29, 1939, 255
  July 21, 1939, 255–256
  August 30, 1939, 258–259
  September 5, 1939, 260
  March 3, 1944, 287
  March 3, 1944 (after), 288–289
marriages *see* Dodge, Edwin;
    Evans, Karl; Luhan, Tony;
    Sterne, Maurice
maternal feelings of, 94 *see also*
    Evans, John
memoirs *see also below* writings
  planning and writing, 92–95

publication and reception, 127–140
menopause, 73–74, 191–192
mother (hers), 39–40, 92, 111 n5, 127–128, 133–134
mother, as see Evans, John
Myron Brinig fixation see Brinig, Myron: Mabel's fixation on
names known by, 1, 31
painting by (*Tulips in Vase*), 6
parents of, xxiv, 39–40 see also above mother (hers)
personality of, xxv
photographs of
   1920s, 13
   1948, 29
   Fifth Avenue apartment, 2, 4
   Frieda Lawrence, Dorothy Brett, and, 26
   New York 1934, 14
   on horseback, 23
   Taos, 7
   Tony and, 27, 30
   with son, 3
pregnancy, 41–42
psychoanalysis see also psychoanalysis
   pioneer of, 45–48
   under Brill, 51–57, 72, 92, 124, 181–188, **307–312**
   under Jelliffe, 49–53, 156–157
relations, various, 128
relationship with son see Evans, John
reviews of work, 130, 136, 138–139, 153, 171 see also below writings by
revives salon, 266–268
slander suit against, 213
summary of life, xxiv
Tony Luhan see Luhan, Antonio (Tony)

Villa Curonia, life at, 43
writings by
   articles for *New York Journal*, 46–47
   Background, 94–95, 110, **127–135**
   "Ballad of a Bad Girl," 13, 84–86, 106
   "Change," 73, 89
   Change of Life, 89, 191
   Conversation Pieces, 181–182
   Doctors: Fifty Years of Experience, 40, 279, 290, 305
   Edge of Taos Desert, 7–9, 63, 168, 170–171
   European Experiences, 40, 103, 136–137, **141–145**, 278
   Family Affairs, 80, 127, 133, 208, 211, 221 n6
   "Golden Mean, The," 233
   Hildegarde: Eight Years After, 206
   "Holiday from Science?," 294
   Intimate Memories, 54, 127, 129, 133, 153, 171, 297
   Intimation, An, 66
   Let's Go Away Together, 293
   Lorenzo in Taos, 12–13, 72, **120–125**, 129, 243
   "Mabel Dodge Talks About the In-Between Times," 139
   "Money Complex, The," 216–218
   Movers and Shakers, **149–159**
      Brill comments on, 124
      Eastman's letter, 57 n1
      Edwin Dodge, 43
      Jelliffe, 52
      Maurice Sterne, 55, 130
      on Brill, 185
      original title of, 137, 146 n3
      Van Vechten, 15
   My Attitude in the Writing of Autobiography, 130

Notes Upon Awareness, 93, 198, 234, **241–244**, 247, 263 n11
  see also *On Human Relations* below
On Human Relations
  begins work on, 163
  Burton's contribution, 208
  Cosmopolitan and, 192, 213
  expanded version, 198, 242
  fire theme, 176 n2
  getting published, 22, 193, 196, 205
  "Money Complex" and, 216
  on artists, 221, 227
  pleasure and reality, 234
  resuming analysis and, 180–181
  sends to Brill, 201
  Thornton Wilder reads, 209
Parting, The, 54–55
Psychoanalysis for Beginners, 22
  see also *On Human Relations* above
Psycho-Analysis with Dr. Brill, 102, 183, **185–188**, 214, **307–312**
Quarrel, A, 54
Statue of Liberty, The, 30, 64, 177 n14, 296
Taos and its Artists, 29, 296
Una and Robin in Taos
  Brill leads conversation, 193, 204
  Brill on, 240, 245
  Brill's photography, 23
  completes, 238
  notes, 248 ns3, 8
  page count, 211
  Una and Hildegarde Donaldson, 207
Water of Life, **218–219**
  attempts to publish, 286, 288
  Brill receives, 238
  Brill's comment on, 245
  Brinig fixation and, 17
  completes, 216
  mountain theme, 260
  page count, 142
  working on, 214
Winter in Taos, 10, 135–136, 145–146, 177 n11, 290–291
Luhan, Tony (fourth husband), **62–66**
  as antidote to Brill, 72
  Brill on, 87, 177 n14
  Bursum Bill and, 74–75
  D. H. Lawrence at Taos and, 73
  death of, 305
  drinking sprees of, 229–231
  Frank Waters admires, 259
  has extramarital affair, 114, 165
  his silences, 235 n5
  Lorenzo in Taos dedication, 122
  Mabel writes of, 295–297
  Mabel's affairs during their marriage, 97, 102, 106–107
  Mabel's feelings about her decision to marry him, 80–81
  marries Mabel, 77
  meets Mabel, xxiv, 62
  need for Mabel, 93
  photographs of, *8–9*, *23*, *27*, *30*
  syphilis and, 77–78
  "Talk of the Town" on, 268–269
  thyroid problem of, 271, 273 n6

Man Makes His Own Mask (Robert Hobart Davis), 197, 202
"Manuscripts of D. H. Lawrence: A Descriptive Catalogue" (Los Angeles Public Library), 175
Marceau, Theodore D., 5
Marcy, Everett
  Brill treats, 103–104, 119, 175

continuing infatuation for Mabel, 232
Mabel falls for, 98, 100, 107, 114
Mabel pays for psychoanalysis of, with D. H. Lawrence manuscript, 97–98
song apparently written by, 236 n12
Marie, Pierre, 33
Marinoff, Fania, 277
Masses, The, 54
May Flavin (Myron Brinig), 201–203, 211 n1
McCrary, Sarah Brisbane, 258, 261
menopause, 73–74, 89, 190–192
Merchant of Yonkers, The (Thornton Wilder), 209
Meyer, Adolf, 32
Mitchell, S. Weir, 233
Monaghan, Marion S., 101–102
Moses and Monotheism (Sigmund Freud), 200 n3
Mukerji, Dhan Gopal, 90–91

Navaho Indians, 290, 292 n12
Nazis, 262 n7
Nemon, Olem, 273 n5
New Mexico Quarterly, 175
New Mexico Sentinel, 189
New York Academy of Medicine, 187
New York Herald, 60
New York Herald Tribune, 141–142
New York Journal, 46
New York Neurological Institute, 37
New York Neurological Society, 18
New York Psychiatric Institute, 82 n2, 147 n6, 235 n3
New York Psychoanalytic Society, 5, 137, 298, 301
New York State Hospital, 194
New York State Pathological Institute, 32

New York Times, 301
New York Times Book Review, 125, 130, 171, 249
New York World, 77, 80
New York World-Telegram, 265–266
New Yorker, The, 27, 171, 268, 293

Oberndorf, C. P., 298, 303
Oedipus complex, 52, 86, 301
Orage, Alfred, 101–102

Palms magazine, 73
Parmenter, Dr. John, 40–41, 43, 279
patient/analyst relationship, xxiv–xxv
Peter Whiffle (Carl Van Vechten), 4, 108
Pike's Peak (Frank Waters), 259–260
Placitas, 259, 264 n31
Police College, 311
Pond, Dr. Ashley
  Brill mentions, 190
  Mabel consults for depression, 294–295
  Mabel's depression and dysentery and, 231
  prescribes benzedrine sulphate for Mabel, 229
  treats Thornton Wilder, 209
  various tests and samples from Mabel, 251–252
Powers, Lillian Delger, 82
Price, Marian, 202
Prinzhorn, Hans, 117–118 n6
Proust, Marcel, 94
Psychiatric Quarterly, 299
psychoanalysis
  Brill's interest in, 33–37
  Brill's quote about, xxvi
  common fears of, 94
  criticism of in *Time* magazine, 18
  early boundaries in, 56, 80, 82

early days of, 31
for analysts, 186
Jelliffe and, 37–38, 49–53
Mabel a pioneer of, 45–48
Mabel acknowledges Brill and, 163
Mabel approaches, 40, 43
Mabel on her early experiences of, 123
Mabel's relations with her mother and, 92
Mabel's writing style about, 192
miscellaneous works on, 46
Pueblo Indian lifestyle and, 66
Psychoanalysis and the Unconscious (D. H. Lawrence), 71–72
Psychoanalytic Review, 37
Pueblo Indians, xxiv, 62, 66, 74–75

Rádo, Emmy, 138, 146 n5, 150
Rádo, Sándor, 117, 137–138, 140, 147 n7
Random House, 192, 199–200 n3
Rauh, Ida
  marriage witness for Mabel, 77
  mentioned in Brill's letters, 98, 106–107, 109
  relationships of, 111 n7
Reeder, Admiral, 111 n5
Rehn, Frank K. M., 110 n1, 111, n3
Reinhardt, Max, 209, 211 n6
Richthofen-Marquier, Baroness Anna Elise Lydia von, 199 n1
Rilke, Rainer Maria, 258, 263 n23
River House, Embudo, 280
Rogier, Joseph, 259–260
Romm, May, 269, 299
Rubin, Isidor, 277
Rydal Press, 290–291

Sachs, Dr. Bernard, 18, 44–45, 233

Sakel, Manfred, 262 n9, 263 n15
Salmon, Thomas William, 275
Salmon Lectures, 275
Salpetriére Hospital, Paris, 33
Salversan, 606, 78
San Geronimo Day, 223–224
Sanger, Margaret, 289, 292 n8
Santa Fe, New Mexico, 62, 285, 288–289
Santa Fe New Mexican, 179
Saturday Evening Post, 54
Saturday Review, The, 239
Schreiber, Dr., 258, 264 n34
Schwarcz, Dorothea, 177 n9
Sea and Sardinia (D. H. Lawrence), 71
Selected Papers on Hysteria and Other Psychoneuroses (Sigmund Freud), 35
Selected Poetry of Robinson Jeffers, The, 199 n2
Seltzer, Thomas, 121
Sergeant, Elizabeth Shepley, 238–239
Shadow and Light (Maurice Sterne), 56
Shadows Flying, (John Evans), 225–226, 261
Shevky, Marian, 114, 165
Shevky, Richard, 114
Sillman, Leonard, 232, 235 ns9, 10
Sisters, The (dir. Anatole Litvak), 176 n8
Slee, James Noah Henry, 292 n8
Smith and Durrell publishers, 293
Soma, Tony, 236 n11
Sons and Lovers (D. H. Lawrence)
  Brill accepts manuscript of as payment for Everett Marcy's psychoanalysis, 97, 119
  handwritten manuscripts of, 26, 98, 175
  Mabel reads, 71
Southwest Review, 294
Spencer, Claire, 134

"Sphinx of Taos Desert" (Elizabeth Shepley Sergeant), 239
Spinoza, Baruch, 34
Steffens, Lincoln, 45
Stein, Gertrude
  at the Villa Curonia, 43
  European Experiences and, 142–143, 145
  Mabel meets in Paris, xxiv
  Mabel perceived to be influenced by, 94
  Mabel's marriage to Tony Luhan and, 80
  Van Vechten and, 15
Stein, Leo
  European Experiences and, 142–143
  Mabel meets in Paris, xxiv
  Mabel reports to on Brill, 92
  Mabel shares interest in psychoanalysis with, 47–48
  Mabel writes to about Brill and abreaction, 110
  Mabel writes to about Brill and Tony Luhan, 87
  on "Ballad of a Bad Girl," 86
  on Lawrence's sadism, 95
Stern, Adolph, 302
Sterne, Mabel Dodge *see* Luhan, Mabel Dodge
Sterne, Maurice (third husband), **59–63**
  almost drowns, 155
  annoys Mabel at a lunch, 138
  attitude to Mabel's memoirs, 130
  Brill mentions, 117–118 n5
  Brill seeks to remove Mabel from, 59
  consults Brill, 55–56
  Mabel's portrayal of, 152
  Mabel's stories about, 54
  marriage to Mabel, 3, 153

  Movers and Shakers and, 124, 155–157
  nature of relationship with, 50–51
  on *Background*, 130
  on *Lorenzo in Taos*, 125
  on *Winter in Taos*, 136
Sterne, Vera, 117–118 n5, 150
Stieglitz, Alfred, 44, 263 n27
Stieglitz, Dr. Leopold, 258, 261, 263 n27–264 n34
Stockbridge Institute for the Psychoneuroses, 236 n13
Stokowski, Leopold, 172, 174, 211 n2
sublimation, 89, 110, 165
Sunday Reference, 125
syphilis, 55, 77–78, 114, 156, 297

"Talk of the Town" (*The New Yorker*), 27, 268, 293
Taoism, 232
Taos
  Brill's attitude to, 68–69, 163
  D. H. Lawrence and, xxiv, 12, 67, 71–74, 83–84, 88, 90, 95
  Jeffers and, 120
  Los Gallos, xxiv
  loses its magic for Mabel, 295–296
  Lotus Dudley on, 66–67
  Mabel chooses as home, 62–63
  marriage to Tony Luhan in, 77
  Public Library, 211 n3
  syphilis enquiry, 114
  Taos Theatre, 202–203, 211 n2
  World War Two and, 294
"Thanatopsis" (William Cullen Bryant), 299–300
theolin, 220, 222 n8
Thompson, Clarence, 88, 107
Time magazine, 18, 201
Tiwa community (Pueblo Indians), 62
Toklas, Alice B., 43, 181, 266, 268

Toomer, Jean, 102, 114, 116
Tregor, Nison, 188, 271, 273 n5

unconscious, the
   appeal of to American avant-garde, 46
   Brill accepts, 34
   Brill makes Freud's views available, 35
   Brill upsets guests at Mabel's salon with talk of, 45
   compelling force, a, 31
   D. H. Lawrence on, 72
   Hapgood on Freud and, 47
   Mabel questions, 62

Valdez, New Mexico, 98
Van Vechten, Carl
   daybooks of, 100
   falls out with Mabel, 151
   Gertrude Stein writes to about Mabel and Tony, 80
   Mabel sends manuscript to, 94
   Mabel's close friendship with, 44
   on "Ballad of a Bad Girl," 86
   on Mabel's writings, 144–145
   Peter Whiffle, 4, 108
   photographing Mabel, 1, *15*
   portrait of, by Robert Hobart Davis, 197
   wife of, 277
Venture (Max Eastman), 108
Vidonian Club, 299
Viking Press, 286, 288
Villa Curonia, near Florence, xxiv, 43

Warde, John William, 263 n10
Ward's Island, New York, 32
Waters, Frank
   Brill mentions, 287
   Brinig works with, 254–255
   Mabel distributes trilogy of, 260–261, 264 n36
   visits Taos, 259
Weston, Edward, 1
Where the Two Came to Their Father, a Navajo War Ceremonial (Jeff King), 292 n12
White, William Alanson, 37
Wickes, Frances, 113–115
Wilder, Isabel, 205–206, 209
Wilder, Thornton
   autographed photograph of, 211
   end of Mabel's salon and, 268
   Finnegans Wake discussed and, 266
   on *Winter in Taos*, 136
   reports to Gertrude Stein about Mabel's resumed psychoanalysis, 181
   visits Taos with his sister, 205–206, 209–210
   writes to Mabel, 267
Witt, Nina, 68, 81–82
"Woman Who Rode Away, The" (D. H. Lawrence), 95
Works Progress Administration, 210
WQXR, Radio, 210

Y.W.C.A., Harlem, 174

Zurich, 33–35